If WOMEN HAVE COURAGE ...

AMONG SHEPHERDS, SHEIKS, AND SCIENTISTS IN ALGERIA

by Dorothy L. Pond

with a
Foreword by Chomingwen D. Pond
Afterword by Mary Jackes & David Lubell

AFRICA MAGNA VERLAG

Impressum

Publisher: Africa Magna Verlag
Altkönigblick 83
60437 Frankfurt am Main
Germany

www.africamagna.de

Design & Typesetting: Africa Magna Verlag

Printed in Germany by: Druckhaus Köthen GmbH, Köthen

Bibliografische Information der Deutschen Nationalbibliothek

Die Deutsche Nationalbibliothek verzeichnet diese Publikation in der
Deutschen Nationalbibliografie; detaillierte bibliografische Daten sind
im Internet über http://dnb.ddb.de abrufbar.

About the Author

*Dorothy (Long) Pond, a 1925 graduate of the University of Wisconsin (B.A., Economics), and
Alonzo Pond, a young archaeologist, fell in love through letters while he was on an expedition in the Sahara.
Immediately after their wedding, they left for another Algerian expedition. She became his partner in
archaeology, tourism businesses, radio broadcasting, and writing. She edited and typed his manuscripts
for publication. She lectured on their travels and on natural history and published childhood memories. When
Alonzo's work kept him away for months at a time, she was the sole homemaker for their children,
Chomingwen and Arthur.*

ISBN: 978-3-937248-41-7

For David and his family, grandchildren for whom this book was originally written.

Dorothy and Chomingwen Pond, ca. 1929

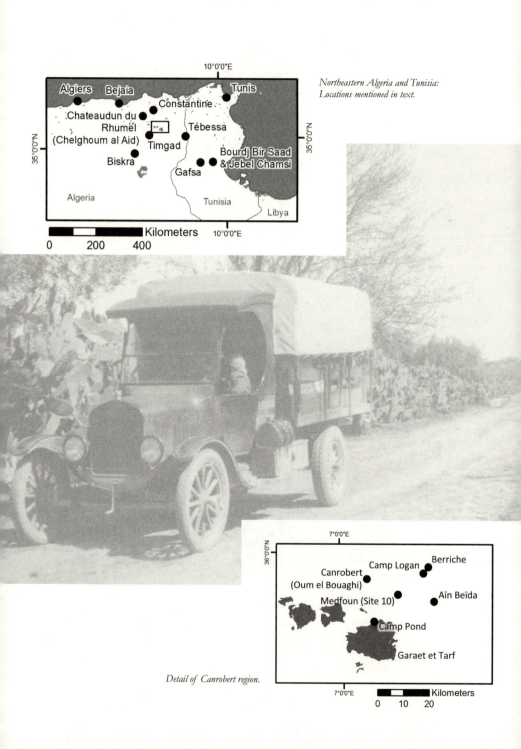

Northeastern Algeria and Tunisia:
Locations mentioned in text.

Detail of Canrobert region.

Contents

Foreword

"IF women have courage," said the sheik — for he wasn't sure they could — "IF women have courage, Madame Pond surely does!"

The words were spoken by *Caid* Khalifa Lamine as he bade farewell to my parents. For four months we had endured — and enjoyed — the rigors of living in a field camp at archaeological diggings on the High Plateau of North Africa. Now it was time to return home to the United States.

"Home" for Mom had been Sun Prairie, then a quiet village surrounded by the rich farmland of south-central Wisconsin. Grandpa and Papa had run the general store, and life revolved around home, school, and neighborhood. Excitement was provided by the community festivals — the Fourth of July picnic, the Christmas program — and by the sporadic appearance of gypsies, those mysterious people whose arrival sent children scurrying indoors to safety, certain that otherwise they risked being "stolen" and carried away forever.

Today we dream nostalgically of such peaceful, small-town life, but for a young girl with adventure in her soul, it could be dull. Some days Mom would sit on her front steps, look down the quiet, elm-shaded street, and quote the heroine of a favorite book: "Oh, if only something *exciting* would come down the road — even if it was only a plaid pig!"

Mom was in her mid-twenties and living in Madison when her "plaid pig" appeared in the form of the still young science of archaeology. It was the heyday of small field expeditions to exotic, out-of-the-way corners of the earth, searching for clues to humanity's prehistoric past.

This is Mom's memoir of her part in that search — keeping house under canvas, rearing a toddler far from the modern conveniences of the U.S., making a home in the semi-arid countryside of Algeria. Here are the challenges she met, the friends she made, the beauty she enjoyed, the strangeness she came to love among the people of northern Africa. Here is her account of her welcome to a "plaid pig."

Chomingwen D. Pond, Ph.D.
Minocqua, Wisconsin, USA
February 2011

Acknowledgments

The Wisconsin Historical Society's Library-Archives Division (Madison, Wisconsin, USA), which houses the Pond family papers and photographs, facilitated publication of this memoir, as did the Logan Museum of Anthropology, Beloit College (Beloit, Wisconsin, USA), which houses archaeological collections and related documentation from the fieldwork discussed herein. Prof. William Green, Director of the Logan Museum of Anthropology, Beloit College, has been especially helpful.

1

How it All Began

It was two o'clock on the 12th of June, 1926, when the doorbell rang in our second-floor apartment. I dashed to the top of the stairs — to be met and kissed by a man I had never seen before. Then we stood back and looked at each other.

Ten months before, a college classmate and neighbor had said, "A boy I've known since grade school has written to say he is going into the Sahara Desert for six months and has no girl to write to. Would you write to him to keep him from being lonely?"

I agreed and for some months had received letters postmarked Timmimoun and Aoulef Arab. I addressed my replies to such places as Tamanrasset and InSalah, Algeria. Now the young man was standing at my door.

We spent all afternoon getting to know each other.

Alonzo Pond grew up in Janesville, Wisconsin, the son of a successful businessman. He had shown an early interest in natural science and then in archaeology. Ambulance driving in France during the War interrupted his studies at Beloit College, but he graduated in 1920 with a Bachelor of Science degree. That led to a scholarship to study anthropology in Paris and do fieldwork in prehistoric archaeology in Europe, and then the expedition into the deep Sahara in Algeria.[1]

---

1. His account of that expedition is told in *Veiled Men, Red Tents and Black Mountains*, published by The Narrative Press (2003).

I grew up in Sun Prairie, Wisconsin, just three houses from open countryside. My only neighborhood playmate was a boy three years younger than I, so I played cowboys and Indians more than I did with dolls. The year I graduated from High School, we were at war and things were so upset that the next year I clerked in my family's general store. The following year we moved to Madison, and I started at the University of Wisconsin. Like Alonzo, I had a break in my studies, so it was 1925 when I received my B.A. in Economics. When the hoped-for teaching position failed to materialize, I took temporary jobs near home. Then in March I moved into a permanent position compiling medical statistics at Mayo Clinic in Rochester, Minnesota.

The afternoon passed quickly. In the evening we went canoeing on Lake Mendota — and became engaged.

When Alonzo asked me to set a date for the wedding, I suggested October.

"That would be a nice month," he said, "but I'm going back to Europe and Africa in July and will be gone a year." We settled on the 20th of July.

Later, when Alonzo told his cousin that he was going to be married, she laughed, "Any woman would marry you for a honeymoon in Europe."

"I didn't tell her I was going back until after she'd said 'Yes'," he replied.

I went back to the Mayo Clinic to resign and pack my things. Alonzo went back to Beloit where he was Assistant Curator of the Logan Museum.

It was a hectic six weeks. I had to buy clothes for a year, and my trousseau included formal clothes for the Captain's dinner on the ship and for the opera in Paris, as well as riding trousers and high boots for archaeological diggings in North Africa. At last, however, my trunk was packed and sent to the ship in New York.

We were married on one of the hottest days of the year. Next morning we took the train for New York, stopping in Chicago and Washington, D.C. It seemed to me that at every stop, dozens of aunts, uncles, cousins, and friends came to the hotel to meet the bride. Even in New York there were aunts and cousins of Alonzo's mother. At last we boarded the *S.S. Orduna* and sailed away.

The Atlantic was as calm as a mill pond that July, and we both agreed we could have paddled a canoe across it and never shipped water. The moon was full and silvered the ripples on the ocean. We never tired of standing on the stern of the ship watching the little phosphorescent animals glowing in the wake of the ship.

The passengers at our table kept wondering if we were newlyweds or not. Finally one of them asked my husband if I was a good cook. He turned to me and said, "Are you?" That settled the question for our tablemates.

As we stepped off the boat onto the pier at Cherbourg, Alonzo said, "Remember, we are *foreigners* now." It was a concept I never forgot.

Such a honeymoon it was! We wandered through Paris holding hands like other lovers and kissed under the dim street lamps. We watched the children sail their toy boats in the Luxembourg Gardens. We went to Père Lachaise Cemetery and saw the graves of Abelard and Heloise, those medieval lovers almost as familiar as Romeo and Juliet. Evenings we sipped coffee at the sidewalk cafés on the Left Bank. We stayed on the Left Bank because Alonzo had his first room there when he went to the University and had been going back there every time he went to Paris, a practice we continued.

In the middle of August we took the overnight train to Czechoslovakia. The trip was a kaleidoscope of European scenes: the Cologne cathedral standing out like a white cameo, its brightly lit steeples towering over the almost dark city at midnight; women in the countryside carrying loads on their heads; the Black Forest with its towering spruces; red geraniums in "window boxes" around the lamp posts in Pilsen; girls at the railroad station calling *"Bier, bitte,"* *"Bier, bitte sehr,"* as they held up full steins of amber liquid with heads like whipped cream.

Prague was the site of more history than I had ever dreamed of. We saw the famous Street of the Alchemists, but I liked the places next to the city wall better. Here, ex-soldiers were given land to build retirement homes. They were only sixteen feet wide, and some were only that long. One made me remember a playhouse I had as a little girl.

At Brno, we met Dr. Karel Absolon, head of the prehistory department of Czechoslovakia. He showed us the digging sites at Wisternitz and Olmutz. On another trip, we followed an underground passage and came out on the floor of a large, sunlit rock bowl. The sides went up and up 450 feet. A clear stream entered the cave a little at one side, ran across the cave floor, and disappeared beneath a rock.

Mrs. Absolon was born a countess and entertained us at their ancestral villa. We entered through a wooden gate carved with peacocks and drove down a wooded road to the summer home. She spoke English, so I did not feel left out of the conversation. Sometimes we got confused, as when I said with assurance that it had rained tomorrow in Prague, and Mrs. Absolon excused herself to "eat" her hungry baby. On the whole we got on rather well, though.

One day while driving through a village, we saw a wedding party. The bride's veil was held on with a wreath of fresh ivy, and small circles of ivy were scattered over the veil.

On to Vienna, where we drove around the Ringstrasse, saw where Marie Theresa lived and where Johann Strauss wrote his beautiful music. My biggest thrill was that night at the theater when four pianists played the "Blue Danube Waltz."

We got to Innsbruck at night, and the mountains seemed menacing, the lights on them so high and scattered, but the next morning it was beautiful with the city nestled in the valley. The mountains went up and up until the tops were lost in the clouds.

The next day we traveled through the Alps, sometimes going through them in tunnels, sometimes going around them in steep-sided valleys. When we reached

Zurich, we found a hotel near the lake. All evening we heard yodeling by young people in the boats.

Geneva was an international city. Its League of Nations gave it world prestige. Its shops were the costliest and filled with marvelous goods. We looked for a souvenir we could afford and finally settled on a little circlet of edelweiss carved in ivory. At sunset, I looked out of my hotel window and saw the lovely alpine rose tint the slopes of Mt. Blanc.

The next day our trip to Chamonix was interesting but scary. We took a cogwheel railway up Mt. Blanc. It seemed to push us up two feet and slide back six inches all the way up. At last we reached the top and enjoyed a lunch in the small hotel there. Below us stretched the *Mer de Glace*, and Alonzo decided to go out on it. I sat on a boulder near the edge of the glacier and heard the crunch of stones as the glacier moved over them, but I couldn't see anything move. I watched Alonzo walking around the broken ice surface and began to worry when he couldn't find his way back. There were deep crevasses everywhere. After a half hour he made his way back to a very frightened bride.

Several days later we were back in France and went down to Les Eyzies de Tayac.

"We must go and see the Maurys. They want to meet you," said Alonzo.

We walked a kilometer down the Vézère River road to the Maurys' home. It was a house with three sides of brick. The fourth side was the stone cliff which went up about three hundred feet above the house. About a hundred feet farther on was Laugerie Basse, a prehistoric site. M. Maury was a Parisian who had bought the site and made a meager living by showing it. A year before, he had followed a little trickle of water high on the cliff side, blasting away 200 feet of rock and finally opening a cave that had never seen daylight. It was a wonderland of stalactites, stalagmites, and helictites. His two daughters were thrilled, as it meant sizeable dowries for them.

"How goes it? How goes it? *M*. Pond and *Mme*. Pond," they all cried and talked together.

We became friends immediately.

Les Eyzies has been called the capital of the prehistoric world. We saw the rock shelter where Cro-Magnon man had been discovered. We saw the caves of La Mouthe, Combarelles, Cap Blanc, and Font de Gaume. We saw where Aurignacians had worked and where Magdalenians had painted bison on cave walls. It was a kaleidoscopic trip in prehistory, and now we were ready to go to work.

Work meant digging in shell mounds in Algeria. The Logan Museum, a teaching museum of Beloit College, needed collections of Stone Age artifacts to illustrate the courses. Alonzo had spent three years in Europe studying and buying collections, but they were expensive and did not always include artifacts to illustrate every culture. The trip into the Sahara had convinced him that North Africa was rich in prehistoric habitation sites and that it would be cheaper and better to collect the tools of Stone Age man by digging them himself.

An agreement had been made between Dr. George L. Collie, Curator of the museum, and the Algerian government to allow us to dig in the prehistoric mounds, dividing the collections made with the Algerian Department of Antiquities. Dr. Frank G. Logan, sponsor of the Logan Museum, agreed to subsidize the expedition.

We took the train from Les Eyzies to Marseilles and boarded the *S.S.Timgad*. The *Timgad* was a special boat for us. The year before, Alonzo had written his first letter to me from her deck. It was just noon when the ship pulled away from the dock. Other passengers who were used to ferrying from Marseilles to Algiers rushed to the dining salon, but we lingered on deck. As the boat glided through the harbor, Alonzo pointed to a castle and said, "That's the *Château d'If* where the Man in the Iron Mask was imprisoned. Someday when we have more time we'll visit the castle and the dungeon."

Our last view of the coast of France was the tall spires of *Notre-Dame de la Garde*, the sailors' church perched high on a peak above the Mediterranean. All afternoon we sat in our deck chairs and watched the blue sea.

"The Mediterranean is just as blue as picture postcards show it, isn't it?" I remarked.

"Yes, they don't exaggerate a bit."

The bright sunshine and the softness of the air reminded me of warm October days back in my Wisconsin home, now so far away. Our ship plowed steadily through a calm sea.

After dinner we stood at the rail watching the moon rise big and golden. From the afterdeck came the haunting strains of a flute.

"It's probably some homesick shepherd boy," my husband said. "He's dreaming of once again driving his flocks out to pasture."

The plaintive tune, the warm breeze, the golden light of the moon on the water, all made the evening one of exciting anticipation for the new country to which I was going.

2

The White City of Algiers

*V*ery early the next morning the *Timgad* slipped between the walls of the breakwater at Algiers. When we woke it was a bright, hot morning. After a quick continental breakfast of *brioche* and *café au lait*, we went on deck with the other passengers to wait for port officials to come aboard. Some of the tourists threw coins over the railing and watched Arab boys dive for them. The boys would dive only for five-franc pieces; they would not bother with copper *centime* pieces.

The third-class passengers, mostly Arabs, were huddled on the afterdeck. Each had a bundle or small trunk. They would be the last to debark. Porters in red fezzes and grimy, white robes ran back and forth along the quay shouting to the passengers on deck and trying to make a deal to carry their luggage.

"We'd better wait until we debark," Alonzo said. "With our two trunks and eight pieces of hand luggage, we'll need a man with a cart."

Above the gesticulating, shouting crowd rose the white city of Algiers, tier upon tier, like a great wedding cake, the top crowned by a tiny fort. Along the shore was *Boulevard de la République*, its colonnaded buildings facing the sea. Just to the right, the tall palms of a park rattled their fronds in the morning breeze.

Once on land and settled in our hotel room, I was eager to start getting acquainted with these new surroundings.

Algiers was an exciting city and my first touch with the Middle East. Like all North African cities, it was a good mixture of Western influence and the culture of the East; even the street names were a blend of East and West. We strolled down the *rue Bab-Azoun* to the *rue Michelet*. We saw the new Post Office, a large, white building in Moorish style. In the next block, housed in a building that reminded us of the arcaded *rue de Rivoli*, was the Algiers branch of the *Galeries Lafayette*, a large Parisian department store.

S.S. Timgad in Algiers Harbor.

As we passed the Post Office, a young Muslim came down the steps. His pleated, white trousers tucked into his high, white boots, his cape-like *burnous* flung casually over his shoulders, and his spotless white turban crisscrossed with black cords made him a romantic figure.

"Do you suppose he's a sheik?" I said, my mind full of Rudolph Valentino in the movies.

"Probably not. Perhaps he's the son of a wealthy merchant."

"Oh." I murmured disappointedly. "But he looks like a sheik ought to look."

We strolled on down the *rue Michelet*. The store windows displayed dresses, purses, and shoes every bit as chic as those I had seen in Paris a month before. In fact, Algiers liked to call itself "The Little Paris."

"Look," I whispered to my husband. "There is a veiled woman."

He looked over toward the window and saw a woman in a long, white robe covering her from her head to her feet. A veil across her face allowed only her eyes to show, and these were modestly cast down. The tinkle of her silver anklets as she walked made a pleasant sound. She, too, was looking at those Paris clothes.

At the end of the street we reached the *Café de Tantonville* and slipped behind a glass-topped table and ordered an aperitif. Three white-turbaned Arabs sat at a nearby table. They were seriously discussing something as they sipped their coffee. First one would shake his head, then another would.

"Could they be plotting intrigue?" I said with my head still full of Hollywood movies.

"Oh. I don't think so. They're probably discussing closing prices of the Paris *Bourse* or the future of the winter wheat crops."

I decided right then to give up Hollywood.

On our way back to the hotel, we stopped at the flower market and browsed.

"What do you want to make the room more home-like?" asked Alonzo.

"Let's have the golden mimosa balls; they'll bring sunshine into the room."

We bought an armful of them and decorated our room.

The next day Alonzo had official calls to make, so while he went to the U.S. Consulate and called on the Algerian Minister of Antiquities, I explored the shops.

At the edge of a little square, I timidly peeked into an open doorway, then walked in to a shop that could have been the setting for an Arabian nights tale. Low divans and tables of dark wood were heavily carved and inset with mother-of-pearl. Red leather cushions, heavily embossed, were tossed carelessly on low benches. Shining brass lanterns hung from the ceiling. Brass trays holding brass coffee pots and tiny cups were placed on small tables. Counters held leather purses embroidered in silver and gold. Glass showcases allowed one to see trays of silver jewelry made in Arabic style set with heavy turquoises and coral. In another case unset topaz, amethysts, and aquamarines sparkled from their velvet cushions. Wide-eyed, I went from table to counter to case. At last I chose two finger bowls deeply etched with Arabic designs, and when I left I said to myself, "I'm coming back another day with lots more money."

The next afternoon we were invited to M. Basiaux's for coffee. Alonzo had met him on his way back from the Sahara in the spring. M. Basiaux had made a fortune harvesting alpha grass and shipping it to England, where it was used in making fine paper. He had just built a new home in Mustapha Superior, a suburb overlooking Algiers. He met us at the door and introduced me to Madame Basiaux.

"I thought it would be pleasant to have coffee on the balcony," she said as she led us through the living room to a small porch which overlooked a large lawn and formal flower beds. As soon as we were seated, she brought out a coffee set and small cakes. We sipped our coffee, visited, and looked out over the city and the harbor to the Mediterranean.

"Where are the girls?" asked Alonzo.

"The three oldest are not home from school, and the younger ones are with their nurse," Madame Basiaux answered.

A few minutes later she said, "Here are the girls."

From the living room doorway came a line of six girls, the oldest first, and down the line. Madame Basiaux presented each of them to me, "Renée, Yvonne, Odette, Paulette, Nadine, and Claudie."

They came forward singly, shook hands with Alonzo and me, and murmured, "I'm pleased to make your acquaintance."

The three youngest were excused to go back to their nursery, but the three oldest girls stayed and had coffee with us.

"How is school going?" asked Alonzo.

"Very well," Renée replied.

Yvonne shook her head. "I don't like school."

We spent a pleasant afternoon. About sunset we took a cab back to our hotel with a promise to come to dinner several days later.

Our next visit was very informal. We were invited to the kitchen, where Yvonne was beating something furiously in a bowl. We looked inquiringly at her.

"Why do you beat it so vigorously," Alonzo asked.

She stopped the egg beater. "One doesn't have to know when Charlemagne ruled to make good mayonnaise!" she answered emphatically.

"She likes to cook, but she doesn't like school," her mother noted.

The villa was large. White walls contrasted with dark ceiling beams and arched doorways. The solid wood furniture was dark and massive. Oriental rugs were scattered over the parquet floors. The house was built on a side hill. The living room, the dining room, and kitchen were on the first floor, the bedrooms on the ground floor. The girls' dormitory was a long, narrow room with three white beds and three dressers along each side. There was a large bathroom at the far end.

Seniority was the rule in this household. When *mamam* was away, Renée was in charge, and if she was gone, then Yvonne took over. Yvonne had only to mind Renée, but poor little Claudie had five sisters to tell her what to do and what not to do. There was a maid and a nurse, but Madame Basiaux kept a tight rein on the household, and every member of the family had her responsibilities.

3

The Casbah

"Come weez me to zee Casbah," said Charles Boyer, but long before he made that phrase famous, the native quarter in Algiers beckoned us. The guidebook had said that it was better to take a cab to the top of the mountain and walk down through the native quarter. All streets led down, and you eventually would come out in the French city.

One afternoon we took their advice and dismissed our cab in front of the fort on the top of the mountain: We entered one of the twisting, narrow streets that form a labyrinth on the mountain slopes above the bay of Algiers.

"Here comes a donkey with loaded panniers," said Alonzo. "Step into this doorway so that he can pass."

The street was so narrow that the loaded baskets brushed us as he climbed the hill.

We had left the bright sunshine for the gloom of the Casbah. The walls were continuous, running along each side of the street as far down as one could see. The entrance to each house was a carved doorway with a heavy wooden door with hammered iron hinges. Infrequently we saw a carved wooden grill high above the street. The second stories were set out and almost touched each other. They were supported by heavy wooden beams set slanting into the house wall. As we walked down the street, we went from dark tunnels into bright sunlight where single-story houses let the light in. The streets were paved with rough blocks of stone. Several hundred years of wear from sandals and unshod donkeys' hooves still had not worn them smooth. Every twenty feet or so was a shallow step. No wheeled vehicle could ever have negotiated those streets.

A side street branched off, and the wall where the two met was a water fountain. We saw veiled women filling water jars. These public fountains were the only source of water for many homes.

We stopped to look into a native café. Through wide arches, we could see white-robed, white-turbaned men, sitting cross-legged at low, green tables. A waiter passed among them serving small cups of black coffee or small glasses of mint tea. Near the back we could see the caller for the seemingly never-ending games of the Arabic version of Bingo.

Again, we stopped before a hardware store, really just a hole in the wall. Pots, pans, and jars were set on mats around the tiny room. The proprietor sat in the doorway. If we had really been interested in purchasing, he would have roused himself to bargain with us, but for mere browsers, it wasn't worthwhile.

Close to the end of the street, near the bottom of the hill, we found the shop of a fabric merchant. There were heavy bolts of damask and lighter bolts of crepe, all in pinks, blues, and yellows. Some of the satins had flower designs in threads of gold and silver, some designs were made with small, pearl beads. It was as if we had been transported to the bazaars of Arabian Nights.

As the guidebook had said, we found ourselves back in the French city, and we slowly made our way to the *Tantonville*, where we ordered a lemonade.

Another day, Alonzo came back to our room at noon and said, "Monsieur Jougla is taking us up on the Casbah tonight. The lady with him will not be Madame Jougla but his mistress."

Monsieur Jougla was a friend that Alonzo had made on a trip to Algiers that spring. He had taken Mlle. S. to a party where M. Jougla had had to appear with his wife.

At nine o'clock that night M. Jougla and Mlle. S. came to the hotel. Mlle. S. was a very attractive, blonde young woman. With them was a policeman.

"It's really not so dangerous," said M. Jougla, "but he is a good guide, and it is always well to have a policeman along to protect one from cheap thugs."

We left the brightly lighted streets of the French city and entered the Casbah. It was dimly lit and we stumbled along the rough stones. The policeman stopped at a heavy wooden door and knocked. It opened just a crack. Our guide conversed in low tones with someone inside, then the door opened wide, and we entered. It was a narrow, dark hallway lit by a single candle. A shadowy form led us up a steep stairway and into a room with many mirrors on the walls and low divans along the side. The only illumination came from candles sputtering in wall sconces. We seated ourselves on the divans, and three musicians who were in the corner commenced to play weird Arab music. Two fifes played the melody, and a drummer beat the rhythm on a small pottery drum with a goatskin stretched over it.

Hollywood could not have done better with a stage setting, I thought.

We were the only patrons, but perhaps this had been arranged.

Soon three native girls, *toutes nues*, came from an adjoining room and took poses in the center of the room. All were accomplished belly dancers, and we were intrigued by movements of abdominal muscles while the rest of the body was still. To our unaccustomed ears, the music had little variation, and the dancing was more contortionist than seductive. A half hour was enough of such entertainment, and we left by the same dark stairway.

Out on the street again, our policeman took us to another, larger café closer to the French city.

"This is called the Spanish House," said M. Jougla. "It is not really a native brothel but more international and caters to ships in port."

Again the policeman rapped, and the door opened wide, and we stepped into a well-lighted room. We sat at a small table and a waiter soon came.

"Champagne for all of us," said M. Jougla.

I looked around the room. The walls were painted with pornographic pictures. There was a small stage at one end, and soon a blonde girl appeared. She was dressed in long, black silk stockings, fancy garters and high heeled shoes. Nothing else. I can't even remember her coiffeur.

Mlle. S. whispered to me, "All the girls wear stockings. It is considered very vulgar to appear with bare legs and feet."

It was difficult to guess the nationality of the entertainer. She may have been English. She neither spoke nor sang, but she did dance for us while we sipped our champagne. Her dancing was erotic for those days, but today it would be considered very mild.[2]

Again we were the only patrons, and apparently our time had been specifically allotted. The policeman got up after we had been there half an hour and finished our champagne. We walked back to the hotel, where we said goodnight to M. Jougla and his charming mistress.

Several years later I told an American friend who had lived in Cairo, Egypt, about the evening.

"Oh, the Spanish House in Algiers is famous, or infamous if you prefer, all along the Mediterranean coast," she said.

All too soon we had to leave Algiers for our diggings on the High Plateau. As our train pulled out of the station, we said *"à bientôt,"* for we knew we would be back at Christmas.

---

2. This was written in 1976.

4

Châteaudun du Rhumel

*T*he train from Constantine paused at a bleak and cold station on the treeless plain. We climbed down onto a deserted platform while our trunks and other luggage were unloaded from the baggage car. The engineer blew his squeaky whistle; steam clouds hid the turning wheels, and we stood alone with our luggage.

As the little train disappeared, a taxi rolled up in a cloud of dust. We piled into the touring car with our suitcases. There were three of us now, for we had stopped in Constantine to meet our French colleague, M. Arthur Debruge. He would work with us throughout the winter. He was a retired postal employee whose hobby was archaeology and who had spent many vacations digging in the prehistoric shell mounds of North Africa. His snapping brown eyes and "walrus" mustache gave him a fierce look that belied his real nature. During the months that we worked together, we came to have a real affection for him, and we called him Debby between ourselves but *never* to his face. That would have been too undignified.

Fifteen minutes later our taxi stopped in front of a small hotel in the village of Châteaudun du Rhumel[3]. The truck with our trunks came, too. As I looked at the solid wooden door with the words *"Hôtel des Voyageurs"* painted above it, I thought, This is the half-way house to the Stone Age, and I wasn't far wrong.

The door opened and a young Muslim came out saying, *"Bonjour, Messieurs, Madame."* He gathered up as many pieces of our luggage as he could carry and led the way into a small bar, on through the kitchen to a courtyard, up an outside stairway, down a short hall and into a room facing the street. While he went down for the rest of our luggage, the proprietor came in.

---

3. Now Chelgoum Laïd.

Left: Alonzo Pond. Right: Arthur Debruge.

"I hope this will be satisfactory," he said. "It is the best room in the hotel." He looked at the shallow fireplace. "Heat is not furnished, but you can buy wood, and the boy will always build a fire when you need it."

We immediately ordered a load of wood.

Our trunks were carried up and put in a corner of the room. By placing most of our other luggage under the bed, we made an aisle from the door to the front window which opened onto a balcony. There was just room for one person to stand in front of the washstand. A small table and two straight-backed chairs stood at one wall. The bed occupied the rest of the room.

"Where is the W.C.?" I asked.

The French had taken the letters for the English "water closet" to designate their toilets.

"Off the courtyard at the foot of the stairs, the first door on your left," answered the proprietor.

Later, when I went downstairs, I found the "W.C." was certainly a misnomer. There was no flush toilet, just a small closet-like room with a tile floor sloping gently from all sides to a hole in the middle. There was no seat. One squatted.

We lost no time in having Tyeb, the young Muslim, build a fire. It was November, and it was chilly. A few days later we discovered that the back of our fireplace was a thin sheet of metal. Our fire heated the room next to us as much as it did our room. We insisted that M. Debruge, who had an unheated room down the hall, move next door and share our heat.

We spent our first day in Châteaudun getting acquainted with the town and making arrangements for a car to take us out to our diggings five miles south. Châteaudun was like all "Main Street" towns with several blocks of stores and offices lining the highway from Constantine to Sétif. It did not take us long to walk past the two banks, two garages, several grocery stores, church, school and town hall.

The two hundred French citizens lived on the side streets. Perhaps there were as many natives, but their houses, school, and mosque were on the edge of town.

The next morning our alarm went off at 5:30. I stretched my arm out from under the down puff to shut it off.

"It's cold."

Alonzo laughed and said, "If we hurry, we'll soon be down in the bar having a cup of hot coffee."

I reached out and pulled my clothes into the bed with me. Using my head for a prop, I made a tent of the bed clothes and dressed in the cozy warmth as I had when I was in grade school back in Sun Prairie, Wisconsin. My high boots had to wait until I got out from under the "tent." My husband kept laughing at me and told me about the winter he and his brother slept out in a tent in their backyard in southern Wisconsin, how they'd wake up in the morning, put on their robes and slippers, and dash through the snow to the warm house.

Soon we were dressed in long underwear, riding trousers, wool shirts, and high boots. Grabbing up caps, sweaters, and jackets we hurried out the door and down the courtyard stairway into the bar where Debby was waiting for us. His trousers were tucked into high boots making them look like knickers. He wore a little round high hat with the brim turned up, and he looked just like a wide-eyed little boy about to start out for a *big* adventure.

A loaf of crisp French bread and a pot of strong black coffee and one of hot milk for *café au lait* soon made the day seem livable. At 6:30 the car horn blared. We picked up a lunch the cook had packed and hurried out to the car. It was the same open taxi that had brought us to the hotel. Debby got in front with the chauffeur, and Alonzo and I huddled down in the back seat.

We drove through a drab countryside. The fields were brown with stubble, pasturage was scanty, and the horizon rimmed us in with brown, barren mountains. The few trees we saw were along the side streets in town or in farmyards where they could be watered by hand. We reached the farmstead where we would be working, and M. and Mme. Deloulle welcomed us. The men went to check out the site of the diggings. Mme. Deloulle and I stayed in her warm kitchen and began to get acquainted.

An hour later the men came in. Madame had made fresh coffee and got out the cookie jar. We all enjoyed a second breakfast, but not too much time was spent over coffee for the workmen were waiting.

"Come, boys," said M. Delloule to his sons, "let's all go out and watch the start of these new diggings."

So, bundled up in caps and jackets, we went out to the gray mound of snail shells and ashes left by the Stone Age campers.

The Delloules were not the first people to have lived on this site. Thousands of years ago prehistoric people used it as a habitation site. They had dined mostly on snails with a roast of wild ox now and then. Today, careless campers throw their fried-chicken bones over their shoulders. Is that a heritage from those ancient people who dropped the empty snail shells around the campfires and built up large mounds?

Just as every housewife sometimes loses a spoon, a knife, or a needle, so these prehistoric people also lost their tools in the ashes of their campsite. It was these tools that we had come all the way from America to collect.

The mound had been worked by archaeologists several times before, so Alonzo and Debby chose an undisturbed section. The workmen had cleared the loose surface soil and debris from the top and were already down to a hard layer of calcite which covered the entire mound. It had been deposited by water leaching lime from the shells and forming an impervious layer on the compact ashes a foot or so below the top of the mound. Beneath that hard crust was the undisturbed campsite refuse of prehistoric man.

A square yard had been marked off on the ground. Alonzo picked up a pick-ax and swung it gently, loosening a shovelful of dirt. He motioned to a workman to take a shovel and put the material on the wheelbarrow. Then Alonzo loosened another shovelful. As the workman put his shovel to the ground, the soil fell away from a flint point.

Excavation of Mechta el Arbi. Debby in right foreground; Alonzo Pond in right background.

"Good," cried Debby. "A good sign." He reached over and carefully picked up the weapon point out of the ground and laid it in a box.

As soon as the barrow was filled, another workman wheeled it to a fine gravel screen that had been set up so that the breeze would carry the fine dust and ashes through the mesh. A third workman threw a small shovelful from the barrow against the screen. The dirt went through the screen, and the shells fell down in front. Debby stood watching ready to retrieve any piece of worked flint or bone that had eluded us at the diggings. Our fourth workman was already waiting at the site with another barrow to fill.

"Stop," said my husband to the man with the shovel. Then Alonzo knelt down, and with a camel's hair brush, he gently brushed away the soil from a bone sliver. It fell into his hand and he held it up. "Bone awl, probably used to make holes in skins to run sinews through. Perhaps for lacing a cape-like garment."

Eleven o'clock came.

"Lunch time," said my husband.

The workmen went home to their huts, and we picked up our lunch basket from the farmhouse and found a spot in the sun beside a large straw stack.

"I wonder what the cook gave us for lunch," I said as I opened the basket. "Oh, bread, cheese, sausage, and tangerines."

"No wine?" asked Debby.

"Oh yes. Here in the corner is a bottle."

Alonzo went to the pump and got a dipper of water to dilute the wine, French fashion.

Lunch finished, Alonzo looked at the straw stack. "This looks like a good place for a nap," he said, as he pulled away some

Alonzo Pond at Mechta el Arbi.

25

straw and made a little niche high enough so the sheep and goats wouldn't nibble at our toes. We crawled into the little shelter and relaxed until 12:30 when it was time to go back to work.

The afternoon's work produced a couple of little flat round pieces of flint a little bigger than a thumb nail. "Scrapers," said Debby. "Used to scrape the fat off of hides."

At three o'clock Madame Delloule sent little Jacques out to say, "Please come in, Madame Pond, and have a cup of coffee."

In the warm kitchen Madame Delloule and I munched cookies and tried to compare our countries by finding customs common to both.

Throughout the winter Madame Delloule was very kind to the young bride in a strange country and in pioneer surroundings beginning a strange work. One day, later on in the winter, she saw me sitting alone on a packing box. She thought that I looked homesick, so she went into her garden and picked a bunch of violets. "Do you have these in your Wisconsin?" she asked as she handed them out to me.

The car came at four o'clock. Tiredly, we climbed in and were soon back at the hotel. As we went through the kitchen up to our room we called, "Tyeb, please make us a fire quickly."

Flames soon were crackling in the fireplace. The day before, we had bought a large enamelware coffee pot. I filled it with water from the pitcher and shoved it close to the fire. We had warm water for our sponge baths.

I changed into a dress. Alonzo put on clean clothes, and we settled down in front of the fire to read our mail. The Paris edition of the *New York Herald* was four to six days late; nevertheless, it kept us up to date with the news back in our country.

At six o'clock we went down to join Debby in the dining room just off the bar. Tyeb brought a soup tureen filled with rich broth, vegetables, and chunks of French bread floating on top. Although this was a small hotel in a "backwoods" town, the Europeans kept to the French custom of dining in courses. Soup plates were removed and were followed by a fish course. After that came a dish of green beans. Then Tyeb brought us roast of mutton, with cloves of garlic stuck into it to hide the "muttony" taste. We had mutton almost every day. It was more than a year after that before I could think of buying a clove of garlic, even to flavor a salad bowl. A canister of oil and vinegar was always on the table, as well as pepper and salt. Dessert was a tangerine for each of us and black coffee.

We lingered over coffee to listen to the men tease Tyeb. He was a handsome young man with merry, brown eyes and a close-clipped mustache. The black tassel on his red fez bobbed as he hurried to keep up with his duties of waiter, chambermaid, potato peeler, dish washer, and errand boy. He had just been married and was still the object of many jokes.

"Tyeb, when you can, will you take a second wife?" asked one of the men.

Tyeb shook his head emphatically. "No! A man is a fool to have more than one wife. They are always fighting."

When we were in Algeria the custom of polygamy was slowly dying out. The Qur'an decrees that each wife must be treated equally in housing, in clothing, in attention paid to her. Many natives were no longer nomads but were becoming urbanized. They had jobs with definite hours, and housing was difficult to find. A house with two or three rooms did not take much housework. The women were bored, and as Tyeb said, they quarreled.

Out in the country there were many sheep and goats to care for and milk; much wool had to be carded and spun and woven into clothes. Grain had to be ground by hand and made into bread or couscous. Pottery utensils were homemade. Among the nomads, we often found two or three wives in a household. They were needed and kept busy.

Remembering that 5:30 comes early in the morning, we left the jovial crowd and went upstairs to our room.

And so we established a routine, and the days went on. On rainy days we didn't go out to the diggings but stayed in our room to wash and sort the collection of artifacts. Some days we just found duplicates of which we already had dozens; other days were red letter days when we found a polished bone dagger twelve inches long or the skull of a prehistoric ox with horns attached, the spread of the horns about five feet.

Archaeologists are incurable optimists. The next stroke of the pick may turn up a beautifully worked dagger or weapon point, or it may turn up... nothing.

Of course, the thing that every archaeologist is looking for is a skeleton of primitive man in an undisturbed deposit that can be accurately dated.

Debby with ox horns.

Child's skull.

One gray winter day I was watching the material as it was shoveled into the wheelbarrow. Debby was at the gravel screen, and Alonzo was wielding the pick.

We were almost at the bottom of the deposit. The pick uncovered a smooth, round object.

Alonzo carefully put the pick away from the trench side. "Where's my brush?" he asked. I took it from our case of tools and handed it to him. He brushed away some dirt. "It's bone."

"Stop work and come quickly," I called to Debby. He came at a run. I pointed to where Alonzo was working. Debby knelt down beside him.

The workmen, too, came crowding around. I motioned to them to keep back so that no surface soil would fall into the trench. Fifteen minutes of careful brushing, and there was a baby's skull!

"It's beautiful," cried Debby. "It's a Stone Age baby."

"Keep everyone away while I get my camera and take pictures of it *in situ,*" my husband ordered.

After many shots in order to authenticate its place in the deposit, Alonzo carefully lifted the skull into a box that I had found.

That night at the hotel we packed it in cotton batting ready for shipment to the States for study. After that, it would be returned to the Ethnological museum in Algiers.

When we released the publicity about finding a 60,000 year old[4] baby's skull, Russell Crouse, columnist for the *New York Post*, quipped, "Alonzo W. Pond has returned from North Africa with the skull of a child 60,000 years old. If he had lived he might have been a big help to his parents."

---

4. Some years later this site (Mechta el Arbi) was dated to 7000-10,000 B.C..

5

Vignettes

*A*nthropologists are interested in everything, no matter what their specialty is. I learned that Alonzo was almost as eager to learn the modern native customs as he was to dig up the Old Stone Age culture. Our cameras went everywhere with us.

Sunday was our day of rest from the diggings. Debby took the bus back to Constantine Saturday night to spend Sunday with his family, so we were by ourselves for the weekend. Our first Sunday in Châteaudun was a bright, sunny day.

"It looks like a good day for pictures," Alonzo said at breakfast.

Loaded down with cameras and equipment, we set out to explore the village. There was not much action. The main street was almost deserted because the European stores were closed, so we headed out toward the Muslim part of town. They would be open, since they close on Friday instead for their weekly congregational prayer and worship. As we passed the school for native children, we saw the boys were working a fenced-in garden. Ten-year-olds were hoeing weeds, working as rhythmically as a line of chorus dancers.

"That looks like a picture," said Alonzo and asked the teacher if he might take a photograph.

"Yes," the teacher replied.

Alonzo put the camera to his eye and focused it. He was just ready to snap the shutter when the teacher gave a command. All the boys turned their backs to the camera just as it clicked. My husband grinned, thanked the teacher, and we walked on. The old Muslim custom of not making an image of any living thing apparently was still believed here. That was not wholly true in the marketplace.

On our first market day, Debby went to the diggings alone, and we loaded ourselves with a movie camera, two still cameras, a tripod, a bag of extra film, and lenses. We resembled the poor little burros with heavily laden saddlebags as they took produce to market.

Filming with movie camera at Châteaudun market.

The market square was on the west edge of town, a half city block, enclosed with a five-foot adobe wall topped with red tile. For awhile we stood outside the gate and watched the herders with their flocks of sheep and goats. As each shepherd passed through the gate, a French official counted the sheep or goats and recorded the number. There was a tax on sheep, but I don't know whether the buyer or the seller paid.

Then we, too, went through the gate, greeting the gatekeeper, *"Bonjour, Monsieur."*

My first impression was a picture in monotone gray. Herds of gray sheep were tethered about the square. A few gray tents were scattered here and there. Several hundred Muslims in tattle-tale gray robes, turbans, and grimy *burnouses* were milling about. Even the gray-brown camels and burros melted into the drabness of the scene.

I looked around and realized I was the only woman in the marketplace. Muslim women never go to market. Whether the French women were there earlier or bought their produce from the grocery stores, I don't know.

"There are some crates near the wall," Alonzo said. "I'm going to climb up and get a panorama of this."

I found myself alone, hemmed in by native men. It was an upsetting experience for a shy, young woman in a strange country, but when Alonzo climbed down from the wall and found his way to me, the crowd dispersed.

The meat market was just to the right. Skinned carcasses of sheep and goats hung on tripods, unprotected from the open air, a dusty gust of wind, or a few flies. All the animals had been government inspected at the time of butchering.

"Here's their version of our hot dog man," said my husband. We stopped beside a young man who squatted before a small fire over which bits of sheep kidney on skewers were broiling on a grate. We were not hungry. Anyway, barbecued kidney is not my favorite snack.

We walked on. "Notice how they tether the sheep." Alonzo pointed to two tightly packed rows of sheep facing each other. A rope was interlaced around their necks so that one sheep could not move without shoving the whole flock.

"Goats usually stand by themselves," he continued. Just then I was butted by a frisky young goat that had gotten away from the flock. A young boy ran up, grabbed the kid by one leg, and unceremoniously dragged him back to the flock.

As we went past the camel market, I saw a baby camel, perhaps only a day old.

"Oh, do take his picture,"

As Alonzo put the camera to his face, the owner came up and said, "Don't take it! If the picture should get torn or punctured, the camel would die."

We missed a good picture so a baby camel could live happily ever after.

There were a couple of skinny horses in the far corner but no one seemed interested in buying them. At the burro market a dozen men clustered around. One was a prospective buyer, and the owner decided to demonstrate the strength of the animal. He made the burro kneel and motioned for two men to get on. By pulling on the halter the owner urged the burro to rise. With very little difficulty the little animal got up, lifting the two men on his back. Then the buyer asked the price; the seller replied. The buyer's arms flew in the air; he shouted and gestured. The owner raised his arms and shouted back. Each man waved his fist in the other man's face.

"Are they going to fight?" I asked.

"No, they're just bargaining."

You could just imagine them saying, "A thousand francs for that moth-eaten carcass?"

"What, you'd rob me of my best and strongest animal. Nine hundred francs."

"Ho, he thinks he's selling a horse," sneered the buyer. "I'll give you five hundred."

"Why you old rascal. I wouldn't take less than eight hundred and fifty."

"That old skin and bones isn't worth more than seven hundred."

"Eight hundred, and that's my lowest."

All this time the men were waving their arms and shouting.

"I'll give you seven hundred and fifty, or you can keep your animal."

The owner brought his arms down, stretched out his hand, and the two men shook hands. The buyer took a leather sack from a pocket inside his robe and passed over some money. Both men smiled and walked over to a tent café where the seller bought cups of strong black coffee. The men seated themselves on the ground and chatted amiably. Buying and selling in Algeria is dramatic and fun, even for the onlooker.

It was late in the season, and the vegetable market had only heaps of potatoes and small piles of green peppers. We found little of interest in that area.

The young boys in the marketplace were not afraid of the Muslim taboo about pictures. Everywhere that Alonzo went with his cameras, especially the movie, the boys ran ahead and turned to make faces at the camera and wave their hands, hoping they'd star in a movie.

"There's a group of children over there. Let's go over," I said.

"It's the candy man. He's the Pied Piper at every fair."

The day before, we had seen the candy man pulling his "salt water taffy" in front of his little shop near the hotel. Muslims love children, and in the festive atmosphere of the marketplace, the dirty little urchins, with their whining "Penny, please," were very seldom denied. For a penny one could buy one of those brilliant pink pieces of sweetness.

Our next stop was the old clothes market. Trousers with patches on the knees, vests, coats with holes at the elbows, and all minus buttons which had been removed to put on newer garments, were all spread out on the ground. Even though World War I had been over for eight years, there was an abundance of old army uniforms. There was even a masquerade costume of blue sateen trimmed with gold braid.

"I suppose that will become the best dress of some young country bride," said my husband.

There were piles and piles of old shoes. Natives wore their shoes until the sole was gone so anything with just a hole was saleable.

As the morning wore on, I got over my timidity and walked boldly around examining blankets. Baskets made of palm fronds were interesting, too.

One night we were startled awake by a police whistle under our balcony. We lay awake a few minutes, but there was no commotion, so we went back to sleep. The next morning at breakfast I asked the proprietor, "What was the whistle for last night?"

"That was one of our night policemen," he answered. "We have three. At certain hours he blows his whistle to let his colleagues know where he is. They do the same. It also tells the local people that he is on the job and that they are being protected." Security in those days was important, too.

Two thousand years ago, North Africa was the granary of the Roman Empire. Under Roman management, extensive irrigation and water conservation projects were built and maintained. After the fall of Rome, cisterns and aqueducts were neglected and fell into ruin. The natives again became herders and oasis gardeners. When the French occupied North Africa, large scale agriculture became important again. The land is semi-arid, and without capital for irrigation projects, it takes a large area to raise a paying crop of grain.

Our friend, M. Delloule, was a tenant farmer overseeing a large farm for an absentee landlord who lived in Algiers. The arrangement was typical of many farms on the High Plateau. It was also characteristic of the oasis gardens owned by Muslims. The landowners were always on hand at harvest time to collect their share of the harvest and make certain that the property was kept up.

Our diggings were near the buildings of Mechta el Arbi, the headquarters for M. Delloule's several thousand acres of dry farm. There was a farmhouse, a few small buildings, and a cluster of native huts, some of them built of stones from nearby Roman ruins. There were no barns or sheds to shelter the livestock, although there were corrals for sheep and goats. Pigs and chickens were housed in small buildings with pens. A few cattle wandered loose near large straw stacks. The straw stacks were the main feature of the farmyard. They were about twenty feet high and more than a hundred feet long. There were five of them.

One morning when we went out to work, the helpers on the farm were plastering the stacks with mud. M. Delloule was overseeing the work. He explained, "Straw is the feed for cattle, sheep, and goats in the winter. They are taken out to pasture every day, but it is scanty, and we have to supplement. When we first put up the stacks, we kept them from blowing away by putting a wire network, weighted with stones over them. Now, we must protect them from the winter rains and snowstorms, so we plaster them over with a layer of adobe. The sun will bake it just as it does the clay of the native huts."

"Where do you keep the grain?" asked Alonzo.

"In silos," M. Delloule responded.

We looked around. We could see nothing except small sheds. There were none of those big cylindrical structures we were used to on Wisconsin dairy farms.

"Here," said M. Delloule, pointing to a piece of level ground with sticks protruding here and there. "Our silos are pits in the ground. The men are opening one over there."

We walked over. Several men had scraped off the surface soil and exposed a cement cover. Then they lifted off the cover, and we saw threshed wheat in the pit below.

"Doesn't it spoil?" asked my husband.

"No, the ground is clay and doesn't let any water sink in unless it is broken up. Last year we had a heavy rain, and when it stopped, there was two feet of water over this area, but not a single grain got wet."

Plastering straw stacks with clay.

We counted eleven sticks indicating eleven silos.

"How big is the farm?" I asked.

"About 1250 hectares," M. Delloule replied.

"Oh. How much is that in acreage?" I asked Alonzo.

He thought a moment. "About 3000," he said.

"It is a little larger than most of the farms around here." M. Delloule said. "Many of the farms have from 800 to 1000 hectares. It takes us three months to plow the soil for planting. Most of the crop is winter wheat, which will be planted in the very early spring and will ripen in June."

We turned away to watch the sheep and goats. About two hundred were being watered at the well. A windmill pumped water into a long cement tank. This well also furnished water for the house and neighboring native families. Soon a little shepherdess came to drive the flock out to pasture. I find it hard to judge the age of any native, but I thought she might be ten years old. She started the lead sheep out toward the pasture, and the rest of the flock followed. Two little black lambs couldn't keep up, so she scooped one under each arm and trudged along after the flock.

Other, younger girls came with baskets. At the corral they swept the sheep droppings into piles, then shoveled them into baskets. We watched the girls as they carried full baskets back near the native huts. They mixed the droppings with water, patted them into large cakes, and plastered them against the sunny wall of the stone huts to dry. They were fuel for the cooking fires.

A few days later we ate lunch on the sunny side of the plastered straw stacks. We were comfortable sitting on loose straw, completely protected from the wind and warmed by the late fall sunshine.

M. Delloule came over to us and asked, "Wouldn't you like to go for a drive? It's a nice day, and I'd like to show you an asphalt mine. In fact, I'd like to have you take pictures. They might interest American investors."

While he went to get his car, we shook off the straw, repacked our lunch basket, and picked up our cameras. Soon we were driving down the valley of the Rhumel River. We saw a tree now and then, but mostly the landscape was treeless and the dull drab of early winter. Several miles from the farm a mountain rose abruptly from the plain. M. Delloule turned off the main road and down a country lane. We stopped at the foot of the mountain where some trenches had been cut into the side of the slope. Here the sun beat directly down and a black substance oozed out.

"The black stuff is asphalt," explained M. Delloule. "During the Great War, we bought the property. Twelve of us formed a company and got the mine into production. When the war ended, it was no longer profitable to work it by the primitive methods we had. None of us could raise enough capital to buy modern equipment, so we closed the mine. Perhaps some of your friends in the States could be interested enough to invest and get it back into production."

While M. Delloule was talking, several little native girls came and began picking black tar from the rock walls of trenches. They plopped the stuff into their mouths and chewed as if it were the juiciest of Mr. Wrigley's choicest product. Later I learned that children in Chicago picked the black tar from pavement cracks as summer sun oozed it out in shining black bubbles. Nevertheless, chewing black tar instead of spearmint doesn't tempt me, even if it is chewed by Chicago children as well as Berber girls in Algeria. I prefer spruce resin from our Northwoods.

That night in the hotel bar, Alonzo was telling about our trip to the asphalt mine. One of the listeners spoke up. "I'm an oil man," he said. "This country is full of oil. I wanted to develop it, but when I went to Paris to get the necessary permits, I got nowhere. I was passed from official to official with no results. Finally I cabled my cousin in Mexico. He's an oil driller. He came over and was enthusiastic. He, too, went to Paris but got the same run-around that I did. The prospects looked so good that he sent to Mexico for two outfits — drills, derricks, everything. They were unloaded at Bordeaux and put on the train for Marseilles. They never arrived at Marseilles. Somehow they got 'lost' between the two cities. Imagine losing an oil derrick!"

"That beats our American story about the man who lost a bass drum," said Alonzo.

Later, we learned that neither the French government nor interested American oil companies were ready to put the field into production. It was thirty years before oil was "discovered" in Algeria.

One Saturday we decided to stay at the hotel and catch up on our correspondence and sorting the collection from our excavation. At breakfast we told the proprietor that we would be at the hotel for lunch.

"Will you please come to lunch a half hour early then, and eat in the bar? The daughter of one of our wealthy citizens is getting married today, and we are serving the breakfast."

We ate early and later watched from our balcony as the wedding party arrived. The bride was dressed in an elaborate white gown with a train and a long veil. The groom wore a cutaway coat and gray, striped trousers. The fathers of the couple and the town dignitaries all wore formal morning attire. Almost outshining the bride in elegance was the local *Caid* (sheik) in spotless white robes and scarlet *burnous*, heavily embroidered in gold.

As we went through the bar on our way out for an afternoon walk, we heard the merrymaking in the dining room. When we came back the guests had left. The bride and groom, in all their finery, were eating a supper at a small table in the kitchen before boarding the night train for their honeymoon in Algiers.

Our dinner that night was leftovers from the wedding breakfast, minus the champagne and wedding cake.

The proprietor confided to us the next day, "The bride's father has a lot of money, but they didn't serve lobster, just fish."

A French evening meal is not complete without a crisp, tossed lettuce salad. It is always dressed and tossed at the table.

Debby fancied himself quite a salad maker. He was meticulous in measuring the oil and vinegar, careful with salt and pepper, but when he tossed the salad, he lifted some lettuce leaves above the bowl with a flourish and dropped them gracefully. Then he brought the fork and spoon crushing down hard into the bowl. The result was a salad limp as green dishrags.

I like my salads crisp, so one day I rebelled politely. "M. Debruge, you make such good salad dressing. Won't you show me how?"

He gave me precise instructions which I followed, but I tossed the leaves lightly, and the salad was crisp as if it were garden fresh. After that it became an undeclared race to see who would reach the salad course first. I won often enough to maintain my interest in crisp, tasty lettuce.

When we had tangerines for dessert, which was almost always, Debby made a basket of his tangerine peel. He carefully cut away a quarter of the skin on two sides leaving a thin strip across the top for a handle. He then loosened the sections of fruit and skillfully removed them without tearing the skin. The result was a pretty little basket that made an interesting conversation piece.

One day late in November, I looked at our American calendar and realized it was Thanksgiving Day. "Let's celebrate," I suggested.

There really wasn't much we could do. We had no cranberries and no turkey, but a friend in France had given us a can of pâté de fois gras. That night when we went down to dinner, we took it along and asked Tyeb to open it and bring us some crackers. "And bring a bottle of champagne, too," Alonzo added.

"What's the occasion?" asked Debby. "Is it an anniversary?"

We tried to explain about our holiday of Thanksgiving.

"But yes," our colleague said. "I know. Many primitive people have a harvest festival giving thanks to God."

So we knew where Americans stood in his estimation.

6

A City on a Mountain Top

We had been digging at Mechta el Arbi for several weeks. Moving thousands of snail shells and scores of wheelbarrow loads of campfire ashes had become routine. Sometimes I thought I never wanted to see another flint scraper or a razor-sharp flint microlith. Even daily sponge baths in front of a grate fire were getting monotonous.

"It would be good to have a tub bath and some kind of meat besides mutton. We've been here a whole month," I told Alonzo as we were lingering over our coffee.

"We'll take the train on Friday night and spend the weekend in Constantine," he suggested.

Constantine is a city built on a mountaintop. The Rhumel River has cut a gorge a thousand feet deep right through the middle. I've come into Constantine both by train and car, but the view I like to remember is one we saw on a hot June day as we were driving in from the east. As we crossed the plain, heat waves seemed to sever the city from its lofty perch and make it appear to be floating on air. White buildings shimmered in the sunshine giving the city an ethereal look. I almost imagined we would need a flying carpet to reach it, but as we got nearer, the mirage dissolved, and the city settled down onto solid ground. Our arrival that November evening was more mundane.

We got off the train at the station near the foot of the mountain. A cab took us up the winding road and across the Sidi Rached bridge to the Hotel Cirta. The little *chasseur* spotted us through the glass door and rushed out to take our bags. We followed him inside, greeted the concierge, registered, and walked to the elevator. Entering the elevator was like going into a big, gilded birdcage. Slowly and jerkily, the cage lifted us past the intricately carved marble columns of the lobby, past the blue-and-white tiled corridor of the second floor to the third floor of the hotel. The bellboy opened the door to a room, a *big* room off of which was a bathroom with a lavatory, a big gleaming white tub, and a *flush toilet!*

"It's wonderful!" I said. "Who's going to soak first?" We flipped a coin and I won.

That night in the dining room the waiter handed us a printed menu. "Beef steak or baked ham, and pastries for dessert!" I exclaimed. We lingered over our dinner, savoring every mouthful.

✍

"Let's walk around the road that encircles the city," my husband suggested at breakfast the next morning.

Constantine is an old, old city. The Phoenicians called it Cirta, their word for city. Guidebooks say that it has been besieged eighty times and captured many of them, despite seeming to be impregnable. The Roman Emperor Constantine rebuilt it and gave it his name, but very little of its old glory remains. The Turks demolished most of it.

A short walk took us to a narrow road with a stone guardrail. We stopped to look out over the plain almost a thousand feet below, miles and miles of red clay with isolated mountain peaks dotting the far horizon. We could trace the Rhumel by the scraggly trees on its banks as it twisted across the plain.

Suddenly a dust storm whirled up out of the plain. We were enveloped in a cloud of stinging particles. Silk stockings were no protection. I tried to cover my face with my handkerchief. Alonzo's blue shirt turned gray.

"I know now why native men wear hooded capes," I said. "Does that finely woven *burnous* keep out the dust?"

"It helps." My husband had ridden more than a thousand miles on camelback protected by a woolen *burnous*.

"Wish I had one," I said.

The wind died down, and we came to a curve where the road turned back into the city. A break in the wall showed stone steps leading down into the gorge, so we turned down the stairway. A rusty iron railing gave one a false sense of security. The steps ended on a narrow path not more than three feet wide. At times we slipped a little as our feet loosened pebbles. Sometimes the trail became a series of iron plates held on to the rock wall by brackets; far below us we could hear the Rhumel River crashing over waterfalls or splashing down cascades. At some places the way led onto a wooden sidewalk with some boards missing. We stepped gingerly over such holes with nothing but air between us and the jagged rocks five hundred feet below. We passed the entrances to small caves.

"These were places of hiding during the many sieges," my husband explained. "They were also used as storehouses for grain during the Roman times."

Sometimes the path went under a natural bridge. There were four of them in the gorge, one of which is twice as high as the Natural Bridge in Virginia. At another point we looked up at the steel span of the Sidi M'Cid bridge.

Sidi M'Cid bridge, Constantine.

"That is the highest suspension bridge in the world," said Alonzo. We could barely see its spider-web-like cables. Finally we got close to the river. Stone steps led down. They were slippery from the spray. We went down cautiously, and the gorge got narrower and gloomier. A thousand feet above we could see just a ribbon of blue sky. There was no one on that canyon trail but us. Perhaps when the tourist season was on, there would be more traffic, but the condition of that canyon trail didn't indicate much use.

After two hours of walking, we came out of the gorge into the sunlight. High above us we could see native houses hanging out from the mountainside supported only by palm-trunk braces. I wondered if a strong wind might not blow them away, but they had been there for perhaps hundreds of years.

Up and up we climbed on the zigzag path out of the gorge. It led to the native quarter. All I could think of was a pile of blocks some little child had tumbled together. At times second stories jutted over the streets to form dark tunnels as we had seen in Algiers. We stumbled on the rough stone paving. Narrow streets branched off at odd angles. Everywhere there were people, but much more colorful than such groups in Algiers. Instead of white turbans, many men wore red fezzes. Jewish and black African women wearing red calico dresses and bright yellow head scarves mingled in the crowd of Muslim women. The latter were voluminously robed and heavily veiled. They could not walk with the free, swinging step of the non-Muslims.

"Why are there wide blue bands painted around the windows and doorways," I asked.

"The natives believe that flies do not like that color, and they won't fly in a window or door painted blue," my husband answered.

Shops were small rooms open to the street.

"Let's stop here," said Alonzo, as we paused in front of a jeweler. Right near the front door a small table held a tray of silver bracelets. "Which one do you like?"

I chose one set with blue glass stones, each setting surrounded by a fine silver chain. Between the sets were gold flowers surrounded by a silver-rayed sunburst ending in tiny silver balls. My husband bargained with the shopkeeper, and soon I slipped the silver circlet on my arm. I still prize my first piece of Arab jewelry.

"Let's visit the old palace of the Bey," Alonzo said the next day at lunch.

We walked into the heart of the French city and stopped before a building indistinguishable from its neighbors. Brown framed windows and a heavy wooden door were set in a whitewashed plastered wall.

"It is now used by the military for offices, but the old harem has been restored and kept as a tourist attraction," my husband explained.

We pushed open the heavy door and were greeted by a young soldier-guide. He led us down a long corridor and unlocked a door. We stepped out into a large courtyard. Although it was November outside, it was spring in the courtyard. The walls were covered with tiles painted with bright flowers. That made it look like a garden all year round. Fruit trees grew in beds along the walls. The blue and white tiled floor reflected the blue of the sky above. In the center was a rectangular pool of clear water.

"The women of the harem bathed with perfumed water in the pool," the guide said. "That door leads into a corridor from which small rooms open off. The many wives and concubines of the old Bey lived in those rooms."

Above the door through which we had entered was a small balcony. "A eunuch with a sharp scimitar always stood in that balcony," our guide said. "He made sure that no stranger entered the harem or that no woman got out either. There were always guards standing outside the main door, too."

We walked on through an archway into a smaller courtyard. At the opposite end was a deep alcove, a platform set up three steps and divided from the open room by three carved wooden arches. Against the wall was a long divan with large brocade cushions.

"It was here that the Bey reclined when attended by his favorites. They would feed him sweetmeats, plump his pillows and hand him his water-pipe. From there he could watch other favorites as they sang or danced before the perfumed fountains playing in the center pool. Every morning the Bey used to appear on the little balcony in that corner where he could see the whole courtyard before he dropped a handkerchief. Whoever caught the handkerchief was the official favorite for the day."

The courtyard was encircled by a colonnade much like the cloisters in a medieval convent. The walls were covered with brightly colored tiles in floral designs. The floor was a mosaic.

Our guide pointed to still another balcony near the entrance. "The musicians sat there. They were the best music-makers in the land. All of them were blinded, of course, so they could not see the beauty of the harem women."

"How many women were in the harem?" I asked,

"The Bey had the four wives allowed by the Qur'an and three hundred eighty concubines," the guide replied.

We turned to leave, but I looked back. I could almost see a group of beautiful, dark-eyed women dressed in diaphanous harem trousers, gold belts, and short sequined jackets dancing around the fountain or sitting on huge cushions embroidered with gold and silver threads. A perfect setting for Scheherazade and her tales of *A Thousand and One Nights*, I thought.

When we were out in the street again we had to stop a few minutes and bring ourselves back from a thousand years ago into the present with its hum of traffic and people dressed in modern clothes.

"Let's shop," I said the next morning. Our train did not leave until afternoon.

We left the hotel and walked through a small park filled with Roman relics. A carved column was prominent, and nearby was a small statue. There were several benches of carved stone, and on one of them three old Arabs in white *burnouses* and turbans sat absorbing the warm sun. They were talking together quietly.

"That's a picture of contentment," I said.

"Yes," said Alonzo. "They may sit there visiting all morning."

"Do they do that every day?"

"Oh, not every day, but often. Allah has looked after them well in this world and probably will in the next. There is nothing for them to worry about."

We went on through the park to the business district.

"I'd like to get some toys for the Delloule boys," I said as we passed a department store. Neither my husband nor I knew the French word for "blocks" so I said, "If you please, I would like some small pieces of wood with colors on them for children to play with."

"But yes," said the clerk as he pulled a drawer open and handed me a box of blocks.

At another place we bought a lace handkerchief for Madame Delloule and a tin of special tobacco for M. Delloule.

Back at the hotel, Debby was waiting for us. We called a cab to take us to the station. Well-scrubbed and with memories of ham, chicken, and beefsteak dinners, we boarded the train for Châteaudun, ready for another month at the diggings, mutton dinners, and baths in a basin.

7

The Pearl of North Africa

"*I* think it is time to close the diggings at Mechta," said Alonzo one evening as we were sitting in front of the fireplace. "Debby and I were talking it over this afternoon. We have a good collection of the snail-mound culture. We haven't found anything new for a week."

"We've been here two and a half months," I reminded him, "and we did plan to dig in two or more sites this winter."

"I've asked Debby to write to Hassinou, his friend in Bougie[5] up on the coast. He'll find out if we can rent a diggings near there. Some years ago Debby lived in Bougie and worked at a site called Ali Bacha. He thought it was an interesting one."

Next morning Debby went to Mechta alone to oversee filling in the trench. We had agreed to restore the site to as near the original mound shape as possible. Alonzo and I washed, sorted, and classified the artifacts. We gathered boxes from the grocery store and packed the collections. Half of the material would go to the Logan Museum at Beloit and half would go to the National Museum in Algiers. Unique pieces, such as a polished bone dagger ten inches long and a beautifully chipped flint knife, would go to America for study and then be returned to the museum in Algiers.

A few nights later Debby came down to dinner with a letter in his hand. "I've heard from M. Hassinou. He has contacted the owner of Ali Bacha, and we can work there. He has found rooms for us in Bougie, too."

"Good," said my husband. "Can you finish filling the trench by the weekend?"

"Easily, probably by Friday."

"You write M. Hassinou and say we'll be on the train Monday."

We worked harder than ever to close up the Mechta project.

---

5. Now Béjaïa.

Debby took the bus to Constantine for a long weekend and promised to meet us on the Constantine-Sétif train Monday.

Saturday morning Alonzo accompanied the truck with our boxes of flint artifacts to the station and got them on the way to Algiers.

"Let's take one more walk around the town," I said at lunch. "Tomorrow we'll be busy packing clothes and books and digging tools." We stopped at the grocery store where I had bought many cookies and candy bars because tangerines never were a sweet enough dessert for me.

"Madame, we've come to say good bye," I said as we entered.

"You're leaving. Then you must come into my apartment and have a farewell drink." She led the way into her living room just off the shop. Her son soon joined us, bringing a bottle of wine. Madame went into the store and came back with a package of my favorite cookies. She opened the box and filled a plate with those thin squares of lemon flavored pastry I had bought so often all winter. After a short visit, we said goodbye and went back to the hotel.

As we were passing through the bar, the proprietor stopped us. "*Monsieur, Madame* Pond, won't you sit down and have a drink with us." Then he called to his wife in the kitchen, "Come, Marie! Come and have a liqueur with *M.* and *Mme.* Pond."

This time it was the Benedictine liqueur that I like so much. "We are sorry to have you leave," he said. "It's been a pleasure having you here this winter."

We thanked him and expressed our pleasure for the friendly service they had given us so long. When we got up to our room I said, "We had better not say goodbye to anybody else today. Two farewell drinks are enough."

On Sunday afternoon we hired a car and went out to Mechta to see the Delloules once more. Mme. Delloule was sorry to see us go. We thought she had a lonely life out on the farm, but she had always seemed cheerful and happy. M. Delloule was already making plans for the spring plowing. Soon there would be another kind of activity around Mechta. As we drove away, the family stood in the doorway and waved to us as long as we could see them.

Monday noon found us on that bleak, wind-swept Châteaudun station platform again, but this time we were aboard when the train pulled away. We walked down the coach aisle until we found the compartment Debby had selected at Constantine and settled down for the four-hour ride to Bougie.

I was not sorry to leave the High Plateau with its brown, bare fields. The small villages we passed through seemed like a few large boxes scattered along the railroad. Ahead of us, the Djurdjura Range with its snow-clad peaks seemed a barrier hemming us in. The train kept climbing and slowing speed somewhat until we reached the pass. Sometimes the roadbed clung to a shelf on the mountainside. Looking out the window, we could see only great layers of rock tilted up on edge going up and up beyond our view. Sometimes we went through short, dark tunnels.

Finally, we came out of the mountains into the valley of the Soummam River. Suddenly it was spring.

Some fruit trees were in blossom. The orange trees were still decorated with golden, ripe balls. The sun broke through the clouds, and we could see the blue Mediterranean sparkling in the distance. We stepped off the train at the Bougie station. The air was soft and warm, caressing us with the gentleness of a baby's fingers.

M. Hassinou, a stocky man in a neat, black business suit, was there to meet us. He wore a black fedora hat instead of the traditional red fez of the Muslim. When the introductions were over, he said, "I've a cab waiting," and led us outside the station to a horse-drawn, open carriage with two seats facing each other. The driver's seat was in front and a little higher than his passengers. Another cab was necessary for our luggage, and a small dray was loaded with our two trunks. We made quite a procession as we started away from the depot.

Our horses plodded up the ramp from the station valley floor to the business section. Bougie, like Algiers, is built on a mountainside. We turned onto the main street and drove past an open square. Stores with colonnaded walks lined two sides, and across the side facing the sea was a balustrade to keep people from falling down the steep bank to the railroad yards and the wharf below. Stone benches were scattered under fig trees around the plaza.

"This is the *Place Gueydon*," said M. Hassinou, and in that far corner is the *Brasserie de l'Étoile*. It is the best place in town to eat, and you can get *pension* (boarder's) rates."

As our driver turned right at the far corner of the *Place*, I noted a street sign, *rue du Vieillard*, "Street of the Old Ones." "What does it mean?" I asked.

"While Bougie was a part of the Turkish Empire," M. Hassinou explained, "it was little more than a supply station for Mediterranean pirates. France sent in a small military expedition which captured the city. When the soldiers began searching the buildings, they found six old men sitting in one room of a house on this street so they called it 'the street of the old men.' That was in 1833."

"Our U.S. Marines have a song about those pirates," Alonzo remarked.

> From the halls of Montezuma
> To the shores of Tripoli,
> We will fight our country's battles
> On the land and on the sea.

"Of course that refers to the Tripolitanian War with the U.S. over pirates holding U.S. ships and citizens for ransom. But that was more than thirty years before the French had to clear the pirates out from Bougie."

Three blocks up this gently sloping street our driver stopped in front of a two-story building. M. Hassinou knocked on the door. It was opened by a middle-aged French woman.

"It is M. and Mme. Pond and M. Debruge," said our friend. "Remember I told you about them last week."

"*Mais oui* (of course)," she replied. "Ahmet, come and get the luggage."

We followed her to a smaller door which opened from the street into a small hallway, then up a long flight of stairs to a hall on the second floor. Then she unlocked a door, "For M. Debruge."

Farther down the hallway she unlocked another room at the front of the house. As she unlocked the door, she waved her hand and smiled, "For M. and Mme. Pond."

I smiled, too, as we stepped into the room. It was big in comparison to our quarters at Châteaudun. A big, round table with two straight-backed chairs stood in the center. A large wardrobe was against one wall and a small desk against another. A settee and an armchair were pulled in front of the fireplace. The bed was in an alcove. There was a short hall to a small room with a washstand and a woodbox for the fireplace fuel.

I was almost ecstatic. "A table large enough to hold our typewriter and reference books, and a wardrobe for our clothes!"

Madame turned to go. "The W.C. is just down the hall."

"Wood for the fireplace?" my husband asked.

"I will order some for you in the morning."

We thanked M. Hassinou for finding such a pleasant place for us and invited him to have dinner with us at the *Étoile* later that evening.

Ahmet made several trips bringing our bags, and he and the drayman struggled up the stairs with our two heavy trunks. Even with our luggage strewn about, there was room to move around.

Later I went in search of the W.C., a small room with the tile floor sloping to a hole in the middle. Two elevated footrests made it easy to squat more or less comfortably, and it was inside and on the same floor as our room. Such convenience! It was a great improvement over Châteaudun.

There was no bathtub in the rooming house, so one of the first things we unpacked was our big coffee pot. It would be our hot water tank as it had been all winter.

I went happily about unpacking and hanging clothes in the wardrobe while Alonzo put the typewriter and books on the table. He opened the French windows and stepped out onto a small balcony. "Come here," he called.

We looked to our right across the roof tops of the city and caught a glimpse of the harbor. To the left, the street led on up and up to the fort on the top of Mt. Gouraya. Later on Debby teased me, because I could not trill my *r*'s when saying "Gour-r-r-aya."

That evening, as we walked down the Street of the Old Men and across the square to the restaurant, we were happy and contented. We were in Bougie! The city called "Little Mecca" and "The Pearl of North Africa." Bougie, a city with some streets so steep that they sometimes became a series of broad steps. Bougie, with its U-shaped harbor ringed with jagged mountain peaks that did indeed provide a shelter from wild Mediterranean storms. Bougie, with its soft, warm climate and its leisurely way of life. It was all ours to live in, to explore, and to enjoy for the next two months.

8

Ali Bacha

*O*ur alarm clock went off at 5:30 the first morning as it always had at Châteaudun. Just after the bell stopped ringing, the notes of reveille floated down from the fort. From then on we, as well as the soldiers, were awakened by the bugle call. A few minutes later, the little baker boy started his peddler's call. From way down the street came his clear voice, *"Brioches. Croissants;"* then a little louder as he came up the hill, *"Brioches. Croissants;"* and finally under our balcony *"BRIOCHES. CROISSANTS."* Then it grew fainter and softer as he moved up the mountain. How we wished we had a pot of coffee and could go down to buy some of his delicious hot rolls for breakfast. We always knew when that call sounded beneath our window that it was time to get up and dress.

The first one up opened the French windows to let in the spring air. Straight across from us on the next street over but a little higher up the slope was a white house with balconies, shutters, and doors painted a dark green. The peach and almond trees in the garden around the house were in full bloom, and their pink blossoms made a delightful picture of spring.

We dressed quickly, eager to get outdoors. As we went past Debby's door we tapped, and he joined us. Our pace was brisk as we walked down the street and across the square to the little restaurant. If the weather was warm enough, we sat outside at a small, glass-topped table to eat our breakfast of hot rolls and *café au lait.*

We didn't linger over our breakfast, for our cab would be waiting. Alonzo picked up the wicker basket which the waiter had packed for us, and we walked back across the *Place* to our carriage.

The horses trotted briskly the mile and a half to our diggings outside the city. Instead of huddling down against the wind as we had at Châteaudun, we sat up straight, enjoying the sun on the blue Mediterranean to our left and the green meadows and blossoming fruit trees of the farms to our right. The horses stopped at a path beside a small creek, and we got out with our lunch basket, our small digging tools, and cameras.

"Be sure to be back by four o'clock," we called to the driver as we started up the path.

We looked up the gentle slope to a white cliff crowned with olive trees a half mile away. Our new diggings were at the foot of that cliff, a much more inviting spot than the wind-swept plain at Mechta. The path followed the stream bank at first. After a little distance, it led across the stream on flat steppingstones. They were always a challenge to us with our bulky loads. Beyond the crossing, we heard the splash of a waterfall as the stream tumbled over a ledge about six feet high. The path climbed by uneven stone steps to a flat rock at the top where we could stop and rest. Willow trees trailed their branches in the quiet pool above the falls; however, we couldn't stop long, for our workmen would be waiting for us. The path angled off from the stream, and we climbed a rather steep slope, passed an open well, and set our lunch basket down under an old olive tree fifty feet or so beyond.

Stone Age man had sought shelter from the cold winds here at the foot of this forty-foot cliff. Big rocks that had broken from an overhanging ledge lay at the base of the cliff. Nearby was a small cave that had been worked out long ago. Above us on the rock face was a shield-shaped opening.

"A Phoenician tomb," said Debby, "Despoiled probably a thousand years ago. Nothing in it."

At the foot of this bluff we opened our trenches. Digging here was harder than at Mechta. The soil was damp clay and the artifacts were covered with an iron and clay deposit. The technique of tossing a shovelful at a gravel screen and letting the wind blow away the dust didn't work. Every wheelbarrow load was pushed to the stream and the artifacts put in large sieves and washed. It was slow work. There were no shells, but there were chipped flints and bone tools. Many of the artifacts were so encrusted with iron and clay that later on, back at the Logan Museum, they were dipped in a bath of weak hydrochloric acid to reveal the beauty of their chipping.

At noon we spread our lunch under the ancient olive tree. "What a beautiful place Aurignacian man chose to live," I said, as we looked out over the broad valley of the Soummam River where it wound its way through the green countryside and joined the Mediterranean a few miles away.

"Yes," said Alonzo, "and he was well protected from the cold winds from the snow-capped mountains back of us. If those tumbled rocks formed a large enough overhang, he was well protected from the rain, too."

At a quarter of four we packed up our things and were down the hill to meet our carriage. It had been a good day.

While we were eating lunch one day, a young girl came to the well carrying two pails. She had come from the house on top of the cliff. With graceful motions,

she attached the pail to a pulley hanging from a rough wooden frame over the well. Gently, she let the pail down into the well and slowly pulled it up dripping.

"Rebecca at the well," I said.

Alonzo picked up his camera and went towards her. At first she was startled and turned as if to run. Then, apparently remembering that she had been sent to the well for water, she quickly filled the other pail while my husband got a good picture that we titled "A Modern Rebecca." It was later published in *The Milwaukee Journal*.

We were reminded many times of Biblical scenes. On another morning as we walked up the path, we saw a farmer tilling his field. The plow was a very primitive one made of two sticks. The working end was tipped with an iron shield; the other end was a curved stick which formed a handle. A pair of oxen was hitched to it with ropes. As the farmer drove the plow across the field, it merely scratched the soil a few inches deep. A small boy walked behind him with a two-tined grub hoe and broke up the lumps of dirt broken out by the plow. The farmer was glad to rest while we took pictures. We did not see the grain being planted, but I'm sure that it was scattered by hand just it had been done for thousands of years. Somehow living in a country with such an ancient heritage gave one a feeling of serenity and continuity.

A Modern Rebecca: A Kabylie girl at the well.

Some days I didn't go to the diggings. The two men could do the work easily, and Bougie was a fascinating place. Between eight and nine o'clock I'd stroll leisurely down to the restaurant, choose a table on the terrace near the balustrade, and order hot chocolate and *brioche*. Then I'd look down the slope to the old Saracen gate, an archway of mellowed brick. Sometimes a loaded burro, with his master following behind, came through the gate. That scene always carried me back to Biblical times. Than I'd look across the railroad yards to the harbor and, in the sheen of the sunlight on the water, I thought I could see the purple lateen sails of the Phoenician galleys as they rode at anchor in this pearl-like gem of harbors.

Since history began, there has been a settlement on the slopes of Mt. Gouraya. Perhaps even before that, there was a fishing village on the shore. The Carthaginians recorded that their ships sought shelter from the Mediterranean storms in this almost land-locked harbor. When the Roman legions swept across North Africa, the city became the most important port on the southern Mediterranean coast. The Vandals harassed the Romans, and later the Byzantines completed the downfall of the Roman Empire in North Africa. Then the Arabs, under the leadership of Sidi Okba, Mohammed's able general, subdued North Africa and converted it to the religion of Islam. The Spaniards purged the country of the Arabs only to be overwhelmed by the Turks, and North Africa became a part of the Ottoman Empire. Under the Turks, piracy became rampant, and the Barbarossa brothers hid their ships in the easily-defended harbor.

When France could no longer put up with the pirate-raiding of her ships in the Mediterranean, she put a stop to it, and in doing so, occupied the North African coast, eventually pushing her way down through the Sahara Desert to the Niger.

I was brought back into the modern world by the cry of, "Shine, *Madame*?"

Five or six little urchins with shoeshine boxes had clustered around my table. By this time I had my favorite boy, and I nodded to him. The others fell back a little and either hung around exchanging banter with him or looked for other customers.

My breakfast over, if I was going back to our room, I'd stop at one of the flower sellers' stalls and buy a small bunch of dew-fresh cyclamen that the young merchant had gathered on the mountainside that morning. Then I'd go back up the hill and spend the day writing letters or mending our clothes. Our balcony was just wide enough to hold a chair. I could sit outside and watch the people in the street.

I was amused one day as I watched the boy who brought our fireplace wood come up the street. The two-wheeled cart was drawn by a slowly plodding burro. The little native boy walked along beside, slapping the burro on the rump every now and then to keep him moving. This day the little driver must have felt the spirit of spring, because the burro had a spray of mimosa blossoms tucked rakishly behind his left ear.

At least once a day, I'd hear the sound of drumbeats and look up the street toward the fort. Following the drum roll, a wave of blue flowed as a company of Zouaves marched past down the hill. Their blue uniforms were reminiscent of the Turkish occupation — baggy, blue trousers were tucked into high black boots; red-fringed sashes swung as they marched; short blue jackets were heavily trimmed with yellow braid; black tassels on red fezzes bobbed rhythmically as heels clicked on cobblestones. It seemed as if every corner of the city reminded one of past glories of this Pearl of North Africa.

One morning, as I glanced down at the harbor, I exclaimed, "Oh, there's a ship flying an American flag." I hadn't seen an American flag for eight months.

"She probably brought over a load of farm machinery and will take phosphate back," said Debby that night at dinner. "There's a lot of phosphate mined in the mountains back of the city."

After that morning, I saw several ships of American registry.

We discovered another treasure in this city. The *Brasserie de l'Étoile* had a bathtub, and we could rent that room by the half hour. Some days after I had finished my lunch, I'd say to the proprietor, "May I make arrangements for a bath, today?"

"Certainly, *Madame*. At what time, please?"

"Would three o'clock be convenient?"

"But, yes. That would be well."

At three o'clock I'd walk down to the restaurant, pay the concierge a quarter, and climb the stairs to the second floor where a maid would meet me and open the door to the bathroom. She'd draw a hot bath, hand me a towel the size of a 5 by 7-foot rug — at least it seemed that big and heavy — then leave and close the door behind her. I'd lock the door, undress, climb into the tub, and soak. The room was mine for half an hour. Not all the perfumed pools of the Bey's harem could come up to this!

Oftentimes I'd go to the stores after breakfast. One day I was looking for scallop shells. The restaurant served us a dish called *Coquilles St. Jacques*, a dish of scallops and mushrooms in a rich cream sauce. It was always served in shells, and I thought it would be a good idea to take some shells home. I found what I wanted on a shelf in a department store. They had been well scrubbed and bleached. In those days prices were not put on merchandise. In some stores one could still bargain; other stores had a sign on the door, "Fixed price."

When a clerk came, I asked the price of the shells. She rattled off *"troisquatrevingtdixneuf."* My college French wasn't up to that, so I thanked her and wandered off.

Later, out on the street, I went past a fish stall. There was a big pile of scallop shells with a sign *"80 centimes."* That was just under four cents in our money, and I bought a dozen. They had been hastily washed when the scallops had been removed. When I got back to our room, I found a small, stiff brush that we used to brush dirt off the artifacts. I washed and brushed and washed and brushed until all trace of the shell's owner was gone. I've had them for forty-nine years and used them many times, but the tiny grooves still hold some sand and grime from the bottom of the sea.

Our American clothes gave us away as strangers in Bougie. The first few weeks, I was followed everywhere I went by boys shouting "Guide, guide." I came to know most of the boys, as they were the same group of shoeshine boys who clustered around me at breakfast. Eventually the boys let me alone, but one day there was a new boy in the group. The next time I started out for a walk, he followed me and kept insisting on being a guide. Finally I was so exasperated that I turned on him and said, "How can you be a guide? You just came a week ago, and I live here."

9

Toudja, a Kabylie Village

M. Hassinou joined us as we were sitting down to dinner one Saturday evening. "Would you like to visit a Kabylie village tomorrow?" he asked.

We accepted enthusiastically. Debby, however, declined. Sunday was his day of rest and besides, he had lived in Bougie some years before, and he knew all he wanted to know about Kabylie villages.

"May I bring my camera?" asked my husband.

"Oh, certainly," was the answer. "We Kabyles, while outwardly accepting the Muslim religion, have our own culture. We are more democratic and outgoing people."

As we left the café M. Hassinou said, "Be sure and breakfast early, for I will call for you at 7:30."

The next morning we dashed down to the restaurant for our coffee and rolls, and when we got back to the hotel, M. Hassinou was waiting with a carriage.

We left the city by the Route Nationale, a good macadam road. As we went along, M. Hassinou explained, "Kabylie is a *département* of Algeria."

"Much like our states," Alonzo said in an aside to me.

"My people inhabited these mountains before the dawn of history. They were here when the Phoenicians came. We have never been conquered. We have never even signed a peace treaty with the French."

"We have the same situation at home with the Seminole Indians," I replied.

Our driver turned right into a country road that climbed steeply. Ahead we could see a cone-shaped mountain whose top was plastered over with small, brown huts that blended in with the mountain color.

"That's Toudja, where we are going," said M. Hassinou, pointing to the cluster of houses higher up on the mountain. He continued his explanation of the Kabyles. "We value our independence. Even now the *gendarmes* patrol the villages in pairs."

I must have looked apprehensive, for he hastened to add, "Oh, I have many friends there. We will be safe. We are an adaptable people. We have had to be, to keep our culture intact after so many invasions. The itinerant merchants that you see on market day in small towns are almost always Kabyles. Many of our men walk five miles down the mountains to work in the Armstrong Congoleum factory in Bougie. They walk back at night, too. Sometimes our people go to Marseilles or Paris to work, but they always come back to Kabylie when they are old or have made enough money to live comfortably."

"Why are the villages always built on the mountain tops?" I asked. "They are so inaccessible."

"That's the reason, or, one of them. Before the French came, the villages were often at war with each other. Mostly family feuds. By building on top of the mountain they could be defended easily.

"Another reason is that the valleys are fertile, and every hectare is needed for raising food. The barren mountains were the only lands that could be used for shelter."

By now we had reached the outskirts of the village.

"We'll have to walk the rest of the way. The village streets are made for men and burros only."

Our driver tied his horse to a convenient tree and settled down to sleep until we returned. Our friend led us up a steep path with houses built close together on the one side and the next row of houses high above our heads on the other side. The street led into a grassy, open square dotted with fig and olive trees. It was market day, and several hundred men milled about. M. Hassinou greeted friends and evidently explained about us, for while we were objects of curious looks, no one objected when we took pictures.

We passed by the butcher with his skinned carcasses — that was familiar from other markets — but we did stop at the sandal maker's. He had a pile of tanned goat-skin squares in front of him, the hair still on them. We watched as a customer stopped before him. The craftsman laid out two squares, and the buyer stepped onto them. The cobbler drew an outline of each foot with a black crayon. The buyer stepped off and sat down to wait for his custom-made sandals. The artisan cut off the excess hide leaving two inches outside the crayon mark. He punched holes on each side and threaded a rawhide lace through the holes. The customer handed the merchant some money, put on his sandals and laced them up, then walked off with new shoes, the hair side outside.

"Oh, look over there," I exclaimed. A small boy, perhaps eight years old, had four lemons spread out in front of him, his sole stock in trade. "Let's buy them. Then he will have a few pennies to spend."

We used the fruit for lemonade at lunch the next day.

"Let's go this way," said M. Hassinou as he guided us down a little path away from the village square. Ahead was the most idyllic nook — a fern-covered rock wall.

Six feet above our heads, water spurted from the mountainside and fell in a fine spray into a smooth rock basin at our feet.

"Feel it!" urged M. Hassinou.

I put my hand into the spray. It was tepid.

"There are warm springs higher up in the mountain. It is here that the village people come to bathe."

The blue sky, the warm sun, the fern-covered walls, warm water falling in a fine mist made this the most beautiful bathroom I have ever seen.

We retraced our steps to the marketplace and followed a path in another direction. Beside a stream tumbling downhill were five small, stone huts, one below the other, scattered along the rocky banks.

"Grist mills. Long, long ago, the Kabyles learned to make turbines to turn their grindstones," M. Hassinou explained.

Flumes made from hollow logs diverted the water from the stream to each building, then rejoined the channel. We stumbled down the steep path and looked in the door of one small house. It was just a stone hut with an open door.

"There are flat paddlewheels underneath, and when I lower this lever, the mill stones are put in gear with the turbine," he continued.

A woman approached with a sack of grain. We stepped aside, and she entered. We watched as she spread a cloth around the turning millstones. Carefully she fed

Flumes for mills at Toudja.

wheat into the center hole, and soon coarse flour sprayed out between the two stones and fell on the cloth. When the grain was all ground, she gathered up the cloth, shook it into her sack, and went away with the week's supply of flour.

As we climbed back to the village square M. Hassinou said, "Toudja's water is very good. In fact, the city of Bougie gets its water supply from the mountains above here. It is piped from springs higher up. On the way home I'll show the ruins of the old Roman aqueduct that brought water to the city of Saldae, the old name for Bougie."

Back again in the marketplace, we saw the olive oil merchant who stood beside several large jugs. Women brought their own containers, and he measured out a liter of oil just as milkmen used to sell milk in earlier days in America. The oil seller was also the fuel merchant in Toudja. Just back of him was a large pile of olive pits. A bushel basketful was only a franc, and the pits made a quick, hot cooking fire.

"This way," said M. Hassinou, and we followed him down still another path. "The olive presses are down this way."

In the midst of a grove of olive trees were two old primitive presses. The stone basins were made of rock from the mountainside cemented together. Each had a frame over it of heavy, wooden cross pieces, held up by rough tree trunks. We stopped before the first one where a heavy, solid stone wheel was suspended from the frame.

"The ripe olives are dumped into this basin. A long pole from the center of the wheel is attached to a burro. As he walks around the basin, the wheel crushes the olives and the pits roll toward the center. The pulp is carried over to this other basin."

We walked over. A hand-carved wood screw about ten inches in diameter was suspended from the frame over the basin. At the bottom was a wide cover just a little smaller than the basin. At the base were four holes in the four directions of the compass.

"When the olive pulp is dumped in here, men put poles in these holes, then push against them as they walk around the basin. This lowers the flat cover and squeezes out the oil, which runs into the stone trough on this side. Some sediment settles to the bottom, and the oil runs into the stone trough just below. From there it is drawn off into big jugs or cans."

"How old do you think these presses are?" asked Alonzo.

"I don't know. They could be a hundred years old. Maybe even older. Some of the olive trees are over a thousand years old."

We shook our heads in wonderment.

On our way back to the village square, we stopped to watch some boys playing Duck-on-a-rock. "Childhood games are alike the world over," I said, as we climbed the path.

It was noon, and the market was almost over, so we started back down the steep road to our carriage. Part way down, M. Hassinou stopped at a door. "I have friends here. A widow and her two daughters. Her husband was killed in the Great War. Let's greet them."

A young woman opened the door at his knock. *"Bonjour.* Won't you come in," she said.

M. Hassinou introduced us to his friends. He must have sent word ahead that we would stop, because all three women were dressed in party clothes and wore a great deal of jewelry. Madame had on a necklace of gold *Louis*, comparable to our five-dollar gold pieces.

"Coffee will be ready soon," she said. "Won't you sit down," and she indicated some straight-backed chairs.

The other furniture in the room was a wooden chest and a white iron bed piled high with blankets. The cooking fire was a small depression in the center of the room with metal strips laid across it to hold the coffee pot. M. Hassinou and his friends carried on a spirited conversation while we sipped cups of strong black coffee. After we had drunk the conventional three cups, which hospitality demanded, we thanked our hostess, said our goodbyes, and walked down to the carriage.

As we looked back at the village, we saw that the roof tiles were held down by rocks, just as we had seen in the Alpine villages in Switzerland.

On the way back to Bougie we saw the ruins of the old Roman aqueducts, but M. Hassinou assured us again that the city water for Bougie was piped down underground now and was not contaminated.

"Thank you, thank you very much," we said as we climbed down from the carriage at our front door. "It was so interesting, and without you, we could never have seen a Kabylie village."

M. Hassinou beamed as he rode away.

10

We Explore

We needed a weekend vacation away from work. Debby took the train to Constantine Friday afternoon. Saturday morning we slept late, dressed leisurely, and strolled downtown for breakfast. We chose a table on the terrace overlooking the bay.

"Two pots of hot chocolate and *croissants*," we told the waiter.

"Am I dreaming," I said, as I glanced out over the harbor, "or is that a three-masted schooner out there?"

Alonzo looked. "That's real. A three-master," he agreed. "She's unfurling her sails and getting ready to leave. She must have come in last night after we had dinner."

We watched as the breeze slowly caught her sails, and the graceful boat moved quietly and sedately out past the lights on the breakwater at the harbor mouth and into the Mediterranean.

We brought our gaze back in across the modern freighters moored to the docks, across the railroad yards with its puffing, bustling engines, to the old Saracen Tower on the slope just below us — a single glance that swept through twelve hundred years of Mediterranean history.

"I suppose that as recently as two hundred years ago, there were watchmen in that tower identifying all the sailing ships as they came into the harbor," I mused.

"There was probably a cannon mounted there, with its barrel pointed directly at the harbor entrance, too," my husband continued the fantasy.

By now the ubiquitous bevy of shoeshine boys had surrounded us calling, "Shine, *Monsieur*, shine."

Alonzo nodded to our favorite, and the other boys dispersed to find other customers.

"Let's go down to the native quarter," I suggested, after we had finished breakfast.

We crossed the square and immediately left the European stores with their colonnaded entrances to follow a narrow street that led down the hill. The street was lined with small shops, their open doorways inviting customers to stop and look. We paused at a hole-in-the-wall shop.

"Come in, come in, *Monsieur, Madame*," a voice called. When our eyes became accustomed to the gloom, we saw the artisan working on native jewelry. He spoke French well and was able to explain his craft.

He showed us a small box about ten inches long filled with white sand. "The sand is from the Sahara. The desert sand makes the best molds."

He laid a flat strip of filigreed metal on the sand, then removed it, leaving a perfect impression. Next he ladled molten metal from a crucible and carefully poured it into the mold. Then he placed a flat cover on it and set it aside to harden. He took other molds from a shelf and poured fancy pins and anklets. Arabic pins are distinctive. They are shaped like our old-fashioned stick pins, with a fan-shaped head of filigree. Sometimes, small, semi-precious gems are set in the fan. I have one with coral and turquoise. A hole is punched in the stem close to the place where the pin joins the head, and a thin wire run through it. The wire is then bent in a three-quarters circle, cut off, and flattened at the ends. When the pin is thrust through clothing, the circle is turned so that it becomes a safety clasp holding the pin securely in place.

The craftsman took the hard strip of metal from the mold, placed it on a cylinder of wood, and with a wooden hammer, shaped it into a bracelet. Then he washed it in a weak solution of acid and the bracelet turned a bright silver color.

"What kind of metal is it?" I asked.

"A mixture of zinc and copper." We bought the bracelet and several pins. It was the kind of jewelry a country woman would wear everyday as she went about her work. I still have it on our trinket cabinet.

Later we strolled back up to the square and stopped in front of a French jewelry store. A delicate gold necklace of green stones and seed pearls was displayed on a velvet tray in the window.

"See how the French have adapted native jewelry styles for their customers," said my husband. "The many pendants with their gems are set on a chain just as the natives set their gold coins. This is much too delicate for a Muslim woman. She wants heavy jewelry, but it is just the right airiness for a French woman or an American one. Let's go in."

We did and Alonzo said, "May we look at the necklace in the window?"

The clerk brought out the lovely piece of jewelry. My husband asked the price. I immediately lost interest. However, he kept looking at it and holding it so the sun shone on the peridot stones and reflected a cool green light. I looked at other things in the store. Finally my husband said "Don't you like it?"

"I love it." I replied. "But it will wreck our budget."

"I'll take it."

When we got outside Alonzo put the oblong box in my hand and said, "A husband may overextend the budget for a gift for his wife when she puts up with primitive conditions and dusty, cold situations at the diggings as you have done."

We went right home, and I wore the necklace all that day.

M. Hassinou joined us for dinner that night. He was a widower, and his housekeeper looked after his seven-year-old son, so he was free to go when and where he pleased.

"How would you like to drive out to the lighthouse on Cap Carbon tomorrow morning?" he asked. We thought it would be a good idea. "Then we'll walk back along the *corniche*. That is the walled path that hugs the coastline. It's about five miles back to the city."

The next morning promptly at 7:30 we heard horses' hooves clattering on the paving stones, and M. Hassinou arrived in the now-familiar two-seated carriage. We climbed in and started up the street.

"Please stop at my home for a moment," M. Hassinou told the coachman.

We stopped before a house higher up on the mountain. M. Hassinou's seven-year-old son came down the walk and handed me a bouquet of jasmine blossoms.

"The flower of the Arab," said our friend.

"Thank you very much, Ahmed," I said, as I took the pretty yellow flowers and held them to my face to enjoy the delicate perfume.

Our road wound up the mountain back of Bougie. At times it was just a narrow shelf cut from the mountainside. At other times it skirted around the ends of steep gullies. M. Hassinou pointed out interesting landmarks at almost every turn as we went along.

"That is the Peak of the Monkeys. People who picnic up there are often joined by wild monkeys who help themselves to the picnickers' lunches. It is said that sometimes the monkeys throw rocks down on passing carriages."

We were a bit skeptical and inclined to remember falling rock signs on American mountain roads. I must have looked apprehensive, for he hastened to reassure me, "Oh, we won't go that close to the mountain."

When the road became steep the driver urged his team on with a soft "EEEEEEEEE — ooooooo."

Cork oak covered the lower slopes, but the jagged peaks above us were bare. The road eventually ended at a narrow isthmus. M. Hassinou dismissed the driver and said that we would walk back to Bougie by way of the *corniche*.

A walled path led along the ridge, which was a little more than an inverted V, its steep sides dropping down to the Mediterranean five hundred feet below. We made our way safely across and climbed a steep, rocky path that zigzagged up the landward side of the cape. The last part was so steep that it was a flight of concrete steps following the contour of the rock.

Cap Carbon.

At last we were on the top. The rock had been leveled to provide room for a cluster of small cottages, and a little higher up, at the very end of the cliff, was the lighthouse. A man came down the narrow road, and our friend introduced us to the keeper of the light.

He was always glad to have company, he said, because it was lonely at the light, although there were eight families living in the cottages. Someone must always be on duty at the light and someone on maintenance. He led us up the path to his cottage. His home was a small house of red brick and white stucco. We went through a small archway into an open court surrounded by the rooms of the house. A narrow colonnade surrounded the court and kept the brilliant sunshine from making the rooms too hot. We followed him up a stairway onto the flat roof that led to the round lighthouse tower.

"We have many ways of communicating besides the light," he said. "We have semaphores for ships that have no wireless," and he showed us a tall, steel pole with cross-arms for signal flags. "I have a telegraph which ties into the national communications system. When ships signal me, I can relay their messages to any place in the world."

We climbed the steep stairs to the tower and the big light with its large, heavy lenses.

"At this point we are 750 feet above the sea. This light can be seen for thirty-five miles at night. Down there," and he pointed to a small light near the base of the rock, "is a small light that is always kept burning. In case of fog up here on the cliff, the small light warns the ships away from the rocky shore."

"Tell them about the heliograph," prompted M. Hassinou.

"Oh, yes. It was on this point that the first heliograph was established. Way back in 1068 a series of mirrors were placed on rocky points along the shore, and messages flashed from place to place."

We finished the tour of the lighthouse and went down the steps.

"Come and see my garden."

"Garden! On this barren rock!" said my husband.

"Certainly. We French need our radishes, shallots and, of course, fresh lettuce." He led the way to a plot of ground about ten feet square, held in place by a stone curb.

"Where did you get the soil?" asked Alonzo.

"I carried it up in baskets on my back. I found dirt in little pockets over on the mainland rock. Every day I filled panniers, such as you see on the burros, put one on my back, and climbed up here. After many days I had a garden four inches deep. It is enough." He thrust a stick into the ground to show us how deep it was. Rows of tiny lettuce leaves and spears of shallots had poked their tips up through the soil, assuring this Frenchman of fresh salad all the year round.

We said goodbye to this dedicated civil servant who worked so hard to bring the convenience of civilization to his outpost. Back across the isthmus we went, where we turned onto another walled path that clung to the cliff high above the Mediterranean.

"This is the *corniche*" said our friend, "named after the famous way at Nice on the French Riviera, but our guidebooks say that ours is more beautiful."

Five hundred feet below us, the blue sea crashed in a white froth on the black rocks. The mountain rose in sheer walls to our right. We took our time, stopping now and then to lean on the railing and just look out over the blue water sparkling in the sunlight.

M. Hassinou knew his part of the country well. "Below us is the *Baie des Salines*. In the spring when tides are high, the water fills those rock basins. The summer sun and wind evaporate the water, leaving a heavy crust of salt. Then in the fall, people come here with bags and scrape up enough salt to last a year. Our people have been doing this for thousands of years."

The path wound around another point and into a cove.

"During the Great War, a German submarine landed in this little bay. The water is very deep. The German sailors dressed themselves in French army uniforms and walked into Bougie to buy supplies. They got away before the French knew about it. This really is a wild part of the coast."

Our path always descended a little which made for easy walking. When we reached the city, we were only fifty feet above the sea. During our five-mile walk we had descended about seven hundred feet.

We made our way back along the wharfs and up through the Saracen Arch to our little restaurant. As we sat on the terrace, we tried to digest the beauty we had seen, as well as the biggest lunch that the waiter could bring.

11

Mosque of the Women

M. Hassinou usually joined us on Saturday nights at the restaurant, so we were surprised to find him sitting at a table waiting for us Monday evening. He greeted us and said, "My mother-in-law would like to have you visit her tomorrow evening."

It is not often that a non-Muslim is invited to a Muslim's home and especially to meet the women of his family. So we really felt privileged and accepted the invitation gladly.

"I'll call for you at eight tomorrow night," said our friend, as he left us after dinner.

Debby had told us that M. Hassinou's wife had died the summer before and that when the year of mourning was over, he would marry Leila, the next oldest sister in his wife's family.

We were waiting at the street door the next night when M. Hassinou came walking down the *rue du Vieillard*. "Good evening, M. and Mme. Pond," he said. "It is only three blocks from here. We can walk."

We took a cross-street. The soft breeze from the peach trees in full bloom in nearby gardens gave the evening a delightful fragrance. Soon we stopped at a white house with green shutters. As in most European and North African cities, the houses were built tight together and touching the walk. Walled gardens were in the back for privacy.

M. Hassinou knocked, and the door was opened by a slender, dark-eyed woman.

"Come in, come in," she invited us.

"I have brought M. and Mme. Pond," said M. Hassinou, and to us, indicating the tall lady, "my mother-in-law."

She led us into the living room and presented her three daughters. Pretty, vivacious girls, they were, with sparkling brown eyes. "This is Leila, the oldest, and Naila, and my youngest, Fatima," she said. "Won't you sit down?"

The room was furnished in a mixture of European and Moorish styles. There was a table and straight-backed chairs. A row of plump cushions lined one wall. In front of them was a low table, perhaps a foot high, made of some dark wood and inlaid with mother-of-pearl. A chest of drawers stood against another wall, and a Singer sewing machine was across a corner. The room was lighted by a kerosene lamp that hung from the ceiling. When I was a young girl in southern Wisconsin, my rural friends often had similar lamps in their homes. At our host's invitation, we accepted the straight-backed chairs. I wasn't sure that I could gracefully make it down on those soft cushions.

The mother and oldest daughter spoke French much more fluently than I did, but they were patient with my stumbling college diction.

After a few minutes of pleasant conversation, the mother said to the youngest daughter, "Fatima, will you please bring in the coffee?"

Little Fatima left the room quickly but was back in seconds with a brass coffeepot and small delicate china cups on a large brass tray. The coffee was very strong and black. We knew from experience that we were expected to add a heaping teaspoonful of sugar to each cup.

Naila, the middle daughter, brought in a plate full of cakes. I had often seen little boys with trays of cakes like these on their heads. They circulated through the marketplace or near cafés, selling them to the men drinking coffee. I had never tasted one. They looked like grease-soaked crullers, so I was surprised, when I bit into one, to find it crisp and filled with liquid honey.

"Mmmm! They are delicious!" I said. "How do you make them?"

Naila explained. "I make a dough of farina and water and force it through a pastry tube. It comes out looking like macaroni. As I force it through the tube, I coil the dough into small circles. These I drop into a pot of hot olive oil and fry them until they are crisp. Then I drop them into a dish of liquid honey and let them stay until the honey fills the hollow center. After that I dry them on a clean cloth."

It was thirty years before I found a recipe in English. Now I can make them, but I've never found a mold that would make a macaroni-like form. I just roll the dough in my hands until it is pencil-thin.

After we had finished our coffee, Leila said, "My little sister is going to be married in May. Would you like to see her trousseau?"

The three girls left the room and returned with arms full of dresses. There must have been fifteen at least. "These are not all of them, just a sample," Fatima explained.

They were all made after the same pattern, a jumper style — sleeveless, with a deep V-neck, full skirts gathered at the waist. There was a white blouse for every dress. The blouses had round necks and full, puffed sleeves gathered just below the elbow. The sleeves and necks on most blouses were trimmed with handmade lace. What the dresses lacked in change of style, they made up for in variety of materials. Dresses for house wear were of ginghams and sateens; afternoon dresses for around home were of voile, dimity, and crêpe de Chine; party dresses were of brocade, satin, and velvet. Dresses for winter were of flannel and heavy crepe, and dresses for summer, of tissue gingham and sheer crepe.

Some dresses were of plain colors, some striped, some dotted, some checked, and many of them were flowered. The brocaded party dresses had the designs outlined in silver and gold threads. The neck and armholes of each dress were bound with silk braid; some had a ribbon rosette or a pearl bead placed every inch on the braid.

"There are bloomers to match each of these dresses," Leila said.

Fatima left the room and came back with an armload of head scarves; some plain silk with a deep fringe; others of brocade with silver or gold fringes. Surely, this bride could never complain that she "didn't have a thing to wear."

When we got up to leave, Madame said to me, "Would you like to go with me to the mosque tomorrow afternoon?"

"I would like very much to go," I answered.

"Would you please come just at noon?"

I nodded assent.

We started down the hall to the front door when Alonzo remembered that he had left his hat in the living room. He turned to go back and surprised M. Hassinou and Leila in close embrace just the way an American and his fiancée would say "good night." We were embarrassed, but they weren't.

The next day just at noon I rapped on the door. Madame and Leila welcomed me. I stepped into the hall while they put on face veils and the long, white *barracan*, which all Algerian Muslim women wear as an outer garment.

"There'll not be many women at the mosque today," Madame said as we walked along. "It is Ramadan, and without food or water, it is too fatiguing for most women to make the long walk."

I already knew about Ramadan, the Muslim month of fasting, when no devout worshipper will allow a morsel of food or a drop of water to pass his lips between sunrise and sunset. For those who must work, it is a real hardship, as we had found at the diggings.

It felt strange to be walking down the street between two veiled women. Now and then, they greeted other women as we met them. How they knew their friends when just their eyes showed, I do not know.

"We're going to a mosque that is just for women," said Leila. "It is a room in an old fort down on the shore. Many years ago a holy man who lived here in Bougie was especially good to the women of this region. When he died his body was placed in a sarcophagus in a room in the fort, and so this has become our place of worship."

"Friday is our Holy Day," explained Madame, "but because the streets are full of men going to their mosques, we women worship on Wednesday when the streets are less crowded."

We entered the fort through the gate in the thick wall, then crossed a small courtyard to an archway that led into a long corridor. We stopped beside an open door, stepped out of our shoes, and placed them with the ten or more pairs along the wall. I was glad that I had American shoes so that I could easily pick out mine when we left. Stocking-footed, we stepped into a small room. High up on the seaward side was a small window through which we could see a patch of blue sky and hear the waves crashing on the rocks below. The white-painted walls were covered with silk flags in pastel colors. Arabic characters on them were embroidered in gold. I suppose they were verses from the Qur'an, their Holy Book. An ornately carved wooden sarcophagus covered with a green and gold silk flag stood in an alcove.

My two friends stepped forward, dropped a kiss on the tomb, and put a few coins in a box placed nearby. I, too, put a five-franc piece into the box. Then we stepped back into the room. We joined the other women seated on the floor. Madame turned toward the wall and prayed, running her fingers over her prayer beads. Leila modestly lowered her head and kept her eyes downcast.

I sat silently until Madame turned back toward the center of the room. She started a conversation with her neighbor. Many beautifully decorated candles had been placed on a small table near the door. Leila whispered to me, "If one has a special wish one wants fulfilled, she may buy a candle and burn it before the tomb."

We did not stay long because more women were coming, and the room was getting crowded. After stepping into our shoes, we walked into the sunny courtyard where groups of women were talking, much as people do after church in America. I couldn't understand the Kabylie dialect, but I imagined family news was exchanged.

"We'll take the back way home," said Madame as we stepped into the street. "That way we won't have to wear our veils all the time. It is too hot."

My friends carried their veils in their hands, and when they saw a man coming, they just held the veils over their faces until we had passed him.

When we reached Madame's home, she said, "Won't you come in for a cup of coffee?"

We went into the cool living room where the women shed their long *barracans*. Fatima came in. She was plainly dressed and had whole cloves stuck in her ears to keep open the holes pierced for earrings. In fact, the women wore a minimum of jewelry.

"Naila, will you bring Mme. Pond some coffee," said Madame as we seated ourselves on the chairs.

Soon we heard a squeal from the kitchen. Leila rushed out but returned with a smile.

"Naila forgot that it was Ramadan and tasted the coffee. Now she will have to keep the fast five days longer."

"But how can you tell whether the coffee is good unless you taste it" said Naila, as she appeared in the doorway with a small, brass tray with the pot of coffee, one china cup, and a plate of Turkish nougat.

While I sat and enjoyed my coffee and sweets, the three girls got out their embroidery and lace work. Several parallel lines were drawn on a thin piece of manila board. The girls made geometric patterns by placing evenly spaced knots of mercerized cotton thread between the guidelines. I have never seen lace like that in any other part of the world.

The family was very gay, teasing one another as sisters do. Madame laughed with them. In deference to me, they spoke French, and I could laugh at their jokes.

The afternoon was too soon over, and I had to leave. I still cherish the memory of one of the pleasantest afternoons spent in Bougie.

12

La Grande Prière

*B*oom! The sound and smoke of the sunset gun at the fort rolled down the mountainside, across the city, and over the valley of the Soummam River to echo back from the mountains across the bay. Officially the end of the day had come.

For half an hour a *marabout* (Muslim Holy Man) had stood at the western gate of the fort. In his hands were a white thread and a black thread. When he held them against the sunset sky and could no longer distinguish the color of one from the other, he signaled the gunner, and the cannon boomed. The sound released the Muslims from their day-long fast.

The city of Bougie was thronged with pilgrims. It has been called the "little Mecca," because it has so many tombs of Holy Men. It was said that there are ninety-nine; only Mecca has one more, and that one is the tomb of the Prophet, Mohammed.

We walked slowly down the street to our own dinner at the *Brasserie de l'Étoile*. As we passed the native cafés, we looked in through their wide-open doors. They were crowded with men sitting on straw mats in front of low tables. Turbaned waiters hurried among their customers pouring cups of thick, black coffee. Boys with large trays of sweet cakes on their heads circulated among the crowds. Soon their wares were gone, and they dashed back to the bakers for more.

Above the clatter of cups on tables and the hum of conversation, we could hear the Bingo caller, "sixty-four under the O," but in the Arabic version. Soon there was the excited cry of the winner and the groans of the losers. On this last night of Ramadan, the crowds were larger and the excitement more intense. Later, when we closed our windows for the night we could still hear the Bingo caller, "Sixty-four under the O."

The Grande Prière, Bougie.

The next day, the day of the *Grande Prière*, was cold and gray. After breakfast we mingled with the crowds of worshippers on the plain below the city. Turbans were spotless, and *burnouses* showed signs of recent washing. Most of the pilgrims were the poorer people who could not afford the *hadj*, or pilgrimage to Mecca. Many of the men had walked for several days to attend the service here at Bougie.

Muslim women in their bright dresses hurried toward the mosque. They were allowed to worship on the flat roof. Later, as we stood on a small slope we could look over the mosque. It looked like a great patchwork quilt, with the women in their pink, yellow, and pale green dresses and head scarves.

As the morning wore on, the men arranged themselves in rows facing the east and Mecca, so many hundreds of miles away. The crowd was almost silent in meditation or murmuring their prayers, rarely speaking to their neighbors, and then, only when necessary and in hushed tones. Each man had a small prayer rug on the ground in front of him.

Precisely at eleven o'clock the head *marabout* descended the steps of the mosque. Behind him were two other *marabouts*, each carrying a green silk flag with verses from the Qur'an embroidered in gold. With stately tread, the three walked to the head of the great crowd of men. The flags were placed in standards, and each man spread his own prayer rug.

The *marabout* bowed to the east, then bent from the waist, dropped to his knees, and touched his forehead to the ground. Then, sitting back on his heels, he folded his hands in meditation. Row after row of men followed him.

While seated in meditation, each man repeated silently the Muslim Prayer.
God is great
God is All Powerful
There is no God but Allah
And Mohammed is His Prophet.

The *marabout* stood up. Three thousand men rose like a great white wave behind him. Once again he bowed, dropped to his knees, and touched his forehead to the ground. Then he sat back into a position of meditation and a repetition of the prayer. Silently the men followed. There was no sound but the rustling of thousands of garments as they folded themselves about the kneeling worshippers.

A third time the *marabout* stood, lowered his head toward Mecca, knelt, and touched the ground with his forehead, then resumed his meditation and his prayer: Finally he stood up and walked back to the mosque, the flag-bearers following him.

Silently the men broke the ranks. Small groups drifted off. Their faces glowed with the inner light of a soul-satisfying experience.

13

We Say Goodbye to Bougie and Algeria

"There's a circus poster! A circus is coming to town," I said, as we were driving back from the diggings one day in late April.

"Let's all go," said Alonzo.

The night of the circus none of the regular diners lingered over their meal at the *Brasserie*. We, too, hurried to join the crowd that straggled down the hill to the plain below the city where a tent had been pitched. The brightly lighted circle with the crowd of white-robed, small boys darting around reminded me of a street lamp attracting a bevy of moths.

We bought ringside seats. The crowd was a motley one, mostly French, but with groups of natives scattered here and there on the bleachers. We could hear the excited voices of the youngsters outside the tent as they raced around hoping to catch a glimpse of the action inside through openings in the side walls. There was just one ring.

Shortly after eight o'clock we heard the familiar notes of the "Sheik of Araby." A man entered playing a violin. He wore a harlequin costume covered with spangles. He walked around the circle and then bowed deeply to the audience. For an encore he played Rubenstein's "Melody in F." We assumed that he was the owner of the circus, or at least the manager. We had never associated well-played violin music with circuses; neither did we expect such quality from a traditionally dressed clown. The act was appreciated by the audience.

A trained dog act followed. There were six dogs of different kinds; some walked on their hind feet, some jumped through hoops, and several danced.

"Just like the pony and dog shows I saw when I was young," I exclaimed.

The ponies were next. They pranced and danced and bowed to the audience. They circled the ring in twos and threes and finally fours. Then the gymnasts in spangled tights tumbled and did balancing acts. Finally the ring was cleared of all equipment. Roustabouts and some performers, still in tights, brought in sections of a steel cage.

"The wild animal act is coming;" said Debby, knowingly, then called loudly, "Here, boy, three boxes of crackerjack. We'll have to have something to entertain us while they put up the cage."

For half an hour they lugged, tugged, and bolted. Patiently the crowd watched and waited. At last the steel bars were in place. A menagerie wagon backed up to the door, and six snarling lions and tigers jumped into the ring. The trainer stepped into his place and banged the steel door behind him. He cracked his whip and fired a pistol. The beasts snarled and bared their teeth.

Suddenly our ringside seats were much too close. I could feel and smell the hot breath of the animals. I drew back.

"I hope they haven't forgotten bolts on that cage," I said.

The big cats sat up and begged, jumped through hoops, rolled over, and did many other acts to the cue of a cracked whip. Now and then an animal would tentatively stretch a paw through the bars. The sharp report of a blank cartridge would make him withdraw it hastily. Finally the cage doors were opened, and the menagerie wagon was right there. The cats were wheeled away, and the perspiring trainer acknowledged the applause. The circus was over.

We followed the crowd up the hill to the square and then went farther up the hill to our rooms. While we had seen the Ringling Brothers Circus with its sophisticated five rings and four stages, all active at once, back in the States, that little one-ring circus in Bougie remains in our hearts.

A few weeks later we were invited to another show of an entirely different nature.

One evening when we were having a late dinner, M. Hassinou dropped in to have coffee with us.

"The place seems to be buzzing with excitement," I said. "What's happening?"

"The guillotine arrived today," M. Hassinou replied.

"The what?"

"The guillotine. It came all the way from Paris." Then he explained.

"A native stabbed a farmer to death. He has had a long and fair trial and has been condemned to death. To the Muslims, the body is sacred, and the destruction of any part of it is sacrilegious. The sentence stipulated death by guillotine. It will emphasize the enormity of his crime and make an example of the culprit."

Being a guest in the country kept me from voicing my horror at the method of capital punishment.

The next day M. Hassinou brought word that, as my husband and I were distinguished guests in the city of Bougie, the *Préfet* of Police would be honored if we accepted seats in the window just above the guillotine. The execution would take place at sunrise the next day.

Alonzo sent back word that we appreciated the honor but that we would be unable to attend.

As we went down to breakfast the next day, we met a very subdued crowd returning from the execution site.

We finally had a good collection of artifacts from Ali Bacha. Nothing new was showing up in the diggings. Summer was near with its unbearably hot weather, and we decided to call it quits.

Our workmen carried boxes of stone artifacts down the hill on their backs to the waiting taxi. We spent several days in our room washing, sorting, and packing bone and stone tools. The collection was divided, some to go to the National Museum in Algiers and some to be shipped directly from Bougie to Beloit College.

We made our farewell calls on the American Consul and on M. Hassinou and his charming mother-in-law and her daughters.

Debby was to take the train back to Constantine, and we would go to Algiers. Our train left first, and Debby came to the station to see us off. His round hat with its turned up brim and his trousers tucked into high boots made him still look like a little boy setting out for adventure. There were tears in his eyes as he shook hands with Alonzo. He leaned forward to give me a chaste French embrace with a kiss on each cheek, but some mischievous impulse made me give him a good American kiss on the mouth. We climbed into our coach leaving him standing on the platform his mouth agape and his eyes wide with surprise.

We had enjoyed living in Bougie and had many pleasant memories of the city. We felt sad as our train pulled out of the station, but we soon grew light-hearted because ahead of us was Paris and then home.

Wisconsin would look very good to us after being foreigners for ten months.

14

We Head for Algeria Again

*A*lmost two years had gone by since we said goodbye to our friends in Algeria. During those two years we lived in Chicago while Alonzo earned his Master's degree at the University of Chicago. After that he had spent six months in the Gobi Desert as the archaeologist with Roy Chapman Andrews and the Central Asiatic Expedition. Most importantly, we had added a third member to the family, a daughter named Chomingwen. Translated from the Ojibwe Indian language, the name means "The girl who smiles." Eventually the name was shortened to Chomee.

When we announced to our family and friends that we were going to Africa again and were taking our seventeen-month-old daughter, they all thought we were out of our minds. And when we added that we were not going to stay in small, country hotels but camp out on the open plain among all those so-called "wild Arabs," they knew we were absolutely crazy.

We had carefully planned it, however, and decided that we would be as warm in a heavy tent, sleeping between eiderdown puffs, as we were in the small hotel rooms heated by tiny fireplaces. Besides, we weren't leaving until the winter rains and snows would be over in North Africa.

As for meals, we could always buy canned goods in the grocery stores and fresh vegetables and meat in the market.

"What about fresh milk?" our friends asked.

"Chomee is allergic to milk," we said. "We are taking a couple of cases of powdered milk with us."

Still shaking their heads in dismay, our family saw us off on the train to Chicago and New York.

We sailed out of New York harbor into the worst storm of the winter. I lay in bed and watched my wardrobe trunk slide across the floor, hitting all four walls of the stateroom, and I didn't care. Chomee, too, was seasick, but Alonzo made it to every meal in the dining salon.

The main salon was just above us. The second day out, I heard what sounded like the grand piano break away from its moorings and crash against the opposite wall. I don't know whether that was the last big wave or whether the captain turned the ship to another course, but after that, the sea gradually became calmer. The next day we were able to enjoy our morning bouillon and afternoon tea sitting wrapped up in our deck chairs and watching whales spout far out at sea.

Chomee was the only child in first class and so had the English nanny and playroom all to herself. After the third day, the purser asked if we would mind if a little girl from second class came up and shared the playroom. We agreed and were happy for Chomee to have a playmate.

We landed at LeHavre and took the boat train to Paris. Paris was cold, gray, and wet. We all got the flu. Chomee was sent to the American hospital. Alonzo and I stuck it out in our hotel room and called in a young Greek doctor who was staying at the hotel. He prescribed "blisters." The concierge went to the pharmacy and bought a dozen little glass cups. The doctor put a little bit of cotton in each cup, lighted it, and clamped it on Alonzo's back. When the oxygen was burned out, it created a vacuum which drew his flesh into the cups. They looked like gigantic goose pimples. This was a form of counter-irritant. I declined the treatment and told the chambermaid how to make a mustard plaster for my back. Soon we all recovered and were reunited as a family.

Alonzo had a cousin, Edith, from Brooklyn, New York, who was attending the Sorbonne that year. One afternoon we were having tea with her in her room. Her roommate, Florence Poyer, sat on the bed; Mahmud, who claimed relationship with the ex-Shah of Persia, was perched on the windowsill, and his cousin stood near the door. We were talking about our expedition in Algeria.

"Why don't you and Florence come down and see us during the semester break?" I asked Edith.

"We thought we'd go to Italy," Edith replied.

"Anybody can go to Italy," said Alonzo, "but only one in a million can go camping in Algeria."

Mahmud, sensing the loss of an interesting companion during vacation, glowered. "I think Africa is no place for American girls."

"Let's go, Edith. I'm getting awfully bored with Paris," said Florence.

We left with a half-promise that the girls would join us in a couple of weeks.

The Mediterranean crossing was as stormy as the Atlantic had been. Algiers, too, was gray and cold. There was no wedding-cake look to the city this time as there had been when I first saw it. Now it was just a jumbled pile of gray, stone buildings.

The year before, while Alonzo was in Asia, the Logan Museum had sent a graduate student and his wife to Algeria to work in the shell mounds. They had purchased a half-ton truck and left it down at Tebessa on the Tunisian border. We were to pick it up before we started our year's work.

The thought of digging in a gray shell mound with workmen in dirty gray *burnouses* and living in a gray tent under gray skies was not at all appealing. We sat discussing the matter in our hotel room in Algiers.

Finally Alonzo said, "Tomorrow we'll take the train to Tebessa where we'll pick up the truck. Then we'll drive back to Constantine where we'll meet Edith and Florence. We'll go down to Biskra and across the desert to Tozeur and Negrine, then back up to Gafsa in Tunisia. Probably by that time it will be spring on the High Plateau, and we can pick a site for our diggings in the *Commune* of Canrobert."

Alonzo had made his official calls in Algiers and had been given permission to dig in any site he chose in the *Communes* of Meskiana or Canrobert[6]. An Algerian *commune* was much like a county. We had chosen Canrobert because of the abundance of prehistoric sites and because it had more French villages which were needed as our base of supplies.

We spent all the next day on the train and reached Tebessa in the early evening. A cab took us to our hotel. We had written from Paris to have the truck ready, but of course nothing had been done on it. It sat in the back of the garage just as it had for the last eight months.

"We will get at it tomorrow morning," the garage mechanic promised.

"It will probably take several days for them to get the truck ready," my husband said to me. "We'll just have to spend the time here at the hotel."

Dr. Collie and his wife had spent a month or so at the diggings last year. Before we left Beloit, Mrs. Collie had given me a letter to Madame Pages, a British missionary in Tebessa. They had become good friends during her stay there.

"I guess I'll send a note to Mrs. Collie's friend," I said. "I'll ask her to have coffee with us this afternoon."

A note was dispatched by messenger to the British mission.

Soon the boy brought back a reply. "Would we please come to coffee at the mission that afternoon?"

It was just a couple of blocks from the hotel, so we walked. The mission had just bought a house formerly owned by a wealthy Arab. Madame Pages met us at the gate to the front garden. She was a stout, middle aged woman with iron-gray hair. She introduced us to her two assistants, both American girls in their late twenties. One was from Pennsylvania and one from Minnesota. Their term of duty was five years, and they were so glad to see some Americans. Tourists rarely got as far east as Tebessa.

---

6. Now Oum el Bouaghi.

We learned that they spent most of their time teaching reading, sewing, and hygiene to native women and children. They also did some simple first-aid work. As we sat on the patio drinking our coffee, I saw a heap of brightly colored tiles off to one side. Madame Pages saw me look in that direction.

"We're having a modern bathroom put in and are having to tear down the walls of the old harem," she said.

"What are you doing with those lovely old tiles?" I asked.

"Taking them to the dump," she replied.

"Oh, may I have several to use as tea tiles?"

"Take as many as you like."

I knew how full our luggage was so I took just two. The blue border and bright red flowers are as bright as when they were painted over a hundred years ago.

The American girls regretfully said goodbye to us when teatime was over.

The modern city of Tebessa is built on the ruins of an old Roman city. When we were there, the old Roman wall still enclosed the city. One entered through that ancient gate with its watchtowers over a wide arch. We enjoyed visiting the Temple of Minerva with its fluted columns and wandering around other ruins where Roman villas had once stood.

The French government had decided to enlarge the post office, and one day we stopped to watch the work. A workman turned over a shovelful of dirt where

Outside the walls of Tebessa.

77

the old steps had been. There was a Roman coin. He picked it up and handed it to Chomee, saying, "A thousand years ago some Roman dropped this. Now it is a gift for a little American girl."

Later on Alonzo was given one of those flat stone lamps from the same excavation. Both of them have a special place in our curio cabinet.

The third day we were at the hotel, the concierge handed a letter to me. When I opened it, I said, "Edith and Florence are arriving at Constantine the day after tomorrow."

"The truck will be ready tomorrow. We'll start as soon as I can get it and stop overnight on the way."

The truck wasn't ready the next day, but the morning after that, Alonzo drove up to the hotel, and we piled our luggage in the back with all the camping equipment that had been stored in it from the previous expedition. Chomee and I climbed into the cab, and off we went to Constantine.

We reached there late in the afternoon and found the girls waiting for us. They had come in a day early.

There were some adjustments to be made on the truck, so the next day Alonzo took the truck to the garage while I went shopping for groceries for a camping trip: cans of peas, beans, peaches, and jam; canned butter from Denmark and canned meat from the Argentine; two dozen eggs and packages of cookies; two dozen oranges and a couple of cases of bottled mineral water. We hoped to buy fresh meat and bread at the villages along the way.

We had planned to start at noon but, as usual, the truck wasn't ready. At four o'clock, Alonzo drove up.

"Even though it is late we'll leave," he said. "We may get only to the outskirts of Constantine but we'll be on our way."

Boxes of groceries, camera equipment, typewriter, and personal luggage were all loaded into the back of the truck which already held cots, gasoline stove, lantern, table, and folding chairs left from the year before.

The girls sat on folding chairs in the back while Alonzo, Chomee, and I sat in the cab. We had taken out the celluloid window between the cab and the back so that we could talk. The truck had a white canvas cover over it which made it look like a modern version of the old covered wagon.

The concierge and the little *chasseur* (errand boy) waved goodbye, and we slowly pulled away from the curb.

15

Biskra

We drove across the long, many-arched bridge of Sidi Rached, then on down the mountain, past the railroad station, and out onto the plain. The sun was bright. At last we were on our way, and our spirits were high. We drove through Kroubs, a few miles from Constantine, and just beyond the village, found an ideal camping site — a grassy little park-like spot beside the road with tall palm trees bathing their roots in a clear, sparkling stream. The only drawback: we had no privacy.

Camping in those days was something that just was not done by Europeans in Algeria. We soon had a small crowd of onlookers. During the next few days we became accustomed to preparing and eating our meals in front of curious Algerians. The girls had never camped before — both of them were city girls from Brooklyn and New York — but they pitched in and did more than their share of work throughout the trip. In our hurry to get away we had just shoved the boxes of groceries into the truck. The equipment left from the year before was way at the back end, the gasoline stove under everything.

Alonzo dug the stove out and set it up on a box of groceries while the girls put up the table and chairs on the ground next to the truck and found the aluminum plates and "silverware." By that time I had ready a meal of fried eggs, canned peas, bread, butter, jam, and cookies.

We washed our dishes in the stream. Alonzo set up the two cots for the girls on the grass close to the truck, and I unrolled our bedrolls on the floor of the truck. Soon we were all tucked in. The moon came up and shed such a bright light that it was difficult to sleep.

I was just drowsing off when I heard voices. Peering through the cracks between the sideboards, I saw two men walking down the road. I woke Alonzo.

"There are two men coming down the road, and one of them is carrying a gun."

"They're probably a couple of hunters," said Alonzo, and turned over and went back to sleep.

A few minutes later I heard a shot, and soon the two men came back. A cloud covered the moon, so I could not see whether they had been successful.

I was up with the sun the next morning. It was five o'clock. The smell of fresh coffee soon woke the rest. We washed in the stream and then sat down to breakfast of oranges, oatmeal, bread, butter, and coffee. By 7:00 everything was packed back in the truck in a more orderly fashion. Soon we were on our way south.

It was spring and the countryside was coming alive. Winter wheat gave the fields a green carpet; apricots and almond trees were in blossom, making frothy clouds of pink and white in the farm yards.

Our progress was slow because the shepherds were just taking their flocks from the home corrals to pasture, and the paved roads were their easiest route. No one was in a hurry. The sheep and shepherd sauntered along. We'd come up to a flock, honk our horn, and sit and wait. The startled shepherd flapped his cape-like *burnous* and shouted at the sheep. The flustered sheep hurried their pace but still covered the road. The shepherd would finally pull the lead sheep off the road, and the flock followed. At last the road was clear, and we could drive on, but for a couple of miles only. Then there would be another flock, and the scene was repeated while we waited impatiently.

About noon we came to a small town.

"Let's stop and buy fresh meat and bread," I said. Alonzo parked the truck, and Florence and I went into the only store. We pulled aside the canvas curtain and went into a small room. The contrast between the bright sun and the windowless interior made us blind for a moment. Then we saw the native storekeeper stretched out on a mat on the floor. He raised his head.

"Do you have fresh meat or bread?" I asked.

"No," he replied, and put his head down on the mat. He was asleep before we could go back out the door.

We drove through the town, pulled off on the side of the road, and ate a cold lunch standing around the truck.

On southward we went. About the middle of the afternoon, I saw a group of farm buildings mirrored in a lake.

"Look at the lake. Those farm buildings have a nice setting. Let's stop and have tea."

There was a car ahead of us on the road. "It's going right into the lake!" I cried. A cloud of dust followed it. Only then did we realize that we were seeing our first mirage.

Farther on we came to a real lake. It was only a pond surrounded by a band of sparkling white. A small caravan of camels was on the shore.

"Camels in snow!" said Florence.

"It does look like it, doesn't it?" said Alonzo. "Would you like to get out and eat some of it?"

He stopped the truck, and we all climbed out and touched it. It wasn't wet!

A few white grains stuck to our fingers. We licked them off. That sparkling white stuff wasn't snow!

"Salt!" exclaimed Florence.

"A mirage and camels all in one afternoon," said Edith. "Africa is living up to its reputation."

Our camping spot that night was not as picturesque as the one we had the night before. There were no palm trees and no sparkling stream, just a level gravelly place between the road and a gully. It was getting late, and we knew we must make camp before it got dark. To the south we could see snow-capped peaks of the Aures Mountains. The wind was chill. We ate a hurried supper, made our beds, and climbed in between eiderdown puffs and wool blankets. With all our clothes on, we slept comfortably.

The next day was cool and gray. We drove through small, gray villages and barren countryside. It was even colder that night. We piled the grocery boxes and hand luggage around the girls' cots to make a windbreak. We were up early the next day, and after a quick breakfast, started on.

"We can't get to the Sahara Desert too soon," said Edith, shivering under two sweaters and a coat.

After several hours driving, we saw a break in the mountain range ahead of us.

"The Gorge of El Kantara," I said.

The Kantara River has cut a narrow channel through the jagged mountain range. The river, the road, and the railroad squeeze through this narrow gap. The road runs close to the river, the railroad on a narrow shelf a little above. We stopped to watch native women washing clothes in the shallow stream, then spread the garments to dry on the gravelly banks. The oasis of El Kantara is squeezed between two mountain ranges; the one on the north protects it from the cold north winds and the mountains on the south, from the hot, drying ones. The size of an oasis is given, not by the number of people who live there, but by the number of palm trees. El Kantara was an oasis of 120,000 date palms.

We drove through the Red Village, the White Village, and the Black Village, named, not because of the color of the inhabitants, but, as we were told, because of the tint each village takes on at sunset. The streets were very narrow, and in places the pedestrians crowded into doorways to let us pass. They were made for donkey, camel, or pedestrian passage, not for modern four-wheeled trucks. Intersections were absolutely square.

"How are we ever going to make this corner?" I asked.

"Oh, back and fill," said Alonzo, and we did. Inch by inch, we made the turn.

The gorge through the south range was even narrower than the one through the north range. Our road crossed the river on a picturesque stone-arched bridge. The Romans had built it first. Then the Arab conquerors had allowed it to fall into disrepair. The French had rebuilt it during the reign of Napoleon III. Now it is part of the Algiers-Biskra National Highway. The gap is so narrow that the railroad had to tunnel through higher up on the mountain.

A misty rain began to fall as we drove through desolate landscape. The road began climbing, and we came to the top of the pass. Alonzo pulled over to the side. He insisted that we get out and walk to the other side of the pass.

"This is Col de Sfa, the true Gate of the Sahara."

What a disappointment! No beautiful curving sand dunes, no feathery palms, no camels, just badlands stretching away to the horizon which was lost in a foggy rain. Damp and dispirited, we climbed back into the truck and drove down the mountain. An hour or so later we were in the city of Biskra.

We'd had our fill of camping and drove up to a hotel. Alonzo took the truck to a garage, while we went up to our rooms. A warm meal, bath, and the prospect of a warm bed that night revived our spirits. After lunch we were out on the streets browsing in tourist shops.

Four days of rain had made Biskra a bedraggled city. No tourist busses had come from Algiers. The merchants were discouraged. Prices were high, aimed at American tourists. In spite of the loss of four days' business, the merchants would not lower the prices. Florence was a good bargainer, but the shopkeepers remained adamant. We came away empty- handed.

"Biskra is an oasis in the Garden of Allah," said Edith, "but where are the sand dunes?"

"They are five or six miles south of the oasis," said Alonzo. "Tomorrow we'll drive out there."

"We've come all this way to see the Sahara, and we just can't go home and say we didn't see any sand dunes," said Florence.

The American Express was our ever present help in need wherever we were. Alonzo went to their office.

"You can't possibly drive a half-ton *camionette* out to the dunes," they assured him. "The roads are too muddy. But we have a tourist bus that makes the trip every day. Of course, they haven't gone the last four days, but we'll send one tomorrow morning."

Alonzo bought tickets and joined us back at the hotel for a good meal that was prepared on more than a two-burner gasoline stove. How good it was to climb into a soft warm bed that night!

The next morning, while we were eating breakfast, a boy from the American Express came to tell us that the bus trip had been cancelled and returned our money. Half an hour later the sun came out, and another boy came to say that they would run the trip in half an hour.

While we were waiting in front of the hotel for the bus, a third boy came to say that the trip definitely was cancelled. Alonzo went back to the American Express Co. Wasn't there some way we could make the trip? Surely a horse and carriage could get through. Could they arrange it?

Shortly afterward a surrey with a team of horses drove up to the hotel. We got in and rolled through the paved streets of the city at a smart pace. When we got to the edge of the oasis, it was another story. The carriage wheels dropped into six inches of mud. The horses strained and pulled against their collars. We did go ahead, but slowly. We got one mile out of town, two miles out of town, three miles, and the driver stopped the horses to rest. One of the team was a skinny old nag, and we were afraid that she wouldn't make it. Her sides heaved, and it seemed as if she could hardly lift her feet. Another hundred yards and another stop to rest and so on for an hour.

At one stop the driver jumped from the carriage and picked a bouquet of yellow and purple flowers from the roadside and handed them to me.

What a paradox! Here we were in the Sahara, in the greatest desert of them all, stuck in the mud, and the driver was picking flowers!

It had been three hours since we had left Biskra. As the horses plodded along a small building took shape against a gray hill.

"There's the café," said Alonzo.

The ground was firmer, and perhaps the horses sensed that the end of the trip was near. They began walking a little faster, and in a few minutes we pulled into the courtyard.

We gave the driver some money for his lunch, and walked into the dining room and plopped into chairs. We had been trying to help the horses by straining ourselves.

"I haven't much food," the proprietor said. "No supplies have come through for four days."

"Omelet and tea?" asked Alonzo.

"But yes," the proprietor replied.

Soon we were sipping hot tea and eating olives and summer sausage, canned green beans, and fluffy omelets. There was no fresh fruit for dessert, but the waitress brought wedges of Swiss cheese and a plate of store cookies.

The sun came out. Our bodies and our spirits revived.

"Now for the dunes," said Alonzo.

We trudged up the hill back of the café, and there was the Sahara in all its majesty. Row after row of sand dunes with knife-sharp, sinuous ridges and long gentle slopes, rippled as a beach. At last the Sahara was living up to its picture postcard reputation.

Chomee was having a great time. She tossed sand, she slid down dunes. This was fun, playing in the biggest sandbox in the world.

Prehistoric station at Biskra: Out among the dunes.

Alonzo, ever the archaeologist, was watching the ground. Suddenly he stooped down and picked up a piece of worked flint. The rains had washed away the top sand, and we were standing on an Old Stone Age campsite. We all began to search and filled our pockets with stone scrapers, weapon points, and flint chips.

Finally Edith said, "I'm getting tired."

"So am I," said Florence. "Let's go back to the café and have some tea."

"You girls go on back," said Alonzo. "I'll pick up a few more flints, and then I'll come."

I decided to stay with my husband, and so the two girls went back over the dunes.

Soon Chomee, too, was tired, but Alonzo wasn't ready to stop collecting.

"I'll just take her back to the café, and I'll order tea for you, too," I said. "I can follow the girls' tracks and make it back alright."

"I won't be long," Alonzo assured me.

Chomee and I started trudging back, following the girls' footprints. It was easy, and we climbed first one dune and then another. Suddenly a strong wind came up. The blown sand stung our faces and our legs like sharp needles. I picked up my little daughter and buried her face in my shoulder. In no time at all, the girls' tracks were obliterated.

"Just up this dune," I thought, "and the café will be in the next hollow."

At the top of the dune, there was no building in sight. Another dune and no café. "We must have wandered farther than I realized."

The wind still tore at us. Down in the hollow we were protected, and I could get my breath, but the blowing sand made visibility almost nil when I got on top of a dune.

"Am I going in the right direction," I wondered, "or am I veering off to the left?" If I missed the building, there would be nothing but hundreds of miles of desert — and no easy way for people to search for us if we got lost among the dunes. The wind would obliterate my footprints as it had the girls'; and if I *was* veering to the left, as right-handed people tend to do when they can't see where they are walking, my trail in the hollows could be missed. There were no identifiable landmarks, just endless hills of sand. How many dunes had we crossed as we went out? I hadn't thought to keep track.

I began to be a little panicky, but I kept going up a dune and down a dune. Then from the top of the next dune, I saw the little café. I ran down the slope and burst into the dining room. The girls were drinking tea and eating cookies.

About half an hour later Alonzo came in. He had been down in a hollow between dunes and had not realized that a sandstorm had come up. When he did look up, he saw that the dunes were "smoking," a thin veil of sand blowing from their crests. Realizing that we would be worried about him, he hurried back.

After he had finished his tea, we started back to Biskra. The sun and wind had dried the roads, and the horses could walk faster. We made the trip back in a much shorter time.

The men at the garage told Alonzo that it would not be possible for us to drive across the desert to Negrine. The normally dry riverbeds were overflowing, and heavy trucks were stranded on the banks waiting for the water to go down.

The trip had taken longer than we had planned. Edith and Florence wanted to go back to France by way of Italy. That night we talked it over, and the girls decided that they would take the morning train to Batna, where they could board the Algiers-Tunis Express and take a boat from Tunis to Naples.

We decided to retrace our route to Constantine and then drive to the little village of Canrobert, where we would pick a shell mound for our diggings.

After dinner Edith said, "The morning train leaves at six o'clock. You won't want to get up that early so we'll say goodnight and goodbye now."

"It has been quite an adventure," said Florence, as we climbed the stairs to our rooms.

At 6:00 the next morning, I heard the train whistle and thought, "Well, Edith and Florence are on their way."

By nine o'clock we had breakfasted, packed the truck, and driven out of Biskra. We climbed steadily out of the desert through the "gate" at Col de Sfa and on to El Kantara. We didn't stop as it was another cold, gray day.

Beyond El Kantara we saw a little train slowly climbing the mountain. At first we thought it was coming toward us, but as we drove along, we saw that it was going in the same direction that we were.

"That looks like a freight train," I said. "I didn't know that two trains left Biskra this morning."

Our road paralleled the track.

"I think we are gaining on it," said Alonzo. "Do you suppose it could be the train the girls are on?"

"Not much chance. We heard their train whistle three hours before we left Biskra. This old truck isn't *that* good."

Steadily we climbed, and just as steadily we gained on the train.

"There are passenger cars, as well as freight cars," I said.

Then Alonzo really pushed the throttle to the floor. "There's a crossing a few miles ahead," he said. "Maybe we can beat the train to it."

"Wouldn't it be fun if the girls were on this side of the train, and we could wave to them?"

Our road flattened out, and we got up to thirty-five miles an hour. The train was going up grade and still crawling. People at the windows began waving to us. We got to the crossing two minutes ahead of the train, but a strong steel gate barred the way. As the train rattled by, there were Florence and Edith waving to us.

As soon as the gate was lifted, we dashed across the tracks and sped to the next village.

"Five francs for watching the truck," Alonzo called to a boy who was lounging nearby.

We hurried on to the platform just as the Biskra Express puffed to a stop. The girls came on to the train platform.

"We have half an hour for lunch in Batna," said Edith. "Can you make it and have lunch with us in the station?"

"We'll try," Alonzo called back, as we ran to the truck.

He tossed a five-franc piece to the boy. We climbed in, and he gunned the engine.

The country was level now. Soon the train caught up with us and passed us. But it had to stop at the next station, and we kept going. On the level, the train could make forty-five miles an hour. Our top speed was thirty-five. We seesawed back and forth over the plain. The train would pass us, then stop at a village, and we'd pass it. All of the passengers were waving to us at each passing.

Finally I said, after watching the kilometers markers go by, "Ten more kilometers to Batna, nine and nine tenths, nine and eight tenths… Nine kilometers to Batna, eight and nine tenths…."

When I said "Four kilometers to Batna," the engine sputtered, coughed, and died.

"Oh darn, we had such a good lead."

"Well, the truck won't run without gas," my husband said. "Looks as if they'll beat us now, but it was a good race."

He got out to fill the tank from the extra cans that we always carried. The train rushed by, the passengers waving madly. We gained a little during the next two kilometers, but the train was still ahead. We came to the outskirts of Batna and had to thread our way slowly through the streets to the station. The train was standing on the tracks when we arrived. We ran across the platform into the café.

"When we saw you stop," said Edith, "we thought you had had a puncture and gave up seeing you."

"We were just out of gas," I said. "I don't understand how we could cover the forty miles from Biskra to El Kantara in better time than the express. We heard your train whistle at six o'clock, and we didn't leave until nine."

"The train whistled at six, but we didn't leave until after seven," Florence explained. "Then the grade was so steep that we just crawled along."

We had sandwiches and coffee together, and again we said goodbye to the girls adding, "We'll see you in Paris in June."

16

Medfoun

We drove on to Constantine that night. Vacation was over. Gray weather or no gray weather, we knew we must start work.

We had obtained government permission to work in the *Commune Mixte de Canrobert*. The next morning, we drove east on the Constantine-Tebessa National Highway. The small village of Canrobert was about halfway to Tebessa. There was a hotel on the main street. We stopped and Alonzo went in to ask about a room.

He came back to say, "There's one on the courtyard. This boy will show you through. I'll drive the truck around."

Chomee and I climbed out of the truck and followed the boy through the bar and out the back door into a courtyard. There were rooms on three sides. The fourth side was a solid adobe wall with a heavily barred gate.

The little errand boy ran to open the gate so Alonzo could drive the truck right up to the door of our room. Then the boy hurried to set up a crib for Chomee.

The W.C. was a small, whitewashed room that opened off the courtyard. As usual, it was a squatty. No seat.

That afternoon Alonzo called on the *Préfet* and made acquaintances in the bar. The next day we drove around the open countryside, looking at shell mounds. At each one, we took samples of snail shells and worked flint by digging a small trench in the ancient campfire ashes. After sampling many mounds for three days, we chose a large one about ten miles from Canrobert. It was two miles off the highway and an eighth of a mile from Medfoun Creek. The mound itself was one hundred feet in diameter and ten feet high.

Late that afternoon, Alonzo was in the bar explaining our work to the proprietor, and adding, "Tomorrow I intend to establish my camp at Medfoun. I need four good workmen."

"Here's just the man you should see," said the owner, pointing to a middle-aged man at the other end of the counter. "He manages the government model farm about five miles out of town. He knows every Frenchman and every native within fifty miles of Canrobert."

Alonzo and the proprietor walked across the room, and Alonzo was introduced to M. Gustave Bernard. After pleasantries were exchanged, Alonzo said that he would need four men, one of whom must act as an interpreter.

"I can find good workmen for you easily," replied M. Bernard. "It is the growing season for wheat on my farm. Most of my men are idle, waiting for the harvest. Come tomorrow morning about 8 o'clock, and I'll have the men waiting for you."

"I will pay top harvest wages, but they'll have to work eight hours a day, bring their own food, and get to the diggings anyway that they can."

M. Bernard proved to be as good a friend as M. Delloule and M. Hassinou were in 1927. He was the man we turned to when problems arose. Madame Bernard was a plump, bustling woman who became a very good friend of mine. They had no children and adored and spoiled Chomee.

The next morning we again packed all our gear into the truck and drove out to the model farm. This was a government-owned farm where natives could live for three years while they learned about modern methods of farming — using better seed and better methods of sowing and harvesting and about better breeding stock for their flocks of sheep and goats.

M. Bernard was waiting for us at his farm gate with four men. He introduced them. "This is Ferrah Djemai. He has done his military service and speaks French well for one who learned it there. He will act as interpreter. He knows a little about cooking

Dorothy and Chomingwen Pond, M. and Mme Bernard.

Chabane.

and will be a good handyman around camp. Brahim is a good worker but speaks only Arabic. Chabane is old, but he is a faithful worker. Mahmout works well under supervision. If these men do not please you when you have tried them, let me know. I can get others for you."

Of them all, Chabane, the faithful one, was to make his place in our hearts. He looked like an old man. He had a scraggly gray beard and was almost toothless. His white clothes were tattle-tale gray hand-me-downs. His identification papers said he was 56 years old. To us he looked to be in his late 70s, but their hard, primitive life ages such men quickly. Chabane lived with his widowed sister in a very small hut on the farm and did odd jobs whenever he could find them.

The four men climbed into the back of our truck and off we went, bouncing on the uneven country lane.

In spite of our assurances to family and friends back home that we would be better off camping than living in a hotel, I was apprehensive.

At that time, no Europeans in North Africa had ever heard of camping; picnicking yes, but camping, NO.

The colonists, as the French farmers were called, retired at night into thick-walled houses, some with bars on the lower windows. Front yards were fenced off

Camp near Medfoun early in the morning.

with squeaky gates. Courtyards in back where chickens, rabbits, and horses and carriages were kept were walled with thick adobe walls, often with broken glass on top. Gates were barred from the inside and sometimes locked. Almost every Frenchman had a loaded rifle or shotgun somewhere in the house. "The natives," they said, "you know they can't be trusted."

Here we were, unarmed, planning to live in a fragile tent a quarter of a mile from a group of native huts. We were five miles from the Bernards', the nearest French family. Maybe I should agree with the local population that Americans were crazy people.

Alonzo supervised setting up our tent about a hundred feet from the shell mound. It held three folding cots, a card table and four chairs, two trunks and eventually a two-shelf bookcase made of scrap lumber. The typewriter, camera equipment, and suitcases went under the beds. A cloth screen window at the end, opposite the netting door, gave us cross-ventilation. Canvas flies could be tied over the door to give us warmth in inclement weather. A canvas awning over the door was extended to cover the kitchen. Packing boxes formed a base for our gasoline stove, and other packing cases made a kitchen table. Two gasoline lanterns provided light; one hung from the roof of the tent, and the other hung outside in the kitchen area. This was to be our home for the next four months.

We had no well and drank bottled Evian water. Our water for washing the dishes and bathing came from the creek.

It took all day to establish the camp, and at four o'clock the men left to walk the five miles back to their homes.

We were all so tired that we slept soundly and were awakened the next morning by hearing voices. Our workmen were back, ready to work. They kept a respectful distance from our tent while I got breakfast and we ate.

After our breakfast the men came to the tent, and Alonzo explained through Ferrah that they were to take the two wheelbarrows, gravel screen, shovels, and suitcase of digging tools up to the mound. Chabane was to dig into the mound and fill the wheelbarrow. Brahim was to wheel the barrow to the gravel screen set up about twenty feet away and throw shovelsful of material gently at the screen. Mahmout was to fill the second barrow and take it to the screen. When there was enough debris back of the screen, he was to wheel it away to a pile that would later be used to fill in the excavation. Ferrah was to make himself useful where he was needed and also to help me around the tent. Alonzo would go between the diggings and screen and oversee the work. At the uncovering of any large piece of bone, the work was to be stopped while he carefully brushed away the dirt with a camel's hair brush.

It was obvious that in the short time we had, we couldn't sift the whole mound so we planned to dig a three-foot trench into one side of the mound hoping to get a complete profile from the top to the bottom.

Alonzo turned to Chabane and teasingly asked, "Where is a good place to start, the west or north side?"

Chabane shrugged. Alonzo took a five-franc piece from his pocket. "Heads from the west, tails from the north," he said, as he flipped the coin. It came up heads. "We'll start on the west."

Leaving an important decision to the flip of a coin appealed to the men, and it instantly established a good rapport with them.

"*Inshallah*," said Chabane, as he picked up a shovel and dug into the mound.

"*Inshallah*" means "God willing." Every morning, the work started with the hope, "*Inshallah,*" "God willing," we'll find something interesting today.

The British have a saying, "If you want to draw a crowd, dig a 'ole." Well, we surely were digging a hole, and we did draw a crowd. By noon, fifteen or more men had come to squat around the diggings. As M. Bernard had said, it was a slack time on the farms, and the men had nothing to do until the wheat was ready for harvest. Our gallery of sidewalk superintendents grew.

We showed our workmen the flints and charred bone, and, through Ferrah, tried to explain how the flints were used as scrapers and awls and weapon points. They understood a little, but the onlookers thought the whole idea was stupid. But they continued to come.

Trench in the escargotière at Medfoun: Brahim in the trench, Chabane at the shovel.

On the fifth day, I said to Ferrah, "Ferrah, why do the men come day after day?"

"Oh, *Madame*," he replied. "The story is that there is a tree of solid gold thirty feet long buried in one of these mounds. The branches on it have diamonds and rubies set in them. You do not know which mound the tree is in, so you have driven around and dug into many of the mounds and have finally decided that the tree is in this big one. They want to be here when you find it."

A solid gold tree with diamonds and rubies! We'd like to find it, too! What an ingenious explanation for our sampling so many *escargotières* (snail-shell mounds) and picking the largest one to excavate!

We tolerated the onlookers for a week, but finally they crowded too close to the trench and pushed surface dirt down into the trench. That is an unpardonable sin in archaeological diggings.

Alonzo said to Ferrah, "Tell them they must stay back five feet from the edge. Tell them that there is no tree of gold and diamonds. We are just looking for small stones. Nothing will be found but what they have already seen. They must keep away."

They did move back, and the next day only five or six came. But there was a young man whom we had not seen before. He became very obnoxious, refusing to stay back from the trench and getting in the way of the workmen. We were all glad when the working day ended and everyone left.

That evening we were sitting in the tent looking over the day's collections. Chomee was in bed and asleep. Someone came to the tent door, pulled aside the flaps, and started to come in. It was the stranger.

"Get out!" Alonzo said, as he got up from the table.

The young man paid no attention but ducked his head to enter.

"Get out of here!" Alonzo repeated.

I could see and hear several of the man's friends gathered out in front of the tent.

By this time, my husband had taken hold of the man's arm and was pushing him back through the door. The intruder was struggling to maintain his balance. Slowly Alonzo pushed him backward. I was too amazed to be frightened, for he was violating his own customs. A Muslim never forces his way into the woman's part of his neighbor's tent or hut. It was a deliberate insult. Alonzo was getting more furious. Finally he pushed the man out of the tent doorway. I could hear the men outside muttering. Fortunately there was a short piece of lumber outside the tent. Alonzo picked it up and stood in front of the tent door. Slowly the young man walked away with his friends. They stopped at a group of huts a quarter of a mile away.

That night we barricaded the tent door with our two trunks.

In the morning we told Ferrah about the incident, and he related it to other workmen. They were indignant.

After breakfast Alonzo said, "I'm going to Canrobert to see the *Caid* of this district."

Later, when he came back, he told me about his visit. At first the *Caid* was rather non-committal and shrugged, but when Alonzo said, "I do have permission from the Algerian government to work here. I can take the matter up with your French superior, and I will, but I prefer to handle this with you as it is in your jurisdiction. However, if you are not interested, I will go straight to the *préfet.*"

At that the *Caid* said, "I will come out to your diggings this afternoon."

After lunch we saw a car coming down our road. It stopped at the group of huts near the creek. A little later the car drove up to our camp, and Alonzo went out to meet the *Caid.*

The greetings over the *Caid* said, "I've just talked to the man who bothered you. He is no good. He is a troublemaker and has just gotten out of jail. I hope I have scared him. If he bothers you again just hit him with a club and come and tell me. I'll see that he gets back in jail."

Alonzo showed *Caid* Lamine around the diggings and explained about our work. By that time I had coffee and cookies ready at a table under the awning. When the *Caid* left, we had a friend, one whom we enjoyed for the rest of the time we were in North Africa.

That night one of the workmen stayed to sleep in the truck, and never again were we left alone at night while we were at Medfoun. For a few days my husband carried his club around with him, and it was always close to the door when we were in the tent. We never saw the troublemaker again.

But there was an aftermath to the incident.

A week later on a rainy night, we were sitting in the tent sorting collections. It was Ferrah's turn to sleep in the truck that night, and he called, "Someone is coming on horseback. Oh, it's the *garde champêtre*."

A *garde champêtre* corresponds somewhat to our game wardens, except that he guards fields, not forests.

Alonzo went out to meet him.

Caid Lamine.

"M. Bernard went to town for mail today, and noticing that you had a lot of mail, he got yours and sent it over by me."

We thanked him and he galloped off.

The first letter I opened was from our English missionary friend in Tebessa.

"Listen to this," and I read, "'I hear from my native friends that you are in danger. If so, please be very careful. Won't you send the little daughter to me until this blows over?'"

We talked it over and decided that the danger was over and we would keep together as a family.

A week later, we got another letter. This one was from our friend in Algiers, M. Basiaux. He wrote, "We have heard that an American family who were digging flints down on the High Plateau has been murdered. I inquired but could find out nothing further. Will you please let me know if you are all right?"

Algiers and Tebessa are 400 miles apart. The story of our

ten-minute altercation with a troublemaker had traveled several hundred miles both east and west of us, and probably north and south as well.

Were we actually in danger? We never knew. We did learn that exciting "news," delightfully exaggerated, travels far and fast without the aid of modern media.

17

A Typical Day

*E*arly mornings at Medfoun were the pleasantest time of the day. The sun had been up for an hour or so when we woke up. We rose up on the cots and looked out the window toward Djebel Reghis, a lone mountain on the horizon five miles away. Sometimes the base was circled with a ring of fog with the jagged, barren peak showing like a stubby finger above.

We dressed rapidly and went outside the door to wash our faces in a tin basin of water from the creek. Once or twice it was so cold that we had to break the ice on the water-pail. Most of the time it was warm enough to set up the folding table under the awning and eat our oranges, bacon and eggs, and coffee outdoors.

While we ate our leisurely breakfast, we looked down the hill to the cluster of native huts on the creek bank. First one man and then another would come to the doorway of his *gourbi* and call across to his neighbor. He might just say "*Aleikum*" (May God be with you). One day we heard that a baby boy bad been born during the night; another "newscaster" announced that he was going to market that day.

Far down our country road we saw Ferrah and Brahim conversing earnestly as they walked toward us. Before they reached our camp, little shepherd boys began going past with their flocks of sheep and goats. Green plants were scarce, and each boy looked for the greenest place to pasture his sheep. As the boys walked along, they called across to other shepherd boys on other knoll-tops. They never seemed to shout but their melodious voices, calling the news, carried more than a quarter of a mile. The air was so clear that they had no difficulty in hearing one another.

These morning "broadcasts" traveled long distances by relay. As the story wafted from shepherd to shepherd, a man passing by might hear it and repeat the story in the marketplace. An itinerant vendor would overhear it and retell it the next day in another market village. So the news traveled. Perhaps this is the way the

Shepherds.

famous "desert telegraph" works. If Ferrah thought the news would interest us, he often translated it.

All of our workmen had gathered by the time breakfast was over. Alonzo took the suitcase with the small digging tools; the workmen picked up the shovels and picks from the back of the truck, and pushed the wheelbarrows. All of them went up to the diggings.

Ferrah gathered up the dishes and washed them while I made the beds and swept out the tent.

"It looks like a good day to wash clothes," I called to Ferrah.

"Yes, *Madame*, it should be sunny all day."

I gathered up the laundry in a sheet and tied it into a bundle. Then I took a bar of yellow laundry soap from the cupboard and sliced off a piece about an inch thick from an 8 by 4 inch bar. I had learned from experience that no matter how large the bar, no soap was ever returned from the laundress.

Ferrah took the bundle of clothes and the piece of soap and trudged down the hill to the creek. He stopped on the near side of the bank and called. Soon a woman came from one of the *gourbis*. Ferrah put the bundle down on the bank and came back up the hill.

I picked up the binoculars and watched. Although I had often seen women doing their washing on stream banks, the process was still fascinating. The laundress sorted the clothes and dipped each in the stream. Then she soaped them well. I could see where all of the laundry soap went. There were several large flat rocks

Dorothy Pond typing; Chabane(?) in background.

close to the water on which the soaped clothes were spread singly. Next the woman took off her shoes, stepped up onto the soaped garments, and did a good Irish jig. Nimbly, she would pick up a garment or pillow case with her toes, turn it over, and dance the dirt from the other side. When there were especially dirty spots, she would rub hard with the ball of her foot. The clothes, danced clean, would be rinsed in the running water of the stream and spread out on the bank to dry in the sun.

Later in the day I would give Ferrah five francs for the laundress and say, "It's time to go down for the laundry."

The woman would see Ferrah coming and rush out to fold the clothes and stack them into a clean sheet. Then Ferrah would carry it back up the hill to our camp.

We had no way of ironing, so the clothes that needed to be flat were pressed the "old navy way" by putting them under the mattress and sleeping on them. When we went to town or to call on friends, we took good clothes from the hangers in the wardrobe trunk. Otherwise we wore wool shirts and riding trousers most of the time. Once a month we sent dry cleaning to Constantine.

The laundry out of the way, I put our portable typewriter on the breakfast table and started to answer the week's correspondence. The plaintive sounds of a bamboo flute floated across the countryside. Some little shepherd boy was amusing himself by learning to play love songs as he lay in the shade of a rock. The tune sounded to me like the one I had heard on deck of the steamer the first day we landed in Algiers.

Once, as I was busily typing, I heard the beat of a drum and louder flute music. I looked up to see a small group of men coming up the hill. One man was holding a drum high above his head and beating it with the palm of his hand. Two other men were playing reed flutes, and a fourth carried a green silk flag. The other men were chanting.

"Who's coming?" I called to Ferrah.

"A *marabout, Madame*."

"What does he want?"

"He's collecting money for a prayer meeting."

"Please call M. Pond," I said, as the men stopped at a respectful distance from the tent.

Ferrah and Alonzo soon came back. Ferrah was explaining.

"The crops need rain just at this time. This holy man is going from hut to hut collecting donations. Those who can, give money; those who cannot, give a few handfuls of grain or dates. Tonight the *marabout* will hold a prayer meeting. Afterwards there'll be a feast of roast sheep and couscous. The donations are to buy the sheep to roast."

"Well, well," I said. "Church suppers in this far away country."

"Tell them," Alonzo said to Ferrah, "that I will give them ten francs if they will march up and down in front of the tent so that I may take their pictures."

They agreed, with big smiles, and while the movie camera whirred, they marched back and forth playing and singing. My husband gave them the ten francs, and they went off to another cluster of huts.

By this time it was almost noon, so I made some sandwiches from the roast chicken we had had for dinner the night before. With cookies and lemonade, it made a good noon meal.

I went up the path to the diggings to say that lunch was ready and to see how things were progressing. Chomee was allowed to play on the path between the tent and the mound. There was always some workman or onlooker who would see that she didn't stray too far away or to find pretty stones for her to play with. I had six or seven willing babysitters around all the time.

"Lunch is ready," I called. Alonzo and the workmen stopped work, and the men went over to sit under the shade of the mound. However, one of them walked a little way from the diggings, and facing the east, said his noon prayers.

"When did Mahmout get so religious?" Alonzo asked.

"Ever since you found the skeleton last week," Chabane answered.

The week before, we had found a skeleton among the snail shells and ashes. Alonzo had carefully brushed the dirt away with camel's hair brushes, and we had wrapped it well. It was now in a box in our tent. We had permission from the *Directeur des Antiquités* of Algeria to take such finds to America for study. We were not sure that it was as old as the baby's skeleton we had found at Mechta el Arbi two years before.

After we had eaten lunch and Ferrah had cleaned up around the camp, I had one of those feminine intuitions that company was coming so I "baked a cake." My cake-making was limited to one recipe, one that my grandmother had used for a layer cake. It began, "cream a cup of sugar with butter the size of an egg ...." The flour that we were able to buy in Algeria was about the quality that my grandmother had used back in the 1890s. It was not as bleached and fine as we could buy in the States.

The first time I had gone shopping in the little grocery store in Canrobert, I had blithely walked into the store and asked for baking powder. My request was met with a blank stare. Finally, I said, "Powder to make a cake rise."

"Oh, yes," said the store keeper, and put a small amount of white powder on a small square of white paper and folded it up.

The first cake I baked rose all right but tasted strongly of soda. By now I had learned to put a little vinegar in the powdered milk mixture and the cakes were edible.

Most of the sugar came in lumps like our domino sugar, but if you asked for powdered sugar, you could get granulated sugar. What we call powdered sugar was called confectioner's sugar. All these things, I learned by experience.

The cake was done finally, baked in two layers in an oven on our gasoline stove. We could always buy Nestlé's cocoa, and I iced the cake with chocolate frosting.

My hunch proved correct, for about three o'clock Ferrah called, "M. Bernard is coming."

Soon a horse and buggy drove up to the tent, and the Bernards got out. Ferrah took the horse and tied it to our truck.

Alonzo had seen them coming and came down from the diggings.

"*Bonjour, bonjour,*" we said as they came toward us. Madame handed me a big bouquet of lilacs, and M. Bernard gave Alonzo a rabbit all dressed and ready for the oven. Alonzo handed it to Ferrah, saying, "We'll have that for dinner tonight."

The Bernards had been in town and brought our mail as well as their gifts.

As we sat down under the awning, Ferrah put the coffeepot on the stove.

"How goes it?" they asked, in the French idiom.

"Oh, it goes, it goes," we replied. "No spectacular finds this week, just scrapers, awls, and snail shells."

"How is the wheat harvest coming?" we asked.

"Very well. It looks like a bumper crop."

Conversation then turned to Roman ruins. North Africa is dotted with them. Wherever we went about the countryside, we saw door frames of native huts made of carved stones taken from villas of ancient Roman cities. Once in a while we would come upon the ruins of a small Roman town tucked away behind a mountain. As we in America drive to a park or zoo for a Sunday picnic, the French in Algeria drive to a Roman ruin.

"There are extensive Roman ruins at Kremassa[7]," said M. Bernard. "It is only fifty miles from here."

"Let's go there Sunday," Alonzo suggested. "We can take a picnic lunch and make a day of it."

Ferrah brought in coffee and my fresh cake. As we ate, we planned the Sunday menu: a couple of roast chickens, bread, cheese, fruit, cookies, and wine. At 4:30 the Bernards left with an "*Au revoir*. We'll see you Sunday about nine o'clock."

While we were visiting, Ferrah had put the rabbit in to roast, and at six we sat down to a dinner of rabbit, boiled potatoes, canned peas, lettuce salad, canned pineapple and the rest of the cake. With no refrigeration, food had to be eaten soon after it was prepared.

After dinner Ferrah washed the dishes, tidied up the kitchen area, and started his five-mile walk home. We read our mail and the Paris edition of the *New York Herald,* four days late but timely enough for us. Chabane curled up in the back of the truck. It was he who stayed most often as our guard for the night. He was glad of a quiet place to sleep and that he need not make the long walk back to his hut.

Soon after dark, we turned out the gasoline lantern, crawled under our down-filled comforters, and were fast asleep.

---

7. Khemissa or Khamisa, near modern-day Souk Ahras.

18

The Picnic

As soon as we went into the Canrobert grocery store the next Saturday, the proprietor said, "M. Pond, I have something I think you'll like. Steaks from the Argentine!"

"Beef!" I said. "It will be a welcome change from mutton."

The fillets were expensive, coming 5,000 miles, but they would be a real treat! Something different for the picnic.

We stopped at the Bernard's on the way home.

"I have the meat for our picnic," Alonzo said. "Some beef fillets shipped in from Argentina. We'll cook them American style."

At 9:00 Sunday morning we drove into the Bernards' farmyard. M. Bernard brought out several baskets of food. Madame Bernard came out with still another basket which she handed to her husband. Then she climbed into the cab with Alonzo, Chomee, and me. M. Bernard sat on a folding chair in the back. We had never replaced the isinglass window, so we could talk back and forth easily.

Our road led through miles of wheat fields now grown into billowing waves of bright green.

"The grain looks good this year," commented M. Bernard.

"It must have looked like this back in Roman times," said Alonzo. "When Rome ruled the world, Algeria was the granary of Europe. It still is, for that matter."

"The Roman cities were larger than our small towns," added M. Bernard. "There must have been more people, merchants, lawyers, grain brokers, and expediters in those days."

"Apparently everybody lived in town. There were no scattered farms as we see them now," replied Alonzo. Then he continued, "I had an interesting conversation with Ferrah the other day. It seems that he and Ahmet have rented some land and planted it to wheat."

Kremassa (Khemissa, Khamisa) arch and rutted road.

"But yes, I know about it."

"He tells me that they hired Tyeb to plow the field and plant the grain. When it is ripe, Tyeb will harvest it."

"That is true."

"When the wheat is sold, Ferrah and Ahmet will each get two-fifths of the money, and Tyeb, for all his hard work, will get one-fifth. Ferrah said it works that way because he and Ahmet have the money."

"That's the way with capitalists all over the world, is it not?" laughed M. Bernard. "But without the capital, the Tyebs of the world would never have the seed to plant, the hoe to break the ground, nor the sickle to cut the grain."

About an hour and a half from the farm, we turned off the *Route Nationale* onto a country road, really just a wagon track across the barren plain beyond the fields of grain. The road now followed along the bank of a dry river bed. Finally, we rounded a spur of a mountain and saw a rock-strewn plain — a few solid arches and partial walls — the ruins of a Roman city. Our unpaved track ended where the old stone paving-blocks of the main city street began.

We left the truck and stumbled along the ruts made by chariot wheels two thousand years ago. We walked under the triumphal arch and climbed the steps to the Forum. At the top of the steps was a beautifully carved stone lectern, still standing where it had been placed so many centuries ago. Stone seats in the public restrooms were in good condition, although the walls were roofless.

The dry climate of North Africa has preserved large sections of the stone buildings. Occasional hard rains and rare frosts have loosened mortar. Hard winds have toppled walls and columns, but "recycling" the building blocks for native huts has done as much as weather to make ruins of Roman buildings. Natives looking for straight-sided stone to frame their doorways have carried off some carved pieces. The cities are gradually being reduced to rubble.

We wandered down the aisles of the theater and onto the stage. Once 5000 people could sit out front to watch and hear the performance.

At last Madame Bernard said, "I'm getting hungry."

We all agreed and started back to the truck. We passed a house with two adjoining walls still standing.

"This will be a sheltered place," I suggested.

Nearby a large building block had fallen to the ground.

"That ought to make a good table," said Alonzo.

We made several trips to the car, coming back loaded with baskets and folding chairs and a box of wood that Alonzo had brought from the camp. There were no trees nearby for firewood.

When we were in North Africa, a Frenchman's idea of a picnic was to cook a regular meal and take it outdoors to eat it. They had no idea of hot dogs, hamburgers, potato salads, or Jell-O molds, which we associate with picnics.

Madame Bernard spread a tablecloth over the stone block. Everyone helped take food from the baskets and set the table.

"You didn't bring a pan to cook the steaks," observed Madame Bernard.

"You wait," said Alonzo. "I'll find one. This is to be a picnic American-style."

It was easy to find flat stones from the ruined walls, and he built a fire on one of them. Madame Bernard set out thin sliced sausages, tomatoes marinated in oil and vinegar, ripe olives, small rolls, and sweet butter, a typical first course of a French lunch.

"Where's the wine?" asked M. Bernard, rummaging in a basket. "Oh, here it is!" He uncorked it and filled our glasses. Another of the Bernard baskets yielded a cold roast chicken, a long loaf of French bread, lettuce and the makings for salad dressing, cheese, and oranges.

From my basket I took the steaks, potato salad, some apricot jam that I had made, several bottles of mineral water, and a cake.

Alonzo brushed away the ashes of his fire and placed the Argentine fillets on the hot stones while Madame Bernard watched skeptically.

We raised our glasses to M. Bernard's toast, "To your health," and began sampling the hors d'oeuvres.

M. Bernard helped himself generously to the apricot jam, put a spoonful in his mouth, and looked surprised. Cautiously he took a hard lump from his mouth.

"Oh, oh," I said. "Little Chomee has been helping her mamma cook." The lump was a flint scraper that Chomee had added to the jam while I wasn't looking.

Alonzo turned the steaks. Fortunately, the French like their steaks rare, really just seared with the middle very red.

We passed our plates, and my husband served us each with a fillet, charcoal crisp on the outside and juicy red within.

"À votre santé": Picnic at Kremassa.

"Delicious," said M. Bernard. "You know I've heard that American Indians cooked their food on hot stones, but I never really believed it."

After lunch we spread our blankets on the ground. The men stretched out while Madame Bernard and I sat with our backs against the stone wall, warmed by the sun. Chomee had a good time climbing over fallen blocks.

"It is possible that 2000 years ago, some wealthy Roman merchant was reclining on his couch in this very spot," said M. Bernard, as he looked around at the broken walls.

"I'm sure his lunch wasn't as good as ours," I said.

But the thought that people like us had lived here several centuries ago, and now their civilization had passed into history quieted us. We, who were archaeologists and were digging into the dwelling places of people who lived so many millennia ago, were especially conscious of the bloom and fade of cultures. Was our own civilization to disappear? Two thousand years from now would someone make a picnic table of a stone fallen from a New York skyscraper? Would some tourist stumble over the rubble under the Arc de Triomphe in Paris? Would they wonder if the people who built those buildings and monuments were like themselves? Those Romans in whose dwellings we were picnicking had running water under those stone toilet seats. They had central heating warming the floors of their living rooms.

Each of us was half-sleep, half-awake with our own musings when Alonzo roused us by saying, "I think it's time we started back."

We packed the chairs, picnic baskets, and blankets back in the truck, cranked the Ford and drove away from ancient Rome.

On the way home M. Bernard mused, "Steaks cooked on hot stones! None of my friends will believe it when I tell them."

19

Tunisian Adventure

We were sitting in our tent one evening sorting the day's collections and were bored. There had been nothing new for a week, just the same old scrapers, awls, and bits of charred bone.

Finally Alonzo looked up and said, "This is Holy Week. Let's take a vacation and drive down into Tunisia. We couldn't make the trip when the girls were here on account of the rain. Besides, I've seen most of the classic prehistoric sites in Europe; I'd like to see the really important one in North Africa, the site that gave its name to the Capsian culture."

"You mean drive way down to Gafsa?"

"Yes. It will be good for us to get away for a while, and I think we can do it in a week."

The thought popped into my mind, "How will Chomee stand the trip?" She was twenty months old now and having fun playing around the tent. Would she be too unhappy cooped up in the cab of a truck during the long days of driving? Food was no problem, as we could carry cases of canned goods and bottled water.

"This is Monday," said my husband. "Let's plan to start on Friday morning."

We telegraphed our plans to M. Albertini, the *Directeur* of antiquities in Algeria. Two days later we got a letter from him enclosing a letter of introduction to a hotel proprietor in Gafsa.

We bought a couple of cases of canned vegetables and fruit and two cases of bottled water in Canrobert. Desert water often contains a lot of magnesium and sometimes alkali. We asked Chabane to stay as guardian of the camp, and M. Bernard promised to drive over several times to see that things were shipshape.

Early on Good Friday morning we loaded a camp stove, a table and chairs, food, bedding, and a few clothes into the back of the truck and set out on the *Route Nationale* for the Tunisian border.

The thought of Easter weekend was in our minds. As we drove along, it was easy to imagine ourselves back 1900 years in the Holy Land. White-robed men rode small burros along the highway. Women in long garments were clustered about the open wells. Some were drawing water and filling clay jars; others were washing clothes on flat rocks. Shepherds were leading their flocks to pasture and letting them stop at small streams to drink.

"He leadeth me beside the still water…" I quoted.

Our truck was the only discordant note.

Late that afternoon we drove into Meskiana. Alonzo said, "We'll camp at the first good place we see."

A grove of trees near the road was an ideal place. We turned off the highway and soon were behind the trees and well hidden from the road.

I warmed up a can of soup and one of vegetables, made some tea and had canned peaches for dessert. It began to drizzle before we had our bedrolls spread out on the truck floor and the canvas cover tightly fastened over the truck. We had just put out the lantern and snuggled down when we heard someone calling from the road, "Come on out here."

We paid no attention, and the call came again.

Alonzo raised up and said, "If you want to talk to me, come back here."

We heard someone walking toward the truck. "Who are you?" said a native voice.

"Who are *you*?" Alonzo called back. Then, taking a flashlight, he went to the end of the truck and raised part of the curtain. There were three natives standing in the rain. One was wearing a red *burnous,* the badge of a *caid* on official business.

"I am the *Caid* of this area," said one.

"*Ah, Monsieur le Caid,*" my husband replied. "If you had said who you were before, M. Pond, the American, would have been more polite."

"What are you doing here?"

"I am traveling to Gafsa with my wife and baby. Nighttime came and we decided to pull in here and sleep overnight."

"I have a guest house nearby that you may use. It is Easter week and a dangerous time to be on the roads," the *Caid* offered.

"We thank you for the offer of the guest house, but we prefer our truck. We will be on our way early in the morning."

"It is so dangerous," the man repeated. "I will send a guard to protect you all night."

"We will be all right. I don't like to put you to that much trouble."

"It is well. He will guard you," the *Caid* insisted. With that the men left.

"I don't know whether we are safer with a guard or without one," I said, as we snuggled down under our down covers again.

"He is probably as worried about what we might do as he is about what anybody might do to us. We are in a forest whose trees are protected. He is responsible for every tree. You know wood is scarce in this country."

I was sure that I wouldn't sleep, but the next thing I knew, the sun was shining between the cracks of the curtains. I looked out. No one was around. We never knew whether we had a guard or not.

About 2:00 in the afternoon we came to the border town of Bou Chebka, just a small cluster of huts, a store, and the customs house. We pulled up beside it, and the inspector came out.

"Have you anything to declare, *Monsieur*?"

"Just our personal things and food," Alonzo replied.

The inspector peeked into the back of the truck. "Ah, you have extra tires for the truck!"

"Three."

"They are dutiable. It will take a while to write the declaration." Then, turning to me, "Won't you and the little one come in while I write the necessary papers?"

Chomee and I were glad to get out of the truck and the hot sun and into a cool room where we made ourselves comfortable in chairs. Chomee had her favorite picture book.

Alonzo answered innumerable questions. The inspector was lonely. He rarely saw Europeans and never had seen Americans. He talked and he wrote and he wrote and he wrote.

"I have no typewriter, and no carbon paper, and everything must be in three copies," he explained.

Finally, an hour later with four pages of legal-cap size paper, each copied twice, the inspector said, *"Voilà,"* and gave us one copy.

By this time Alonzo was wondering just how much duty we would have to pay. All of that work would certainly cost.

The inspector continued, "The duty is ten francs."

We smiled. That was forty cents in our money.

The duty paid, we climbed back into our truck and drove on through semi-arid country. We saw more isolated Roman ruins than we had in Algeria. There were fewer small clusters of native huts than on the Algerian side of the border, and the villages were farther apart. As the sun dropped toward the horizon, the distant mountains turned a deep purple. Through the clear air they looked like the painted background on a theater curtain.

In the late afternoon, we came to a small cork oak forest on the edge of the village of Feriana. "This looks like a good place to camp," my husband said. He drove off the road and pulled the truck in behind some trees so that we were sheltered from the road.

Feriana was the most interesting oasis I had seen. Whitewashed native houses lined each side of the narrow street. Back of the houses were the gardens and olive orchards, each separated from its neighbor by a cactus hedge.

Logan Museum truck in the oasis of Feriana.

Supper over and the dishes washed, we decided to stretch our legs after sitting all day. We walked down the road and stopped at an open gate to peer into a walled garden. In one corner was a palm-leaf hut much like our Indian wigwams back in Wisconsin. A little yard with a cooking fire in front of the hut was set off from the garden by a fence of straw matting. In front of the fire, an old woman squatted, watching the couscous cook in a pot hung from a tripod over the blaze.

"It makes me think of Macbeth and the witch scene," I remarked.

"She's probably a poor old woman with no home and is allowed to live in the garden if she will scare away the birds."

"She looks enough like a scarecrow to do that."

Just then we heard a dog growl. Native dogs are vicious! Alonzo picked up Chomee, and we hurried back to our truck.

Next morning, Easter, we ate breakfast at a table under a cork oak tree. The dishes were washed in some of the extra water we carried for the truck's radiator. Soon everything was stowed away and we pulled out onto the road. It was sunny as we hurried on our way.

Just before noon we drove into Gafsa. The European part of the city was new. Nearby was a fort with crenellated walls. I had not seen one like it since we were at Carcassone in France.

We inquired directions to the *Hôtel de la Gare* and a few minutes later pulled up in front of a modest hotel. Alonzo went in and got a room for us. A little *chasseur* came out for Chomee and me and our luggage. He showed us to our room and said, "Dinner is at seven o'clock."

After lunch was over, Alonzo went in search of the proprietor. As with most small hotels, the owner was manager, chef, and tavern keeper. He was in the kitchen wrapping hams in heavy brown paper. "It keeps the juice in the meat," he explained.

Well at El Guettar: An ox pulls the skin bucket.

Alonzo presented his letter of introduction from M. Albertini in Algiers.

"I'm just too busy overseeing Easter dinner," M. Rey replied, "but afterwards, I'll talk about it."

We spent Easter afternoon walking around Gafsa. It had a hurry and bustle atmosphere that we had not seen in North African cities outside of Constantine.

We returned to the hotel for dinner. The brown wrapping paper did indeed "keep the juice in the meat." It was delicious.

After dinner was over, M. Rey came and sat down at our table. Over a cognac, he read M. Albertini's letter. "Yes," he mused, "I knew M. Boudy who dug at the site of Capsica [Capsa]. Used to stay here at the hotel for several months every year. Ah, he was quite a character. I'll see if I can get some guides for you tomorrow. I think you can drive your truck out there. We'll see." With that he turned to other customers.

When we went into the dining room the next morning for breakfast, the proprietor greeted us. "I have a guide waiting for you outside. He is an old man and has only one eye, but he knows the way to the prehistoric site. He does not speak French, so I have another, younger man who will interpret and who can help if the truck gets stuck."

After a breakfast of coffee and French bread, we were ready to go. The guides sat on chairs in the back and could talk to us through the window.

A good macadam road led to the oasis of El Guettar. We stopped at the edge of the oasis to see an irrigation pool filled by a one-ox-power engine. The well was an old one with a sunken roadway slanting to several feet below the top of the stone curbing. A frame of stone pillars and palm-tree trunks supported a cross-arm from which a pulley hung. A rope about fifty feet long passed through the pulley. A large-mouthed ox-hide bucket attached to the rope was let down to the water. Another, shorter rope was attached to the long, narrow neck or spout of the skin bag. The other end of each rope was attached to the collar on the ox.

When the bucket was full, the ox walked up the road away from the well. The rim of the full bucket rose up above the well. The shorter rope pulled the neck, or leather spout, down to a trough extending away from the well curb to the irrigation basin. Well water flowed into the system.

The ox was turned back down the path to the well. The skin bucket dropped to water level again, and the long spout folded back like a closed valve keeping the bag full until the ox again pulled it to the surface.

Our good road ended just beyond the oasis. The guide told us to turn right on a camel trail. A camel trail looks like five or six cow-paths running in the same direction, but they are not parallel enough to fit the four wheels of a truck. Large humps of camel sage add humps to the trail. In fact, it looks something like a hummocky marsh, except the ground between the humps is solid. The paths wind around the hummocks. The result was that the four wheels of the truck were never at the same level at any time. There were no shock-absorbers in those days.

My husband's training as an ambulance driver in World War I came in very handy. In 1917 he had driven Model T's over shell-torn roads on dark nights with no lights. Now, he negotiated the camel trail with skill.

At times we had to cross dry riverbeds. There was no good approach to them, but Alonzo and the guides took shovels and tossed gravel until we had a gentle enough slope to get down into the streambed and up the other side.

One time we drove down a valley. "The villages are on the mountain slopes above on each side of us," said the guide.

We looked up but could see no houses.

"They live in caves hollowed out of the rock."

"Troglodytes," said Alonzo.

"The villages are fortified," continued the guide. "Sometimes they take shots at each other across the valley."

"I surely hope it is a time of peace," I said. "I don't want to be caught in a cross-fire."

We covered the twenty-five miles in three hours. It was very good time for a truck on the camel trails we had been following.

Our guide indicated that we should stop at the *bordj*. The *bordj* is a building constructed by the military when troops were occupying the country. Now they were used as rest houses for travelers.

We much preferred our truck to the *bordj*, because we knew that the truck was clean and uninhabited except by us. We made camp beside the *bordj*. Within ten minutes, a crowd of natives gathered. While we were eating lunch, a man brought his ten-year-old son to us. The boy had a badly infected leg. We were not used to doctoring either the natives or ourselves, as we had always been close enough to a village to use the services of the French doctors. The boy had a dirty rag around his leg which was oozing pus. I boiled some rags, washed the sore with soap and water, made a bread and milk poultice, and bound it on the sore.

"Come back tomorrow morning, and we'll look at it again," said Alonzo, as the man and his son left.

After lunch, Alonzo and the guide walked off to see the site of M. Boudy's diggings. It was near the ruins of Capsa, an old Roman city, so the culture was named the Capsian.

We had purposely parked near a well so that we would have water for washing our faces and hands and for dishes. We drank bottled water. It wasn't long after Alonzo and the guide left that the women from the nearby huts began to gather at the well. It seemed as if every water jar in the country was empty and needed to be refilled. They seated themselves about twenty feet from the truck in a semi-circle. None of them spoke French, and I spoke no Arabic, so communication was limited. Every once in a while one of them would come up and touch something in the truck. They were especially interested in our daughter's folding stroller and my typewriter. I demonstrated as best I could.

When one woman saw our twenty-month-old daughter drinking from a cup, she found a tin can that we had discarded from our lunch and tried to get her daughter to drink from it. The experiment was not a success. I found out later from the guide that the baby was only three months old.

A native man who could speak French walked up. I was soon deluged with questions from the women. They wanted especially to know what we fed our daughter. She was so strong and healthy, much stronger than native babies at twenty months.

"Mashed vegetables and chopped meat and cereals," I answered.

The women shook their heads; they nursed their babies until they were two years old.

Next they asked, "Do all European women wear shirts and riding trousers as you do?"

I tried to explain that in the cities we wore dresses, but that they were much shorter than those the native women wore. These people had never seen even a French woman. Most of them lived their entire lives in this small valley. They had never been to Gafsa, and few of them had even been to El Guettar. There was no use trying to tell them that we lived in a country so many thousand miles away.

Alonzo and the guides came back, Alonzo with a collecting sack full of worked artifacts. After supper the men gathered around and asked him questions. As soon as it was dusk, we all turned in. The guides slept on the ground under the truck on a few old blankets that we provided.

When we got up the next morning, the man and his son with the sore leg were back. The leg was better. Again I boiled cloth and made a poultice.

Alonzo said to our guide, "Tell him we'll take him and his son into Gafsa to the French doctor. He will treat his son. Otherwise, I am afraid the boy will lose his leg if not his life."

The father spoke almost no French and but managed to say the doctor would want money. At that time, we could not contradict him, but later we did learn that there would have been no charge. The man was probably afraid of the city. At any rate, he refused our offer of a ride.

Then our guide who was blind in one eye asked us to treat his blind eye. Regretfully, we confessed that blindness was beyond our curative powers.

Our trip back to Gafsa was uneventful. We bounced from one hummock of camel sage to another and arrived at the good road at El Guettar with both axles and all four wheels intact.

When we got back to the hotel, we found that our host had been inquiring around about prehistoric sites. Someone told him about caves back in the mountains, and he knew that prehistoric people lived in caves. "Would you like to go?" he asked us. It sounded worth a try.

20

Way Out Beyond the Mountains

*T*he next morning M. Rey said, "I have found two guides who will take you to the caves. They are waiting outside."

After we had packed some food and personal luggage into the truck, M. Rey introduced the men. "This is Mahmout. He was born near the caves and knows the way. The other man is Tyeb. He has never been in that country, but he speaks French and will translate Mahmout's directions."

The two guides climbed into the back of the truck and Tyeb, the French-speaking guide, told us to drive out on the road to El Guettar. A mile out on the good macadam road he said, "Mahmout says to turn onto this country road."

Alonzo obediently turned onto a wheel-track lane. Another mile and Tyeb said, "Mahmout says to turn here."

"There's no road or camel trail," replied my husband. The guides conferred.

"Mahmout says you just go off across the country towards those distant mountains. That's where we are going."

Alonzo turned the car off the road and drove over a gravel plain with sparse humps of camel sage. Farther along, we came to a dry streambed.

"All out with the shovels," Alonzo said. Both guides grabbed shovels and dug away at the bank until we had a gentle slope down on one side and up the other. Chomee and I waited on the bank with the guides while Alonzo took the truck across. Then we crossed, stumbling over the stones in the dry streambed.

With its passengers aboard again, the truck bounced along over the plain. Our tracks made a serpentine trail as we dodged large rocks and humps of camel sage. The mountains did not seem to be any closer. Dry riverbeds were scattered a mile or so apart, and at every one we got out while the men built a road across. As we pulled up on one bank Alonzo stopped the car and said, "I had better look this one over carefully."

The banks were ten feet high and quite steep; the streambed, narrow. He walked up and down and finally came back to the truck. "The bank is a little lower farther upstream. I think we can build a road, and down there is a large, flat rock on the other side. It slants steeply but I think we can climb it. I don't see any other way of crossing."

He took the guides up to the place he had chosen. "We will shovel enough to get the car down the bank at an angle. The streambed is sand. When I get the car down, you stand behind it, and if the wheels almost stop, you *push*."

Chomee and I had to ride that time because the bank was too steep a scramble for her or for us to carry her. We three got into the car, and Alonzo negotiated the down slope into the sand at the bottom. In low gear the engine faltered, and Alonzo yelled, "*Poussez!*"

The men rushed forward and pushed; the car kept moving. The streambed was too narrow to turn the truck at right angles, so Alonzo started up the flat rock on an angle. I hardly dared to breathe. All four wheels rolled onto the rock, and we kept moving but the slant was so steep that the truck began to slide sideways down toward the streambed. Alonzo pushed the accelerator down to the floor; the truck bounced ahead, and the front wheels struck level ground.

In those few seconds, a vision of a pile of people and an overturned truck in the riverbed flashed through my mind with the thought that maybe 2000 years from now, archaeologists would dig our bones and a heap of twisted metal from a heap of sand. Would those future scientists speculate about us, as we did about the ancient bones we uncovered?

The spurt of energy carried the whole truck up onto the level ground, and we stopped to catch our breath. I had been frightened, Alonzo apprehensive. Chomee was too small to be concerned. If we had been stuck in the stream bed, it would have taken several days to dig our way out.

Alonzo and I looked at each other and smiled with a sigh of relief. Our guides scrambled up the rock and got into the back of the truck without comment.

It had taken a lot of water to keep the engine cool, and most of our spare water was gone. We drove along over arid countryside.

"Is there water near?" Alonzo asked.

When Tyeb asked Mahmout, he just shrugged.

A camel caravan was approaching. We stopped the car so that the camels would not be frightened. They walked past us with their noses in the air as if to say, "What are you doing here? *We* are the transportation of the desert. We can go six days without water. Can *you?*"

I would have traded the truck for a camel just then.

We found that our guide had made the journey on the back of a burro. He had no idea that country a burro could travel over fairly easily would be so nearly impossible for a truck.

We passed little shepherd boys who left their flocks and fled in terror to their huts. They had never seen a car. Women peeped shyly from the doorways as we chugged past.

The radiator boiled. Our water cans for the truck were empty by now. "Well, here goes," said Alonzo, as he poured two bottles of Evian water into the radiator. "I hope we find a waterhole soon." Depleting our supply of drinking water could pose serious danger for us humans in the desert.

"*Inshallah*," said Mahmout.

Allah was good to us, and in another half mile we came to a waterhole. It was small, the water fit only for camels to drink, but it was *water*. The guides filled our empty five-liter water cans and empty Evian bottles.

Before us stretched a beautiful field of green. Our spirits lifted.

"We must cross it," said our guide.

"We'll drive right down the middle," and Alonzo put the car in gear. We drove ten feet and the car stopped. The wheels had sunk six inches into the loose soil. We tried again and got another few feet before the radiator boiled, and we stopped. Alonzo got down to look.

"It's loess, wind-blown dust." He thought a moment. Then he said to me, "You drive, and the men and I will push. Whenever the radiator boils, you stop." So foot by foot we pushed the car across the field. Finally we were at the foot of the mountains.

"Where are the caves?" Alonzo asked.

Through our interpreter, Mahmout replied, "Just around the mountain." We had gone much farther than M. Rey had said the distance would be, but we were again on rocky plain and the going was not too bad. We drove around the foot of the next mountain and stopped. The guide shook his head, and Tyeb said, "He says it is around the next mountain."

We drove on. At the foot of the next mountain Mahmout and Tyeb consulted. "He says it is surely around the next mountain."

We were hot, tired, hungry, and becoming irritated. I was a little frightened. "Maybe Mahmout just wanted to see his family," I suggested. "Maybe there aren't any caves."

"Well, if the caves are not around the next mountain, we'll stop and camp overnight and go back tomorrow," Alonzo replied.

We went around one more mountain. Mahmout pointed to a pass in the mountain range, and Tyeb explained, "He says the caves are there, but we had better camp near the wells."

A few hundred feet farther on, we pulled up at the "wells." They were large, hand-dug basins lined with plaster; one was about ten by eighteen feet, the other somewhat smaller. The water in them was eight feet deep. They were really cisterns which caught the runoff from the surrounding country and now were only half full. The natives insisted they were not built by the Berbers, but "had always been there."

As we began getting supper, a band of men approached. One of them spoke to Alonzo. "I am the *Caid* of this country. You are welcome here. What is your business?"

The *Caid* had been to Gafsa and had seen cars, trucks, and European women, for he showed no curiosity about us. He spoke French well.

My husband explained that M. Rey had suggested that we might be interested in exploring the caves in the mountains and had supplied guides. He also explained that we were interested in digging in places that were inhabited hundreds of years before.

"Yes," answered the *Caid*. "I know the caves well. They are three kilometers from here. Tomorrow morning I will send my horse and groom to take you there." With a ceremonial handshake and the touching of the back of the hand to the lips, he and his group left us.

We were all tired and made our beds in the truck early. As before, the guides slept under the truck on old blankets which we had.

When we awakened the next morning, the *Caid's* groom and his horse were waiting. After breakfast, Alonzo took one of the gasoline lanterns and digging tools and mounted the horse. The groom led, and our two guides followed.

Before they were out of sight, I began to hold "open house." People came from all over the valley.

Some of the men were shepherds. Quite a few had done their military service and spoke French. Muslims love children and spoil them. One shepherd brought a week-old puppy for Chomee to pet; another brought a young goat, and still a third, a young rabbit. Chomee loved the animals and talked and patted all of them.

At noon Alonzo came back. "The caves are probably Roman. They are hand-dug, but there were no artifacts in any of them. Probably were plundered hundreds of years ago. I think the 'wells' must be of Roman origin, too. Anyway, I'm not interested in Roman archaeology; it's much too modern."

Alonzo gave the groom a few francs and asked him to thank the *Caid* for the loan of the horse. We had our lunch, and as we were packing our gear into the truck, the *Caid* came to call again.

"May I ride into Gafsa with you?" he asked.

We were not enthusiastic about having another passenger in the back of the truck, but he had been so courteous, we could not refuse. He got in with our two guides. When we got to the loess valley, we found that by following our wheel tracks exactly, we made fair time. Every once in a while our guide would point to a different place, but the minute we left our wheel tracks, the engine labored, and we had to go in low. Finally they learned that we must not deviate even an inch from our former trail.

We came to the waterhole and again filled our spare water cans. I had been dreading the trip back over the gullies and especially the one where we had almost slid to the bottom. While we were filling our water cans Tyeb said, "The *Caïd* says that if we drive about a kilometer across the country, we will meet with a camel trail that will take us to El Guettar."

Bouncing along over rocky terrain was much better than crossing all those dry streambeds. On this route we never had to cross one. We did cross the end of a salt lake, which at this season, was as hard as a gravel road. The camel trail, which a week ago would have looked impossible to us, looked like a good road. We reached El Guettar in an hour.

Tyeb spoke through the window. "The *Caïd* would like to be let out here."

We stopped, and the *Caïd* climbed down from the truck and came around to the cab. "Thank you for the ride into town. May Allah bless you with many sons."

I wasn't sure I appreciated his blessing, but we were so grateful to him for showing us a better road that we again thanked him for his hospitality.

"I wonder why our guide didn't know about that better road down to the mountains," I mused.

"Probably he walked from there into Gafsa and knew no other way."

M. Rey was disappointed that the caves were not prehistoric as we had hoped, but then he brightened and said, "*Monsieur, Madame,* you are the first Europeans to see that country since the Romans were there. That is really something, is it not?"[8]

And we agreed that it was really something.

---

8. During World War II we read of British Army cars and American jeeps meeting in the shadow of Djebel Chemsi (Jabal ash Shamsi), the mountain near the "wells."

21

Native Hospitality

We were well aware of the native custom that it is bad manners to inquire about the women members of a Muslim's family. However, as we got to know Ferrah better, we found he was not reticent about his family. In fact, he spoke proudly about his wife and mother. He had lived among the French long enough to answer our questions without resentment or curtness.

He explained that he and his young wife lived with his widowed mother and his eighteen-year-old brother on the government farm.

"My wife is young," he said. "I married her when she was twelve years old, and she came to our *gourbi*. My mother taught her to cook and spin and weave. We did not consummate the marriage until she was fourteen."

"What does your wife weave?" I asked.

"Saddlebags and small rugs. Now she is learning to weave a *burnous*."

I knew that a *burnous* was the acme of accomplishment for a native woman. The large cape with hood must be woven in one piece, and the swing of the cape must be just right.

"Would she weave something for me?" I asked.

"Yes, she would be glad to."

The conversation was dropped at that time, but about a week later Ferrah said, "Tomorrow is my day off. Will you come and have tea with us?"

"We'd be very happy to come," I said.

That evening, before Ferrah started for home, he asked to borrow some spoons for tomorrow. "We don't have enough for company," he said.

"Certainly," I said.

He went off with three spoons. Later, when I knew Ferrah better, I became sure that we also furnished the tea and sugar for the tea party. We did not mind.

Such fringe benefits always have been accepted. (Forty cents a day was top wages in Algeria at that time, but it is difficult to compare wages in different cultures.)

The next afternoon we drove over to the Bernard's, left Chomee with Madame Bernard, and inquired the way to Ferrah's *gourbi*. It was not far from the farmyard, but we drove the truck to his home. The small, stone hut was in a courtyard surrounded by a wall. A crudely fashioned wooden gate gave entrance to the place. We were immediately surrounded by a group of barking dogs. We stayed in the truck until Ferrah came and drove them away.

"Enter, enter, *Patron, Madame*," he said, opening the gate.

We climbed down from the truck and followed him through the courtyard. A small, very frightened young woman stood at the *gourbi* door to welcome us. She was dressed in a magenta-colored brocade dress with a wide, dark blue belt clasped with a silver buckle. Silver chains dripped from her bright yellow head scarf. Four pairs of silver bracelets completed her jewelry.

I was amused at one decoration in her head scarf. The week before I had broken one of our aluminum spoons and had thrown the pieces on the trash pile. The bowl of the spoon was sticking up from a fold in the scarf, just as we would place a pin or ornament.

"Nada," said Ferrah, "This is Monsieur and Madame Pond."

We offered her our hands, and she shook them, but her hands were as cold as ice. Behind her stood Ferrah's mother. We were introduced to her, and Ferrah invited us inside the hut.

"Please sit down," he said, indicating two packing cases apparently gotten for the occasion.

We seated ourselves while Ferrah and his wife squatted, tailor-fashion, on the floor.

I looked around the room. A large loom took up half the space. Underneath it were several bags. A wooden chest was along one wall with a small set of shelves above it. A pile of neatly folded blankets was stacked in one corner. These were the only furnishings in the room. The bare floor was swept clean.

Native housekeeping is very simple. Their beds are blankets spread on the bare floor. Most blankets are woven six feet wide and eight feet long. At night the one or two blankets are spread on the floor. The family lies down on the top half of the blanket and pulls the other end up over them. In the morning the blankets are shaken out in the courtyard, neatly folded and placed in a corner. The floor is swept and *voilà*! The cleaning and bed-making are done for the day.

Ferrah's mother quietly slipped from the room. Neither she nor Nada could speak French, so our talk was with Ferrah. I smiled at Nada now and then to show that she was included in the conversation.

Soon Ferrah's mother came back with a teapot. She took two cups and a glass from the shelves and poured the tea. Ferrah handed the two cups to Alonzo and me and took the glass for himself. Again Ferrah's mother left the room and brought in a plate of cookies. They were made of home-ground millet, chopped dates, and water. These were slightly gritty as the mortar in which the grain was pounded was old and the dough had picked up fine particles of stone. Nevertheless, we ate them.

After the customary three cups of tea, Ferrah said, "Nada, show *Madame* some of your weaving."

Nada took some saddlebags from the chest. The natives love bright colors and mix orange, red, apple green, magenta pink, and yellow into their blankets and rugs. The designs were geometric and reminded me of our Navajo rugs except for the brighter colors. We admired the saddlebags and asked Ferrah about weaving.

He spoke to his mother who took some raw wool from a bag. Then, with two carding combs, she pulled the wool straight and into a fluffy white handful. After she had made several wisps, she attached one to a spindle that was an inch thick and a foot long. Twirling it, she dropped it toward the floor and fed it with twisting wool fibers. When it reached the floor, she picked it up, and rolling the spindle from the palm of her hand to her shoulder, rolled the yarn onto it. She dropped it again, feeding the wool evenly to it. She did this several times, every time adding to the yarn already on the spindle.

She kept talking to Ferrah who translated. "In the spring when the sheep are sheared, the women gather at each other's houses and have carding bees. It is a social time for them. They sit around the courtyard, each with her own pile of wool and spin, both yarn and gossip."

"Do you make your own dyes?" I asked.

"No, each village has a commercial dyer. We men take the wool in and have it dyed."

I had often seen the dyers on the edge of the villages. There were always hanks of red, yellow, green, and blue yarn festooning the walls and hanging outside to dry.

"Would your wife make a small rug for me?" I asked. "Something the size of a saddlebag but not folded together into a sack."

"But yes. She would like to."

"But please use a dark red background with figures only in dark blue and yellow. No pinks or greens."

"That is well. She will do it as you want it." We settled on the price and paid down a little. Perhaps Ferrah could not have afforded to have the wool dyed.

We got up to make our farewells and shook hands with Ferrah's wife. By now she had gotten over her nervousness. Her hand was warm, and she was smiling. Ferrah's mother, too, was at ease.

As we went out the door, we saw the kitchen: a little lean-to made of stone and barely four feet high. A hole scooped from the ground was for the cooking fire. There was scarcely room under the shelter to squat. All the meals were prepared here no matter how inclement the weather.

Again Farrah drove away the dogs. We climbed into the truck and drove off.

The next day Ferrah was back at work, and our spoons were back in the cupboard.

Several weeks later, Ferrah brought the weaving to me: a small prayer rug with a background of ruby red and sapphire blue triangles outlined in gold. It was just what I wanted and makes a nice wall hanging, adding warmth to our living room and bringing memories of the months spent in Africa.

Ferrah's wife Nada weaving a rug for Dorothy.

22

Entertaining Nobility

"*Madame*, someone comes," called Ferrah.

I looked from the tent door and saw a long, black car driving up the dusty trail that led to our diggings and our camp. Alonzo had left a few minutes before to go to Canrobert.

"Do you know whose car it is?"

"No, *Madame*, it is a strange car."

The car pulled up near the tent and a tall, white-haired, white-mustached gentleman got out and said in French, "Good afternoon, *Madame*," as he handed me a note. "We met your husband on the road."

I unfolded the paper and read, "These people are Polish. Show them our diggings and serve them tea. I'll be back as soon as I can."

Reassured, I extended my hand and welcomed the gentleman to our camp. "We don't often have visitors here from outside the area."

"I am Lucien Godziszewski, and this is my wife."

If the note had not said that they were Polish, I would have taken her for an English woman. She was slender, blonde, and dressed in well-tailored tweeds.

"Good afternoon, Madame," she said in English. "We have heard about you, and my husband is writing a book about our travels in Algeria. He would like to include you and your husband in his book."

"That would be very nice of him. Would you like to see our diggings?"

"Yes, very much," M. Godziszewski answered.

I showed them the trench we had dug into the *escargotière* and how we sifted all the dirt to separate the worked flint tools used by Stone Age man in Africa. I found they had quite a good knowledge of Stone Age cultures. In fact, most Europeans are much more knowledgeable about prehistory than Americans are.

After walking around the diggings and seeing the collections of artifacts, I asked, "Won't you have tea? My husband will be back in a little while, and he will enjoy talking to you."

They accepted, and I placed chairs under the awning of our tent and put on the teakettle. We had Russian tea, which we kept for special occasions, and I almost always had a homemade cake on hand, because French friends drove out from the village for afternoon visits.

Alonzo soon returned, and we settled down for a chat. Madame Godziszewski had spent some time in London, which accounted for her good command of English and her English tweeds. During the visit we exchanged cards. I put theirs on the table without glancing at it.

Our afternoon tea was always somewhat primitive as we had only aluminum plates, cups, and "silverware." Nevertheless, we spent an enjoyable afternoon. After they left, I picked up her card — and gasped!

"Madame Lucien de Godziszewski, Née Princess Giedroyc," it read.

"She was a princess, and we served her tea in aluminum cups!" I wailed.

Alonzo took the card, read it, and added, "Maybe she was born a princess, but she is also a book agent. See, at the bottom in small print, *"Agente pour Encyclopédie Britannica."*

⤶

A week later another strange car drove up and stopped before our tent just as Ferrah and I were getting supper. My menu consisted of bacon, eggs, and succotash, and I had already cooked the bacon.

Alonzo had come out of the tent and was walking toward the car. I heard him shout, *"Monsieur le Comte Bégouën!* It is good to see you! Come in, come in."

I stepped forward to greet him, too, for he was an old friend of Alonzo's, and I had been at his chateau several times. He was a well-known French archaeologist and head of the Department of Prehistory at the University of Toulouse, France.

"This is a pleasant surprise," said Alonzo.

"I sent a telegram from Algiers asking you to meet me at four o'clock at the hotel," replied the Count.

"We don't go to town every day for our mail and didn't go today. I'm so sorry not to have received it," Alonzo said.

"It is no matter. When you weren't there, I inquired directions and drove out."

"Come and see the diggings before it gets dark," Alonzo said and led him toward the snail-shell mound.

When they left, I told Ferrah, "Put another folding table next to this table, and we'll stretch this oilcloth as far as we can. Dinner must be served one food at a time, except the meat and potatoes may be served on a platter together. Each food must have its own set of clean silver and clean plates."

Chabane was staying in the truck for the night. "We haven't enough dishes to last through the whole dinner," I told him, "so you must wash dishes for us between courses. For now, peel these potatoes and cut them up fine so they'll cook quickly."

An hour later the men came back from the diggings. Count Bégouën was very complimentary on the way they had been planned and handled. We sat down under the tent awning and had an aperitif, then pulled our chairs up to the table.

Ferrah brought in bowls of steaming cream of tomato soup, and then hovered around to clear the table. Omelets, succotash, mashed potatoes and cold roast beef, lettuce salad, canned pineapple, gruyere cheese and crackers followed. Each was brought in separately, and Ferrah laid clean plates, forks, knives, and spoons before each of us. Out on the fringe of light from the gasoline lantern, I could see Chabane, a shadowy figure, sloshing dishes through dishwater and wiping them. Ferrah was eagerly waiting to place them back on the table.

After the meal Ferrah brought black coffee, and Alonzo got out a bottle of my favorite Benedictine, and we sat around visiting. While the men talked about archaeology, my thoughts went back to the luncheon we had had several months before at the Bégouën chateau.

We had been staying at Toulouse and had hired a cab to take us out to Montesquieu-Avantès, the Bégouën estate in the Pyrenees. We swept up the circular drive and stopped before the chateau. As we stepped out, the heavy wooden door emblazoned with the Bégouën coat of arms opened, and a butler ushered us into the foyer where the Count and his two sons were to greet us. We were seated in deeply carved wooden chairs. I had time to look around. Across the room was a large fireplace with a marble mantle. Persian rugs covered the floor and Japanese screens of rice paper and lacquer were placed around the walls. The heavy, dark wood tables were ornately carved and held curios from around the world.

A carpeted stairway led to a second floor and a balcony. Doors, probably leading to bedrooms, opened onto it.

Soon *Madame la Viscomtesse* came down the stairs accompanied by her companion, an English woman. As soon as we were introduced, the butler announced lunch.

We sat down at a long refectory table. The dining room chairs were also of a heavy, dark wood, leather upholstered. The Bégouën crest had been tooled into the leather on the back of each chair. I was seated between the two sons, a viscount and a baron. I had studied French for two years at college and spent a winter in Algeria, and could get along with tradesmen and the Delloules, Bernards, and Debby, but I was lost when it came to the scholarly French of the two young men. Madame Bégouën spoke English, so I was able to take part in the conversation.

The dinner service was of white Haviland china banded in gold, with the Bégouën crest on each piece. Silver forks and spoons also bore the crest, and the table knife handles were of ivory, with the crest stamped in blue.

Our luncheon was impeccably served by the butler, and there was no noise of dishwashing from beyond the heavy kitchen door. Our first course was sautéed mushrooms and diced meat on toast. Then followed courses of buttered green beans, roast chicken, and endive salad. Dessert was a cake with a very soft creamy frosting. We finished the lunch with a plate of fresh fruit. A native red table wine was served with the dinner and a sweet champagne with the dessert and fruit.

I was jarred from my reverie of the chateau luxury back to the primitive tent in Africa when I heard Count Bégouën say that he must get back to his hotel. He was an adaptable guest, and I am sure he enjoyed our hospitality as much as we did the luxury of his chateau.

As he said goodbye to me, he raised my hand to his lips and kissed it. Alonzo said I didn't wash my hand for a week.

23

Market Days

*A*lgeria had a good system for market days. They were strung out like days of the week. Tuesday was market day in Canrobert. Monday had been market day at the nearest town west, and Wednesday was market day in Aïn Beïda. If one missed the market in one town, he could always go the next day to a nearby town. It was convenient also for the itinerant merchants. They started out with a full load on Sundays and carried less and less as they sold goods. Friday afternoons they headed back home for a new stock. By then they had very little to carry over the long route.

While at the hotel in Canrobert, before we opened our camp, we were awakened about four o'clock Tuesday mornings by the rumbling of the big produce trucks coming in from the coast. Carrots, potatoes, and onions were all dumped in heaps along the curb. Soon afterward, we heard the bleating of sheep and goats as they were driven to the market corral. Burros brayed as the more affluent natives rode them into town.

Shortly after eight o'clock the main street was thronged with French and native pedestrians. They all carried *gouffin* — large, round baskets woven of palm fibers. We had our own *gouffins* and wandered down the street. Most piles of fruit and vegetables bore signs quoting francs per kilo, but the customer usually bargained. Alonzo was excellent at bargaining and could always buy cheaper than I could. The natives liked to deal with him, because he knew their ways and could almost but not quite out-bargain them.

"You buy the potatoes, carrots, onions, and oranges, and I'll buy the meat." I usually said to him. The meat price was fixed, and one could rarely bargain with the butcher.

Alonzo wandered along the street, usually offering half of the stated price for a dozen oranges or three kilos of potatoes. The merchant would demur but finally

Sheep market at Canrobert.

Canrobert market vegetable stall and customers.

come down a little. Alonzo would up his price a little. Eventually they'd come to terms, Alonzo getting the produce at a few centimes less than the posted price. Both merchant and customer enjoyed the spirited contest.

The butcher put a long rack with meat hooks on it in front of his shop just for the day. Quarters of fresh meat hung from the hooks. One enterprising merchant had a wire screen over his meat to keep the flies off, and it was there I usually went for our weekly quarter of mutton.

One of my most embarrassing experiences occurred at the beginning of our expedition. Alonzo and I went alone to market where we separated, he to buy the vegetables and I to buy the meat.

At the butcher's rack I pointed to a quarter of meat and said, "I'll take that one." It really looked nice and fresh. A good buy I was certain. The butcher wrapped it and accepted my money.

Back at camp I handed the package to Ferrah saying, "We'll have this roasted for supper," and then went into the tent.

Soon I heard Ferrah call, "*Madame,* what kind of meat did you buy?"

"Mutton, just as I always do."

I heard him clear his throat and sensed that something wasn't right, so I went out to the kitchen.

"*Madame,*" he said rather apologetically, "when a sheep is killed the butcher leaves a little bit of wool on the end of the tail to show that it *is* a sheep. When a goat is butchered, the tail is skinned clean."

I looked at that clean, fresh, hind quarter of "mutton." There was *no wool* on the end of the tail!

That night we chewed and chewed and chewed on roast goat.

Beyond the produce market the old-clothes man spread his wares along the curb. Trousers with patches or holes in the knees vied with slightly worn vests and shabby coats. Often there were army uniforms of khaki or *poilu*[9] blue. Many of the natives had done military service, and they were glad to get back into the loose robes and *burnouses*.

There were always a few hand-woven blankets for sale. Never many, because blankets were woven for family use. Now and then, when a family needed cash, a good blanket was woven especially for sale. One day I saw one I liked. I went to find Alonzo.

"Come and look at this blanket. It is different from any I have ever seen before and very clean."

When the merchant saw us coming he held up a large blanket, white background with narrow red stripes. The border was stylized camels in purple and green against a dark red background. When he saw we were really interested, he said, "This blanket comes from Souk Ahras, near the Tunisian border. It is a special design of theirs."

Alonzo bargained, and I proudly carried home my Souk Ahras blanket. Now it is spread over the davenport only on special occasions.

On another day I stopped in front of the jeweler. He was an itinerant merchant traveling from town to town. Most of the goods on his trays were zinc and copper alloy such as I had bought in Bougie, but once in a while he had something

---

9. French soldiers in WWI.

worthwhile. This day he had a pair of silver filigree bracelets. Again I pulled my husband away from his produce bargaining and led him to the jeweler. The bracelets had been worn and had the satiny patina of wear and age on them. I took those home, too, and wear them sometimes.

At the edge of the market, the barber and the tooth-puller set up shop. They were traveling artisans who made the weekly markets as regularly as the produce merchants.

A native disliked to be seen without a fez or turban, but when his hair got too long, he sat on the ground in front of the barber and had his head shaved. If he could afford it, he also had his mustache and beard trimmed right out there in the public marketplace.

The dentist was really only a tooth-puller. Most French and well-to-do natives went to Constantine when they had their teeth filled. The French doctor in town pulled teeth for those who couldn't wait. For a few francs, the wandering dentist would pull out rotten teeth and roots without benefit of an anesthetic. The relief was worth the pain.

It wasn't always warm in Algeria on the High Plateau, and one day we woke in our tent and looked out to see a half-inch of snow covering the ground. That day we broke the ice in our water pail before we washed our faces. It was market day, but when we went to town, there was only one pile of produce on the curb, a load of carrots.

Another market day I especially remember. We took the Bernards to Aïn Beïda, along with Larbi, their handyman, and Ferrah. We all had errands to do separately. Madame Bernard, Chomee, and I went one place, and the men split up. We were to be back in an hour.

Alonzo gave Ferrah some money to buy lettuce, radishes, and oranges. "Be sure to be back in an hour," we told him.

Within the hour Madame Bernard, Chomee, Alonzo, and I were back at the truck.

"Gustave will be along soon. He has one more errand to do," said Madame Bernard.

We waited ten minutes. Ferrah came back empty-handed.

"We're leaving right now," said Alonzo.

"I left your groceries back at the grocery store. I'll go and get them right now," Ferrah answered and walked away.

We waited. A little while later Larbi came back with another native from the Experimental Farm who wanted a ride back.

"Larbi, will you please find Monsieur Bernard and tell him that we are ready to leave," said Madame Bernard.

He left. Then we looked up the street and saw M. Bernard standing on the corner talking with two men. Alonzo started the truck, and we drove and picked up our friend, but the three natives were gone. Larbi and his companion soon came back but there was no Ferrah. We drove to the outskirts of town and stopped.

A few minutes later Ferrah came running, swinging our basket of groceries. He climbed aboard over the tailgate.

Alonzo and M. Bernard were furious, but Madame Bernard and I giggled like schoolgirls. It was almost the same situation as two families gathering up their straggling children after a picnic back home in America.

Market days were fun. Most of the men from the farms around went, and very often the women, too. They all congregated at the café to talk over the week's news; the men standing at the bar and the women seated at the tables. It was a social occasion, and everyone seemed to enjoy it, but we had so much work to do at our diggings that Alonzo and I never had time to become a part of the café society.

24

Au'voir to Algeria

June came and with it the heat. We watched the natives on the creek bank get out their summer tents. The roofs were made of strips of woven goat hair sewn together. The tent covers, put up on four-foot tent poles, made a bit of black shade against the burning sun. The circulation of air kept the natives cooler than their windowless huts would. At night, a matting of palm-leaf stems was unrolled around the edge of the shelter to insure privacy.

The harvest season was at hand, and our workmen left for the fields. We had to close the diggings and sort the collections. As we had done previously, the artifacts were divided between the Museum at Algiers and the Logan Museum. Faithful Chabane, who was too old to do much of the harvesting work, stayed to fill in the trenches.

The heat of our light canvas tent became almost unbearable, so M. Bernard offered us his granary as a shelter. It was a small, thick-walled building, and while it had no windows, the heavy plastered-over-brick walls kept out the worst of the sun's heat. We moved all our belongings to the granary and set about packing up. It took only a couple of days to pack the collections and truck them to the station at Canrobert. Our two trunks were sealed and sent to Paris. M. Bernard offered an unused building in which we stored the camping equipment. We got our hand luggage down to one suitcase apiece, the typewriter, and camera case.

The Bernards had received an invitation to a cousin's wedding in Constantine, but there was no place for them to stay so they decided not to go. Then Alonzo suggested that they go with us. "We'll put them up at the Hotel Cirta. They can go to the wedding, and we'll have a room with a bath."

On Saturday morning we drove out in the truck to get them. Back in Canrobert, we parked the truck and took the train. We thought the train would be cooler and less fatiguing than the long, hot ride in the truck.

How good the great, white building of the Hotel Cirta looked! We were able to get the room we always had with a *bath*room. We got similar accommodations for the Bernards.

At dinner that night our waiter said, "We don't serve a noon dinner on Sunday during the summer. The chef and his assistant go out to a small country café by the lake. If you would like to go, I can take your reservations now."

"Dinner by a lake sounds interesting. Let's go," I said. We made reservations and later asked the concierge to have a cab for us the next day.

The Bernards were away to the wedding festivities long before we were down to breakfast.

The cab was waiting for us at eleven o'clock, and we drove five miles through semi-arid country to the "Café beside the Lake."

The lake proved to be about the size of a large duck pond. We were accustomed to lakes like Mendota in Madison, Wisconsin. However, we realized that in this arid region any bit of water surrounded by greenery was a welcome spot to people of Constantine. This one was rimmed with pine trees.

We went into the café and greeted the proprietor. "Luncheon will be served at one o'clock," he said. "There is a path around the lake. Perhaps you would like to walk around it."

We dawdled along the path taking pictures. The pine needles on the ground felt soft to our feet.

Eventually we joined the other diners on the terrace. The owner had built a pergola over it, and the large grape leaves shaded it from the sun. Peacocks spread their gorgeous tails and strutted nearby.

Such a lunch as we had! The waiter brought us ham and pickles, radishes, and olives as a first course. We took our time with that. Then he brought us fresh fish and after that roast beef and mushrooms and a good gravy. The next course was fresh green beans in butter. Then he brought the main course of roast chicken and gravy, and lettuce for a salad. Last of all the waiter brought little cakes with fresh almonds, ox-heart cherries, apricots, and peaches. All of this cost just a dollar apiece!

We took the cab back to Constantine to the hotel and rested.

About five o'clock I suggested that we go out for a lemonade. We found a café near the hotel and seated ourselves at a glass-topped table on the sidewalk.

"Two lemonades and a grenadine with water for the little one," ordered Alonzo.

When they came the drinks were lukewarm. "Have you any ice?" I asked the waiter.

"But, yes," he replied and disappeared. A moment later he returned with two ice cubes — one for each lemonade.

When the check came it read, in French, "Two pieces of ice, two dollars."

"It was worth it," I said.

The Bernards came in soon after dinner. Monday we took the train back to Canrobert, and Alonzo took our friends back to their home.

The next day we went to say good-bye to the Bernards. There were tears in Madame Bernard's eyes as she hugged and kissed Chomee.

"It won't be too long before we see you again. We're coming back next winter," I said.

Alonzo stored the truck in Canrobert in the local garage, and the three of us took the train for Tunis.

25

Ten Days in Italy

We had decided to make a quick trip through Italy. Alonzo had been there several times, but I had not, and he wanted me to see the country. The best way to get there was to take the train to Tunis and a boat across to Naples.

This was the first time I had been on a Continental sleeping car, and the experience was different from the U.S. sleeping cars. The berths were placed across the cars the same way as the compartments with the aisle along one side instead of down the center as they are in the States. Chomee and I took the lower berth, while Alonzo took the upper.

I never sleep the first night in a sleeping car, so I lay awake all night. But it was June, so there were not too many hours of darkness and I was awake when we went through Souk Ahras about dawn. I was glad to see the town where my good blanket was made. It was just like the many North African towns I had already seen.

The train finally got to Tunis, a Muslim city with the Arab population more prominent than the French. It was ruled by the Bey of Tunis. There were French hotels and department stores, but the Muslims had control, and there was less evidence of European influence than in Algiers.

When we went down to the hotel lobby after lunch, we were told that we could not leave the hotel for an hour.

"Why?" I asked.

"Because the Bey is going to ride through the city, and the streets must be clear for half an hour before he comes and stay clear half an hour afterwards."

Security precautions. So we went back to our room to nap until the Bey had gone by.

Later we went out and discovered the *Souks*, the name given to the Arab market. They were much more interesting than the *Souks* at Algiers. The streets were narrower and had louvered roofs to keep out the hot sun. We browsed around the shops looking at brass work and pottery and eventually, the Place of the Silk-Makers. At one shop I found hand-woven pieces. One especially caught my eye. It was gray-green in color and shimmered with a silvery sheen when it rippled. It made me think of moonlight on water. It was dress-length, too. We bargained, and I took it with me.

The next day we saw the Palace of the Bey, its steps guarded by life-sized statues of lions. Books written 150 years ago tell of lions roaming wild in the mountains. I was glad that the only lions today were of marble.

The harbor was an interesting mixture of steamboats and sailing ships. Trans-Atlantic steamboats unloaded farm machinery; sailboats loaded up with bulk cargoes. It was a busy port and near enough to the downtown to be visited easily.

Our boat for Naples left in the early evening, so we went aboard soon after sunset and were asleep before the boat left port. When I awoke in the morning and looked out of the porthole, we were close to shore. I saw Dutch windmills just back from the water's edges.

Where the Bey holds court, Tunis.

"Look! We can't have sailed all the way to Holland overnight. Where are we?"

On deck we asked the steward. "Trapani, *Signora*, we are coasting along the shores of Sicily."

"The windmills look like Dutch ones."

"*Si, Signora*, but they are in Trapani."

A few hours later we docked at Palermo, Sicily. We hired a cab for an afternoon of sightseeing while cargo was unloaded from our steamer. Our driver took us to the monastery of Monreale where we walked through the old cloister and the gardens. It was picturesque and peaceful.

"Our next stop is the catacombs," said our guide, as we got back into the car.

"We don't want to spend any of this beautiful day walking underground and looking at skulls," I said.

The driver thought a moment. "I have a friend who is caretaker for the estate of an Italian nobleman. The owner is away just now. I could take you there, and you could walk around the lawns."

"That's much better," I replied.

We drove several miles along the coast and stopped at a closed gate. The gatekeeper came out and greeted our guide as an old friend. A few lira changed hands, and he opened the gate. We were welcome to walk anywhere on the grounds, the gatekeeper assured us, but we must not even try to enter the house. Our driver and the caretaker settled down in chairs near the gate for a good visit, while Chomee, Alonzo, and I strolled down a path across a beautiful, wide lawn.

The path led off to some trees, and we found ourselves in one of those custom-made grottoes for which Europeans seem to have an affinity. A large pile of gray concrete had been dumped in a shady spot, the outside of it roughed and hacked to resemble a weathered outcropping of stone. The path led us to a room inside the simulated rock formation. The ceiling had been molded into artificial stalactites, and there were several openings through which we could look toward the sea. There were stone benches around the walls.

"A perfect place for hiding secret agents on a dark night," I said.

"Or," Alonzo added, "on a moonlit night, for a fleeting kiss or more intimate moments with one's *petite amour*."

After half an hour of wandering about the estate we went back to the gate, and our driver took us to the ship. We had a good dinner and went to bed, very tired people.

The next morning we woke up in the very busy port of Naples. It took all morning to get off the boat and get settled in a *pension* high above the bay. From the balcony we could see the sulphurous yellow plume of smoke from Vesuvius. Three weeks before our visit, the volcano had erupted and shown the world just what pressure lies beneath our seemingly solid earth. The afternoon was spent in getting tickets to Vesuvius, Pompeii, and Capri.

Next morning we boarded the train to Vesuvius. Our compartment was not crowded and Alonzo stretched out, putting his feet on the opposite seat as was commonly done on American trains at that time. An Italian in the compartment said, "Mussolini doesn't allow people to put their feet on seats." Alonzo sat up straight.

From the station at the foot of the volcano, we took a funicular as far as we could go up on the cone, and then walked to the top of the outer rim. Alonzo carried Chomee on his back.

"If any of you want to go down as far as the inner cone, we will take you down," said our guides. "It is safe now, but you must stay on the path. The cinders are hot on either side." Even from the rim we could see wisps of steam coming through small vents in the floor.

Mt. Vesuvius crater, the sulphurous smoke pouring forth.

"You go, and I'll stay with Chomee," I said to Alonzo.

A middle-aged couple from Australia was standing near us and overheard me. "We'll look after the little girl, and you both go. We don't want to walk down, the footing is too unstable."

I accepted their offer gladly and left Chomee with them.

I have a picture Alonzo took with the guides helping me as I stumbled over the hardened lava.

Chomee was glad to see us when we got back. It was probably scary for a twenty-two-month old to see Mommy and Daddy go off down that still-smoking path. The next Christmas Chomee got a cuddly kangaroo doll from her Australian friends.

On the trip to Pompeii we took Chomee's little three-wheeled stroller. Alonzo had been there several years before and knew how tired Chomee would get stumbling over the uneven cobblestones. It was still quite a job to push the stroller and avoid the ruts worn in the stone pavements by ancient chariot wheels. Alonzo was always behind the party. Several times, the guide waited impatiently for him to catch up. Finally I said, "My husband has been here before and knows all this history. Please don't wait for him."

But the guide always waited, apparently afraid he would lose one of his party.

I was impressed by the evidence of gracious living in the Roman villas. Many had one or two courts which were inner rooms open to the sky. Marble benches and small statuary were placed around the court. There were flowering shrubs here and there, and always in the center was a fountain or a reflecting pool.

"Reminds me of the Pompeian Room in my Aunt Mame's home," said Alonzo. "Now I know where she got her idea."

There were beautiful mosaics in some rooms and at the home of Glaucus, the Athenian, the floor pictured a chained dog in dark colors.

At one of the Roman villas, Alonzo whispered to me, "Lag behind, and I'll show you something the guide didn't show."

I slowed down, and we waited until the rest of the group had gotten outside. Then my husband led me behind a screen where we saw a very bawdy picture, its colors as bright as the day Pompeii was covered with ashes from Vesuvius.

"I expect Mussolini doesn't allow tourists to look at it," Alonzo said as we hurried to rejoin the group.

The guide was very annoyed with us. He knew why we had stayed behind, but he couldn't say much without raising an unwanted curiosity among the other tourists.

When the guide finally led us back to the Italy of today, we realized that for a little while we had wandered in a beautiful city, its gaiety, its daily life stopped at the height of its glory eighteen centuries ago, but still preserved intact, even to loaves of bread in the baker's oven.

The third day we left Naples on an early morning boat for Capri and the Blue Grotto. Our deck chairs were next to those of a very attractive couple, and we could not help but overhear their conversation. The man, a middle-aged gentleman in a well-tailored suit; the woman, still young, probably in her late twenties. Her black hair and brown eyes contrasted with her beautifully embroidered white wool coat. She would have been an outstanding figure anywhere. She wore long white gloves, a characteristic of well-dressed ladies at that time. It was clear to us that the girl had met her companion at a party in Naples the night before.

During the decade after World War I, many impoverished European noblemen were seeking wives among wealthy American girls, and American girls were quite eager to marry a European title.

"I was married very young," said the lady, "very young and had no idea what I was getting into. My husband was an Austrian nobleman. After I was married, I found out that all he wanted was my money. He left me alone for long periods at our castle in the country. When he was home, he often struck me. At last I could not stand it any longer and left him. I settled in an apartment in Rome. Since then I travel a lot."

She took off her long white gloves. "Do you like them? I found a little shop in Rome where I buy them by the dozen pairs."

Whether her story was true or whether it was made up to impress her companion, I don't know. In any case, it made an entertaining way to pass the time as we watched the old houses of Sorrento slip past.

When we reached the island of Capri, the ship went past the port and on to the Blue Grotto. A flotilla of small boats waited at the foot of the railed stairway lowered from the ship's deck. Each boat held only two or three passengers besides the oarsman. Our boatman got into line and rowed toward the cave. At the entrance as each wave receded, a boat slipped into the cave.

Inside it seemed as if we were suspended in a big aquamarine. All light came up through the blue water on which we floated. The white limestone walls of the cavern were tinged with blue. Suddenly one of the boatmen started the song, "Napoli." The others joined him in the romantic aria. As the echo died away the boats slipped out one by one as a receding wave gave them clearance at the opening. Our boat was the last. As soon as we were alone in the cave our boatman asked, "Will you please give me a tip, *signor*?"

"I thought Mussolini had abolished tipping."

"I know, but I have a wife and eight children to support."

Alonzo gave him a few liras.

The big boat took us back to the port of Capri where we went ashore. We took a cab around the island and finally stopped for lunch at Anacapri. We found a table on the terrace overlooking the harbor. It was a romantic setting where we could relax and dawdle over lunch until time to take a cab back down to the boat. We found our deck chairs and slept most of the way back to Naples. Sightseeing can be tiring despite the fascination of new experiences.

The next day we took the train to Rome. St. Peter's was the lodestone that drew us, along with several thousand tourists. The great semi-circular colonnade in front of the church seemed endless. We finally reached the broad expanse of steps, climbed them, and found ourselves inside the church. The majesty of St. Peter's cathedral seemed to dwarf the crowd as well as the speech of the guide. But I did hear him when he said that the big toe on St. Peter's statue had to be replaced every few years because it was worn off by the kisses of devout pilgrims.

Then a tour of the Vatican. The glory of the Sistine Chapel was never diminished for me. That ceiling by Michaelangelo is superb! I never heard anything the guide said and didn't care. Just to look at the painting was joy enough. The Vatican gardens were beautiful. Some of the statuary and many of the paintings were certainly worth more time than we gave them, but it was the Sistine Chapel that has lasted in my memory all these years.

We wandered around Rome. We saw the Tiber River and Hadrian's Tomb; the Victor Emmanuel monument, whose glistening whiteness reminded me that not everything was old in that ancient city; the Trevi Fountain, where everyone tosses coins in the belief it guarantees that one will come back. I never did return but little Chomingwen did. Twenty-five years later, while hurrying to catch a train, Chomee remembered that she had not renewed her wish at the fountain. She had the cab driver go around that way so that she could toss more coins into the magic fountain.[10]

---

10. Thirty-five years later her plane from Sierra Leone landed at the Rome airport, but she did not get into the city to renew the promise again.

We took a streetcar to see the Coliseum. From the street it looked immense. When we got inside, we found that Mussolini had not yet found time to clean it up. The arena was grass-grown, and piles of rubble still covered the lions' dens.

We left Rome with regret but ahead lay Florence! Florence and the Ponte Vecchio, the Goldsmith's Bridge. We browsed among the jewelers' tiny shops on the bridge but bought nothing there. We were saving our pennies for the straw market just off the bridge. There we found baskets and handbags and hats. I had never seen crocheted straw hats before and bought several decorated with flowers crocheted into the brim instead of braid.

Chomee was too young for art galleries; Alonzo had been there before and gets museum fatigue easily, so we passed up the hundreds of paintings. Instead, we took a cab across the Arno and up to San Miniato. We stood entranced in the square before the copy of Michaelangelo's *David*. The original was in a museum in Florence. No weather could harm it there. Then we walked to the terrace railing and looked across the Arno to the striped dome of the *Duomo*.

A man came over to us and said, "Good afternoon," in English. We replied, and he said that he was an American priest just visiting in Italy. After a few pleasantries he asked Chomingwen's name. When I told him and explained that it was an American Indian name, he said, "That reminds me of a story." A woman brought her baby girl to be baptized. "What is the baby's name?" asked the priest. "Hazel," responded the woman. "With all the saints names to choose from, and you name her after a nut," the priest exclaimed.

I gathered that the American priest disapproved of giving a white girl an Indian name. But we like its poetic significance, as well as the sound of the word.

Back in the city again, we had the cab driver take us past the children's hospital that has the Della Robbia plaques set in the outside walls. It was beautifully symbolic of a children's hospital.

From Florence it was on to Venice.

Even in the heat of the summer we loved Venice. The chugging motorboat that took the place of a trolley didn't detract. We found a little *pension* and settled ourselves. The islands of Murano and Burano drew us like a magnet. The glass-blowing and lace-making were techniques entirely new to me. The glass was especially interesting. The dark blue or purple glass with its banding of gold and its flowers was exquisite; the mosaic beads blown into vases and the shapes, intriguing. We bought a perfume atomizer and a vase. Later in the afternoon we saw a coffee set of deep purple glass with a banding of gold. Should we buy it? The dealer assured us that they would pack it and ship it to us. But it *was* too much for our slender budget. Regretfully, we left it and have been sorry ever since.

Back at St. Mark's Square we fed the pigeons and stopped for cooling drinks at a sidewalk café. At sunset we hired a gondola, and our gondolier guided us under the Bridge of Sighs, the Rialto Bridge, and down little side canals. It was the quiet end to a wonderful day.

As all pleasures must end, so did our ten days in Italy. I remember, though, the warm air that caressed one's cheek like a soft kiss. I loved Italy.

We boarded a train for Paris, intending to get off at Milan and see the cathedral. A framed picture of it with all its statues had been in our living room when I was a girl, and I had always wanted to see it. As our train got nearer to Milan the countryside looked hotter and hotter, and when the train finally stopped, we stayed aboard. Late June in Italy was too hot.

We saw the sparkling lakes of Como and Maggiore from the train and had a fleeting glimpse of Isola Bella. At noon we had a heavy Italian lunch in the diner, several courses of pasta with tomato sauce, and vegetables cooked in olive oil. The train did not stop at the French border, but that night we had a French meal of clear soup, veal chops, lettuce, and fruit. The same chef, the same waiter, the same dining car, but a different country and distinctly different food.

Next morning we were in Paris. Paris in summer was a little America or Germany. Everywhere we saw tourists. Every Parisian who could, left for the mountains or the coast or even a country house. We stayed only long enough to make official arrangements for an expedition the next year in French North Africa and book passage on the next available ship. Southern Wisconsin, with its blue lakes and green woods, would be a welcome sight to us.

26

The Start of Our Third Expedition

The problems I had faced in keeping a toddler and my husband healthy and well fed while camping in Algeria were minor beside the challenges of this new expedition. Now it meant planning to keep twenty-one Americans well fed, well housed, and reasonably happy. Fourteen of them were college boys.

The results of our digging in two or three snail-shell mounds a year were puny compared to the number of prehistoric sites in North Africa. What Alonzo wanted was a comprehensive picture of this culture of Snail Eaters. We needed to increase our work force.

During a conference with Dr. Frank G. Logan, our sponsor, and Dr. George L. Collie, Chairman of the Department of Anthropology at Beloit College, Alonzo proposed that we take college students with us. They would pay their own transportation over and back and provide their own spending money. The Museum would provide housing, food, housekeeping equipment, workmen, and tools.

The plan was adopted. I think it is interesting to note that Beloit College was the only college that did not give academic credits to its students who accompanied us, while Northwestern, Wisconsin, and Minnesota Universities all gave full semester credits to their participants. Later, Beloit was one of the first colleges to insist that students take a term off for work or research in their fields between enrollment and graduation.

After our return from Europe in 1929, we had a brief vacation at a cottage on Lake Koshkonong in southern Wisconsin. Then we plunged into the planning details for 1930.

When Beloit College released the publicity that we wanted college *boys* to go with us, the girls set up a clamor. Why couldn't they go? We answered that we were going to a Muslim country where girls were sequestered. Our research itself presented enough problems, and we couldn't add social conflict. Among ourselves, we agreed that we had enough responsibilities without adding the possibility of puppy love and of couples mooning off from the diggings instead of watching gravel screens and collecting artifacts.

When Dr. A. E. Jenks, of the Department of Anthropology of the University of Minnesota, heard of the plan, he wrote to ask if he, his wife, and two graduate students might join us. We finally arranged with the French and Algerian governments for them to dig with us and live in our camp, but to manage their own project, collections, and housekeeping duties.

Tents, stoves, and gasoline lanterns were ordered and shipped to us in Algiers. Alonzo had seen and used French camping equipment on his trip in the Sahara and decided that American tents, stoves, and lanterns were superior.

We also ordered a Ford car, one of the first station wagons made. It was to be assembled in France at the Ford factory and to be waiting for us when we arrived at Algiers.

I spent my time making lists of the number of cots, tables, folding chairs, blankets, sheets, pillows and cases, pots and pans, aluminum plates, cups, and "silverware" that we would need. These could all be purchased in Algiers.

By the first of December our roster of the expedition was complete. George L. Waite, a freelance photographer whose work often appeared in *The Milwaukee Journal*, was our official photographer. Robert Greenlee was a graduate student from Northwestern University. R. Lauriston Sharp and John Gillin were graduate students, and Sol Tax and Alvan Small, undergraduates, from the University of Wisconsin. The Beloit group was Charles Nash, Kenneth Williams, Virgil Moen, Daniel Riedel, Robert Voight, Edgar Roberts, and Robert Krieger. Mason Dobson, son of the *Beloit Daily News* publisher, was to graduate from high school at mid-year and was given the trip as a present from his parents. Dr. and Mrs. Jenks, with Lloyd Wilford and Ralph Brown, graduate students, from the University of Minnesota, were to join us. Alonzo, Chomee, and I finished the list.

George L. Waite, Alvan Small, Mason Dobson, and the three Ponds sailed out of New York harbor the last week of January on a cruise ship bound for the Mediterranean. The rest of the group was to join us in Canrobert the first of March.

As soon as we turned south from the cold New York climate, the weather was warm, and we enjoyed our ship with deck games, swimming in the ship's pool, bouillon at eleven. Chomee, who was 29 months old at that time, says she remembers sitting in a deck chair and having the steward hand her a cup of bouillon and crackers. Horse racing, tea in the afternoon, fabulous meals, movies, concerts, dancing in the evening, and a bedtime snack of fruit and cheese — all of these we enjoyed. Except Mason. Mason was seasick.

After six days at sea, the ship docked at Ponta Delgada, Azores, for an afternoon of sightseeing. When the little boats came alongside to take us into the dock, Mason was the first one in the boat and the first one to step ashore. I think he spent the whole afternoon walking, hardly taking his feet off solid ground.

We and George L. took a cab and drove around the island, stopping at a pineapple plantation and driving up on the mountain so that we could look down on the tiny pink, blue, yellow, and pale green houses, truly an artist's delight.

Our next port of call was Funchal, Madeira. When we got off the small boats onto the dock, the local "cabs" were waiting for us. They were surreys with the fringe on top, only these were two-seated sleds drawn by oxen. The seats were cretonne-covered, and the cretonne canopy had a long white fringe. Although the cobblestones in the streets had been worn smooth by many years of use, men ran beside the vehicle placing greased rags under the runners so they would slide easily.

We rode in them to a funicular which took us three thousand feet up the mountain to the Esplanade where we ate lunch. At times the clouds came in from the sea and covered the mountaintop, and we could see nothing, but they soon melted away. After lunch we slid down the mountain. Our tourist brochure said it was a "thrilling, dangerous ride, two and a half miles long."

The sleds were waiting for us outside the hotel. Each had a wicker seat mounted on wood runners. We tucked Chomee in between us, and our two guides ran along beside us. Sometimes they pushed, sometimes they pulled, until the slope got steep and they could stand on the runners. If they thought we were going too fast, they held the sled back. The slide had been built with ridges and hollows evenly spaced and paved with smooth pebbles. The sled hit only the tops of the ridges. Our speed was not great, but the hairpin turns provided plenty of thrills. Two and a half miles and three thousand feet lower, we got out of the sleds near the main street of Funchal.

We still had a couple of hours to spend wandering the city, and of course, shopping was a must. We bought several pieces of embroidery and a small native costume for Chomee which, a few years later, she wore to kindergarten for a "show and tell" session. She did so well with her little travel lecture that she was invited up to the 7th and 8th grades to repeat it.

Our next stop was Gibraltar. The *Rock* doesn't look at all like the Prudential ads until you get onto the Spanish side. We were interested in the great cement patches near the top which catch and channel rain water into cisterns. At one time the fortress was able to store enough water for its needs.

I had been looking forward to shopping in Gibraltar as it was a free port, and I had hoped to buy French perfumes and some oriental silks, but it was Sunday, and being a British possession, all the stores were closed. We did have a trip through the passageways that honeycomb the rock and saw obsolete cannon pointed seaward. The modern installations were higher up and were closed to the tourists.

The next day we debarked at Algiers. Our vacation was over, and for the next five months we worked almost eighteen hours a day.

Our stoves, tents, and lamps were waiting for us, and we managed to get them in duty free if we would take them out in six months. The car was also waiting for us on the dock, but it had been assembled in Spain, not France, and the cost and duty were $3000. In 1930 that was much too high a price for a Ford. We refused the car and bought a chassis from the Ford dealer in Algiers. Then, after looking at the car on the dock, he hired workmen to build a body for us. It would not be ready for several weeks, so he obligingly loaned us a sedan.

The next few days were busy purchasing cots, folding tables and chairs, pots, pans, blankets, and sheets—all things needed to set up a camp for twenty-one people. Cases of canned vegetables, fruits, and jams were added to the pile of goods waiting shipment by train to Canrobert. We bought several cases of American breakfast foods: oatmeal, cornflakes, shredded wheat, all exported from the Canadian factories, because duty was less than for U.S. shipments.

We made our official calls and renewed our acquaintance with the Basiaux family.

Finally, late one morning we started off for Bougie. In the Atlas Mountain passes, we drove through a blinding snowstorm. The road was narrow, and our visibility almost nil, so we were slowed down. Evening came, and we were still eight miles from Bougie when we had a blowout. As we had not intended to be on the road that late, we had no flashlight handy, but Alvan and Mason soon had the tire changed, and we pulled up in front of the *Étoile* where we had had so many good meals three years before.

Apparently I was overtired and an easy victim to the flu, so I spent the next two days in bed and saw nothing of my beloved Bougie but the four walls of my room.

Alonzo renewed his friendship with M. Hassinou and took George L., Mason, and Alvan to the Hassinou home for coffee.

Then, since it was the end of Ramadan, we left George L. at Bougie to photograph the *Grande Prière,* and the rest of us drove on to Constantine through intermittent snowstorms.

I had not recovered from the flu and decided to stay a few more days in Constantine. Alonzo, Alvan, and Mason drove down to Canrobert. It was almost March 1, and camp had to be ready. I had expected Alonzo to come back for me because much of our personal luggage was left at the hotel, but two days later I got a telegram asking me to take the noon train the next day. Hurriedly, I packed, but there was still a mound of clothes left plus the typewriter and briefcase. Fortunately Alonzo had left his old blanket bathrobe, so I put it on the floor, dumped all the leftover clothes in it, and tied it up. When I got on the train I felt like a nomad with all his worldly goods tied in a bundle.

There was no one to meet me when I got off the train at Canrobert, but the station was close to the village and two natives offered to carry my luggage to the hotel. The hotel owner, who was also our friend, greeted me and quickly showed me to a room.

Alonzo came soon, and we spent the night at the hotel. The next morning we drove to our camp at Aïn Berriche.

27

Camp Logan

*A*ïn Berriche was twenty-five miles from Canrobert, and as the three of us climbed into the car Alonzo had brought, he said, "We'll stop at the Bernards' on the way out. They're eager to see you and Chomee."

Twenty minutes later we turned into the country road that led to their place. "We are going to see Mme. Bernard," I told Chomee. "Do you remember the nice lady who gave you cookies last year? She always gave you two, one for each hand."

Madame Bernard rushed out, her arms wide in welcome, as we stopped in front of the farmhouse. Alonzo lifted Chomee from the car, and she walked shyly up to Madame.

"*La petite* Chomee, how she has grown!" cried Madame. "And Mme. Pond, how are you? Come, we will go inside and have some cookies."

M. Bernard came from the farmyard back of the house, and we settled down in the living room, ready for a second breakfast coffee.

"The little one is hungry," M. Bernard said, and reached out to pass the plate of cookies.

Chomee sat up straight and reached out her right hand, then looked up at M. Bernard and, smiling, asked "May I have two?"

"But yes, and two more when those are gone."

Alonzo and he began talking business.

"This year we will need Ferrah as a full-time interpreter. That means that Dorothy will need another handyman. I will need at least fifteen workmen. Can you get them for me?"

"Perhaps not all fifteen, but eight or ten. I'm sure you can hire other labor from around your camp."

"I like the men you have trained here at the farm," Alonzo continued, "but it is too far for the men to walk back here every night, so I'll need three local tents for them."

"I'm sure I can arrange that. I think I can rent them from the highway department. When the natives work on the road, their jobs are too far away from their homes, and the department furnishes tents. I'll see about it tomorrow."

Madame Bernard and I were having a good visit, but Alonzo was anxious to get back to camp. We said "*Au revoir*," and got back into the car. Chomee had a cookie in each hand.

After several miles we turned off the *Route Nationale* and onto a secondary road that led to Aïn Berriche. We drove half a mile.

"Here we are," said Alonzo, and turned into a field.

Fifty feet off the road was a single tree and under it, an open well with a three-foot stone curb. The water from this well was to be our supply for drinking, washing clothes, dishes, and ourselves during the next five months.

Several hundred feet back of the well were three green tents: one for Alvan, one for us, and one for Mason. Thoughtfully, Alvan had set up three cots in our tent, and I lost no time in making up the beds and stowing our equipment underneath.

Piles of cots, tables, chairs, boxes of bedding, and canned goods were stacked outside Alvan's tent, which later became the mess tent for headquarters.

Alonzo had already hired Ferrah, Ahmet, and our faithful Chabane. Under Alvan's supervision, they were busy erecting the other seven tents. Eventually there were two rows of five tents, staggered so that when we looked out the back window, if any of us had time to, we looked between the tents to the barren plain beyond. Sidi Reghiss still stood aloofly on the horizon, a reminder that a rock of ages would still be there when our frantic rushing was over with.

As we sorted the equipment, we could find neither kitchen nor dining room supplies — only the four knives, seven forks, and seven spoons which had been left from last year. Lunch that day was bacon, eggs, bread, and canned jam.

The next morning Alvan went to Canrobert. Although Aïn Beïda was closer to camp, our friends were all in Canrobert, and we decided to keep that as our trading center. Alvan came back with three of our students, Laurie Sharp, John Gillin, and Bob Greenlee, who had come in two days early. He also brought four telegrams.

The first was from Algiers, notifying us that the station wagon was ready. The second was from George L. He said he would be on the Saturday evening train and wanted to be met at Canrobert. The third was from the Jenks. They had bought a car in Algiers and were driving down leisurely. The fourth was from eight of our boys who were in Constantine. They wanted to come straight to camp.

The next day was Friday. Alonzo and Mason started early for Algiers, stopping in Canrobert to reserve rooms at the hotel for the eight boys over the weekend. Alonzo also sent a telegram for them to come on to Canrobert.

In the next two days, the four American boys and three workmen put up the rest of the tents and distributed the cots, tables, chairs, stoves, and lanterns. A carpenter

The 1930 crew. Back row, left to right: Ralph Brown, Lauriston Sharp, Virgil Moen, Robert Greenlee, Edgar Roberts (holding Cous Cous), Alvan Small, Dorothy Pond, Robert Krieger, Alonzo Pond, Robert Voight, Ken Williams; Front row, left to right: Charles Nash, Lloyd Wilford, Mason Dobson, Sol Tax, John Gillin, Chomingwen Pond, Danny Riedel.

in Canrobert was busy making sorting trays for the artifacts. I had my hands full overseeing the cooking for all of us.

Saturday evening Alvan took the truck to town and met George L. The two of them managed to persuade the eight disgruntled boys, who wanted to come to camp immediately, that they were better off at the hotel until Monday. Cooking equipment still hadn't come, nor had we been able to buy enough blankets in Constantine. Alonzo and Mason would bring more from Algiers.

The long fast of Ramadan was over, and our workmen went home to celebrate. Sunday, George L. built a darkroom from a packing case. When he put it in the corner of his tent, there was just room for him and Mason to get out of bed and dress. The rest of us spent a quiet, lazy day. It was the last that we would have until the middle of June.

Alvan went to town on Monday morning and brought the boys to camp. Still no box of pans and plates. Since there were only seven forks, we ate in shifts and washed dishes in between. My letters home say that we lived mostly on eggs.

Tuesday night, Alonzo and Mason drove in from Algiers, a total of three hundred miles. It was quite a drive for a new car and, in fact, for anyone in those days of macadam roads and top speeds of 40 to 50 miles an hour. They brought the blankets!

Wednesday the Jenks drove in. We had hired Larbi, the *garde champêtre* of the year before, as their handyman.

Our cooking equipment and "silverware" arrived at the depot in Canrobert. It had been missent and had been sitting in a freight depot until a tracer was sent and located it. On one of his trips to Canrobert during the week, Alvan had picked up three conical, white canvas tents for the workmen.

M. Bernard sent over Malmar to be my handyman. The last two boys arrived on Thursday. Except for workmen, our camp personnel roster was complete at last.

Our camp chart looked like this:

Three workmen's tents were at the left and farther away.

About seventy-five feet back of the second row, Alonzo had had the workmen dig two holes. Planks were laid, one on each side of the holes. Tarps were put up enclosing three sides of each hole. These were our toilet facilities. By common consent, we agreed that whenever one hole was occupied, the occupant would hang his hat on the front pole that held the tarp. The hat could be seen from the back row of tents. That plan worked well, and no one was embarrassed by intruders.

For bathing, sponge baths were the most popular, although some of the boys put on swimming trunks and had their tent-mates pour pails of water straight from the well over them.

Malmar, my handyman, proved unsatisfactory. He didn't like taking orders from a woman. He was lazy and impudent. Still, I had to have some help and tolerated him as best I could.

Camp Logan.

We frequently butchered sheep. Our American personnel were familiar with chops, roasts, and stews, as well as the liver and the heart. Our local workmen were also accustomed to eating the entrails, the stomach, and the head. We gave these vitamin-rich parts to them as a free bonus. Alonzo explained to Malmar and all the workmen that they must cook their own food over open fires just as they did at home.

One day Malmar cooked his share of the intestines in my pastry oven. That put it out of commission for two days while it aired. Just two days later, I opened the oven to put in a cake. There was the skinned head of a sheep, its eyes staring and teeth bared. It was the last straw. I called Alonzo. Malmar was paid off and started walking home.

By Saturday morning of the first full week, the camp was organized, and everyone knew what he was supposed to do. Alvan was camp manager and sole driver of the truck. He also sold postage stamps, candy, and cigarettes to the American boys; cigarettes and bread to the workmen, all at cost. He kept track of what each workman owed so that it could be taken off his paycheck at the end of the week. Mason was to keep the stoves and lanterns filled and in good repair. He also helped George L. when needed. George L. had his hands full with his photography. He not only took pictures but also did his own developing in the packing-box darkroom.

Each team of two students had workmen and tools assigned to them, and three test trenches had been opened. Dr. Jenks had his diggings well started.

My job was to plan the menus for the week, make out grocery lists, apportion the food for each tent, as well as try to keep up with the correspondence.

Saturday afternoon we put up a flagpole. Protocol decreed that the French flag should fly above the Stars and Stripes, but the boys would have none of it. We compromised. We purchased two French flags and put them up with the American flag in the center and a couple of inches lower. Below the three flags was the Beloit College banner. Alonzo had carried that across the Sahara attached to his camel saddle in 1925-26.

We called the site Camp Logan, in honor of Dr. and Mrs. Frank G. Logan, who financed the expedition.

28

Harassment

This year it was not the natives who bothered us; it was a trio of officious French bureaucrats.

The Tuesday that Alonzo and Mason were in Algiers for the new car, I discovered that I needed something in town. Aïn Beïda was so close that I decided to go there instead of Canrobert where we were well-known. Alvan was busy and George L. had to develop his films of the *Grande Prière* that he had taken the previous week in Bougie.

I had tried several times the year before to learn to drive the Covered Wagon, as we now called the truck, but advancing the spark and retarding the gasoline flow, or was it the other way around, proved to be too intricate a maneuver for me. John Gillin volunteered to drive me to Aïn Beïda.

We had planned to be gone less than an hour, so I decided to leave Chomee at camp under the watchful eyes of Alvan and Ferrah.

At Aïn Beïda, John and I finished our shopping in a few minutes and came back to the truck to find a policeman waiting for us.

"Will you please come with me to the police station?" he said to me.

"I'm sure I won't be long," I told John, and followed the man to the police station about a block away.

We entered a room where the police chief sat at a desk. "Where are your official papers?" he asked.

"My husband has gone to Algiers and has taken our papers with him."

"Oh? Then we must wait for the mayor."

So we waited a half hour, three-quarters, a full hour. I was getting furious. Finally the mayor sauntered in.

"*Madame*, we need to see your papers."

Again I explained that Alonzo had taken them to Algiers, where we were purchasing a new car.

He hemmed and hawed.

I was almost speechless with anger, but I said, "We do have permission from the Algerian Government to work in Algeria. Furthermore, I have a young daughter back at camp who needs me. It is her lunch time. I must get back to her."

"Well, you may go now, but when your husband comes back, have him bring his papers in to me."

I walked back to the truck fuming. Back at camp I told Alvan about it. He immediately drove to the Bernard's and took M. Bernard back to the police station at Aïn Beïda. Alvan later told us that he sat in the truck while M. Bernard walked into the police station, his mustache bristling. The shouting of two angry people could be heard out on the street.

On the way back, M. Bernard told Alvan to tell me not to worry but to try and avoid going in to Aïn Beïda if I could.

When Alonzo came back, he didn't pay any attention to the request, and we did our shopping in Canrobert.

One day the little *gendarme* who had charge of our district dropped in for coffee. The year before, we had sometimes befriended him by giving him a ride when we met him walking along the road because his motorcycle had a flat tire, or he had unexpectedly run out of gas. As we were sipping our coffee in the mess tent, Alonzo asked, "What was all the fuss about when my wife went to Aïn Beïda a couple of weeks ago?"

The *gendarme* smiled and shrugged. "Oh, you know. *Madame* dresses a little unconventionally when she goes to town sometimes. She wears riding trousers and high boots. The police chief and the mayor are new at their jobs, and they want to impress their constituents with their efficiency. *Madame*, as a foreigner, seemed like fair game. It was nothing but a desire to impress."

Usually I did wear dresses in to town, but when I was in a hurry, I didn't bother to change. The next time I went to Aïn Beïda, I made sure that I wore riding trousers and boots and a flannel shirt.

Alvan was my chauffeur this time, and when we returned to the truck, there was the policeman waiting for us.

"Your husband hasn't brought his papers to us."

"No! He doesn't have to. We are not under your jurisdiction. Our papers have been cleared by the *Caid* of Canrobert and Sidi Reghiss, the mayor of Canrobert, the *administrateur* of Canrobert, the *Préfet* of Constantine, and the Governor General of Algeria. You have no authority over us. When I come to town, you are not even to speak to me. Also, you are to keep all these little urchins from climbing on my truck."

With that, Alvan and I drove away, leaving the policeman open-mouthed and the crowd of bystanders grinning behind their hands.

29

Days at Camp Logan

"Roll out, boys. R-r-r-roll out." Alonzo walked down the rear row of tents. The alarm had gone off at 5:20. By 5:30 Alonzo had dressed and was out walking the *rue de l'École*, which the boys had named the alley between the tents. How the boys hated to hear that call. There were groans and mumbles from each tent.

Komici had come to replace Malmar. He was the right man for the right place. He had once worked in the kitchen of a French restaurant, and he didn't mind taking orders from a woman. While I was getting dressed, I could hear Komici putting the coffee over the fire in the kitchen. The kitchen was under the awning to the mess tent. Then he set the table for six of us — cups, plates, silverware, and an orange or tangerine for each one.

"You snuggle under the covers a few more minutes," I admonished Chomingwen. "Mama'll be back to dress you."

I always cooked the breakfast bacon myself out of respect for the Muslim taboo on pork. I also carefully washed the skillet afterwards so that Komici would not have to handle a contaminated utensil. While the bacon sizzled, I got Chomee dressed for the day.

I could hear Alvan, who slept in the mess tent, getting dressed. A few minutes later he had picked up an empty cup from the table. "Please, Komici, a cup of coffee," he said sleepily.

"Immediately, M. Small, immediately," my helper replied.

Alvan had learned the French *poilu*'s trick of adding a shot of *rhum* to the morning coffee. He carefully carried the cup of black coffee to his bed, rummaged underneath to get the bottle of *rhum*, poured a slug into his coffee, and sipped it. He brightened up immediately, and by the time the cup was empty, he was at the table peeling his orange.

I went back to the kitchen and turned the bacon. Komici had put eleven eggs on to fry with vegetable shortening.

George L. and Mason wandered in from their tent and sat down at the table. Mason, who had a typical teenage appetite, started right in on the bacon and eggs. Komici brought two loaves of French bread and two cans of jam and set them in easy reach of the hungry boy.

Larbi was busy getting breakfast for the Minnesota group.

No one lingered over breakfast. There was no sitting out in the sunshine, sipping coffee, and listening to the little shepherd boys calling their news as we had done at Medfoun. No time to watch the ring of mist dissolve from around the mountain, Sidi Reghiss. Camp Logan had to move on a more rigid schedule.

At breakfast the plans for the days were announced. George L. went to his darkroom to develop films. The day before he had taken color pictures of women carding and spinning wool. Mason started his rounds of the tents collecting stoves and lanterns. It was his job to clean and fill them every day. Alvan went to Canrobert almost every morning with letters to mail and pick up mail. There were usually some provisions to get. If it was market day, I'd hand him a grocery list that usually read: 200 eggs, 400 oranges, 50 pounds of potatoes, 20 bunches of carrots, 20 loaves of bread, 10 pounds onions, and anything else that looked good.

"Alvan," I said, as he went toward the car, "don't talk too long with Georgette, because I need some of these things right after lunch. I want to make two cakes."

The doctor's pretty teen-age daughter, Georgette, always went to the post office for the mail as soon as the Covered Wagon drove into town, and somehow she and Alvan wound up leaning over the yard gate to her home. Alvan picked up French very fast while he waited for the incoming mail.

At 6:45 A.M., fifteen workmen assembled in front of the mess tent, which was also called headquarters tent. Each picked up his wheelbarrow, a pick, or a shovel. The boys came from their tents with collecting bags and sometimes canteens of water. A line of men started out on the path to our diggings, an eighth of a mile away. Dr. Jenks and Alonzo walked along at the end of the line.

Komici washed dishes. I made our beds and swept the tent. Komici then cleaned the mess tent. Larbi took care of the tents for Dr. and Mrs. Jenks and their students. Our boys were responsible for their own housekeeping. Each team got its own meals and did their own dishes, sweeping, and bed-making.

Twice a week, I gathered up the headquarters laundry for George L., Mason, Alvan, and my family, and gave it all to Komici. Larbi washed the Minnesota contingents' clothes. The two men would go down to the well and haul up pails and pails of water, splash some over the clothes, soap them, rub them, rinse them, and spread them on the ground to dry.

The well also was used by the natives who lived nearby, so one man always stayed with the clothes until they were dry. If they were left alone, a sheet or two might "blow away" and be missing. It was just a case of "these people have so much, they won't miss one piece," but when the nearest source of supply was Constantine, one piece gone *was* missed.

I usually started on the never-ending typing of correspondence and reports. Letters home, a carbon this week to my family, next week to Alonzo's. Letters to Dr. Collie and Dr. Logan, reports of interesting finds to M. Albertini, *Directeur des Antiquités* in Algiers.

I didn't have the time to spend with Chomee that she wanted, and she often came to me and said, "Love Chomee!" I'd give her a hug and say, "Bring a book. I'll read to you." She would bring a picture book, and I'd start reading Mother Goose or Alphabet books, but never for very long.

George L. would call, "I need help, and I can't find Mason."

Maybe Alvan would drive in with groceries that needed to be put away.

Or Komici would ask "*Madame*, what will we have for lunch?"

Our morning reading always was interrupted. "I'll read later in the day, Chomee. See if you can find some pretty stones to play with."

One day Alonzo came home with a little, white, three-week-old puppy. He was all white, fluffy fur except for two bright, black eyes and the tip of his nose. What should we name him? The whole camp gave suggestions. Someone suggested Lax, a contraction of Logan African Expedition, but as the puppy wasn't housebroken the name seemed too apt. We settled on Cous Cous.

Chomingwen and Cous Cous.

Couscous is the staple food the natives use in place of potatoes or rice. It consists of small pellets of ground winter wheat or semolina. The wheat is ground in stone mortars into coarse flour. The flour is then spread on a large tray, sprinkled with water, and rolled with the flat of the hand into tiny balls. Then it is sun-dried.

Every day a handful or two is placed in a pottery steamer over boiling meat. This steam filters through the couscous, fluffing it and softening it into digestible bits. To serve, it is heaped into a bowl and surrounded by cooked vegetables and bits of meat. Each diner spoons some into his own bowl. He adds vegetables and meat and pours the meat broth over it. Most natives like the addition of red pepper, so the sauce is as hot as Mexican chili.

We thought the fluffy, white puppy was as pretty as a plate of fluffy, native couscous. Also, it was a name Chomee could pronounce. Chomee loved the puppy and would run around camp with him, saying, "Puppy dog, don't bite my bloomers." Often she carried him, apparently preferring to carry him upside down with his tail tickling her nose. She had learned it was easier to catch and hold him by his hind legs.

Cous Cous wriggled his way into everyone's heart. Edgar took the sleeves from an old sweater and made a chic doggy sweater for the puppy. Alvan allowed Cous Cous to sleep on his sheepskin beside his cot. One night he heard someone outside his tent, and Cous Cous growled. Alvan snapped on his flashlight, and there was Cous Cous facing the door, the fuzzy white hair on his back standing up straight. He was growling a fierce puppy growl. They did not hear any more noises and both went to sleep.

At 11:30 all of the boys and some of the workmen came back to camp. The boys got their own lunches, and the workmen ate their bread and dates near their tents. Some of the workmen always stayed at the diggings as guards for the tools. They had carried chunks of bread and handful of dates in their pockets when they left in the morning. We often lunched on sandwiches, coffee, and fruit.

Sometimes at lunch George L. would say, "I'd like to get some pictures of women carding and spinning wool today."

Then Alonzo or Alvan would drive him and Ferrah to a native village. Ferrah had many acquaintances around the country and could always be relied upon to locate whatever George L. needed to photograph.

After I had tucked Chomee in for a nap, I often made several cakes. This year I remembered to bring a can of good, American baking powder with me. I also made pies for the whole camp. One letter to folks at home states that I made four custard pies that day and "apparently they were alright, because no one came to the mess tent for bicarbonate of soda afterwards."

We missed the Bernards dropping in for coffee as they did at Medfoun, but a forty-mile trip was too long for them except on a Sunday with a special invitation to dinner.

About three o'clock I usually started apportioning food for the next day. Bread was piled at one end of the table in the mess tent. Roast or chops or neck meat for stews was apportioned into five piles, one for each of the boy's tents; only one kind of meat for each day. Eggs, oranges, cans of vegetables, and jam were doled out, always the same variety for each tent. Slabs of bacon were piled next to the meat. Boxes of American breakfast foods and cans of condensed milk were given by Alvan or Alonzo, because some of the boys were inclined to hoard.

At four o'clock the line of workmen returned, each carrying a shovel or pick or pushing a wheelbarrow. The boys followed with their collecting sacks full of artifacts and their notebooks full of data. Alonzo tried to be at the diggings at the end of the day to take care of any special piece — a needle-sharp bone dagger or a beautifully chipped knife. Those, he brought back carefully wrapped in tissue paper and carried in small wooden trays.

From then on, for the next two hours it was hustle and bustle. Boys were going to the well to get water. The smell of cooking mutton permeated the air. The tent-mate who was designated cook for that week was busy frying or roasting meat. Larbi scurried around getting the evening meal for the Jenks and their two boys. Komici was hurrying to set the table and keep an eye on supper.

The six of us sat down to dinner about 5:30. Mason was always hungry, and when there was one serving left on a platter, he would pick it up and pass it quickly in front of each of us, saying, "No one wants any more of this, do they?" Then he would scrape it off onto his plate.

None of us went hungry, but sometimes I served unfamiliar dishes. I remember one time when I made a Roquefort cheese dressing for the lettuce salad. Mason took a bite and said, "Who put soap in the salad dressing?"

Mason took his share of ribbing with good grace.

After dinner Komici always got some workman to help with the dish washing; perhaps he paid him an extra franc.

Alvan put the portable record player on the table and got out stamps, cigarettes, and bread. Whoever wanted any of these things came in during the next half hour. The boys settled down to sort their day's collections. I put Chomee to bed and went next door to help Alvan. Alonzo started making the rounds of the tents. He checked the boys' work every night, helping them to decide whether an artifact was a worthless flake, chipped by jumbling with another stone, or a real tool, chipped by hand.

Mason played the record player. We had brought several dozen records from the States. When Alonzo and Mason were in Algiers, he purchased four or five recordings of native musicians and singers. Whenever we played these records, the workmen gathered just outside the tent door, and we could see the smiles of pleasure on their faces.

At nine o'clock we all went to bed except Alonzo and the boys with whom he was working. It was always 11:00 and sometimes 11:30 before he came back to our tent.

Sunday was a day of relaxation. The workmen were paid at five o'clock on Saturday night, and most of them went home. Sunday everyone slept as late as they wanted. We had told the boys before they left home that there would be no way of going to church. Sunday mornings the boys used as wash days for their clothes as well as their bodies. Some boys washed their sheets and pillow cases, and aired their blankets by spreading them out on the tent roofs. Then they hauled water from the well and washed their personal clothes. Other boys never took their beds to pieces the three and a half months they were there.

There were some "Do not disturb" signs on the tents, signifying that bathing was in progress. Other boys just went to the well in their bathing trunks and had their tent-mates pour pails of water over them.

We organized softball teams in the afternoon, and there were footballs to kick around.

We soon learned that Sunday was to be "At Home" day. Everyone who had a car and lived within fifty miles of camp came to see the Americans camping out on a shell mound. Car after car drove up, and people introduced themselves. We showed them our tents, stoves, lanterns, and air mattresses. Amateur archaeologists were shown some artifacts.

Special friends, such as the doctor and his wife from Canrobert, the hotel keeper, and the proprietor of the grocery store were invited to have coffee.

Once a month we organized a day's trip for the boys to some Roman ruins. Some of us always stayed in camp, however. We had too much valuable equipment to ever leave it alone. So the days and weeks went on, one much like the other.

Sunday softball.

30

The Days Were Not Always Humdrum

The days were not always humdrum. There was the day that I cut up the pig. The camp had been living on mutton for six weeks. We bought sheep live from the farmers near us. Often they were delivered to us, thrown over the back of a horse. We tethered them away from the tents and when we needed fresh meat, Komici, Larbi, or Ferrah killed and dressed them.

One market day, Alonzo met M. Bernard at the hotel bar.

"Does any farmer around here raise pigs?" Alonzo asked.

"But, yes. There are two who do. There's one of them down at the end of the bar now."

Delivering sheep to camp.

M. Bernard, with Alonzo in tow, walked over to the man. After the introductions and small talk about weather and crops, Alonzo said, "Do you have any hogs for sale?"

"Yes, yes, *Monsieur*. I have good ones, but I'll need two weeks to fatten them for market."

"Good. I'll order one now. When it is ready, you can send word through our friend, the hotel keeper." Our nights had been cool and the days comfortable.

Two weeks later the hotel keeper told Alvan that the pig was ready to be slaughtered. The farm was on the road back to camp, so Alvan stopped in and left word that he would pick it up the next day.

Alvan and Alonzo both went to market the next day and brought home a 200-pound dressed hog.

At Camp Logan, the pig was put in the little station wagon and all the doors locked. It was the only "meat chest" big enough to hold it. We were not afraid that the natives would take it, because the meat is unclean for Muslims, but that a stray dog might come by.

The next morning we got up to a blazing sun. When we sat down to breakfast, we knew it was going to be a hot day. Without ice or refrigeration, we had 200 pounds of pork to be eaten in a hurry.

I looked around the breakfast table. "Alonzo, will you cut up the hog this morning?"

"You know I've got an appointment with the administrator at nine o'clock."

"Alvan?"

"It's market day, and if I don't get in early, all the eggs and oranges will be gone," he replied.

"George L?" I asked hopefully.

"I'm sorry, Dorothy, but with this hot weather I've got to develop the color pictures I took yesterday. The negatives will spoil, and some of them were of almond trees in blossom. This heat will brown the blossoms and I won't be able to get other pictures."

Mason had his never-ending job of filling and repairing stoves and lamps.

A few minutes later the camp was deserted except for Komici, Chomee, and me. Alonzo and Alvan had obligingly carried the carcass to the mess table. I had never even sawn pork chops off of a loin roast.

After the breakfast dishes were washed, I said, "Komici, you'll have to help me."

Komici was shocked! "But *Madame*, I have never even touched pork! At the hotel they didn't ask me to. Our religion forbids us to touch pork. It is unclean."

I rummaged through the cupboards and found a pair of clean canvas gloves and gave them to Komici. "Now there's no one around to see you. If you put on the gloves, you won't be touching the pig. Then you can hold the animal while I saw."

"Only for you, *Madame*, would I do this."

"Thank you very much, Komici. We can't let this meat spoil. Now you hold it tight while I saw."

Komici was careful that his garments didn't touch the meat. For two hours I hacked away with a butcher knife or sawed. Then I divided the meat into seven piles. The Jenks had asked to have a share. At noon, when the boys came back, I called them together and said, "Take your share of the pork. Cook some chops this noon. Put the rest in the coolest part of your tent. All the meat must be cooked by tomorrow night. It will keep better if it's cooked."

That noon the whole camp smelled of frying pork chops. We all ate cold, cooked pork for a week.

Several days later, Alvan started to build a doghouse for Cous Cous. He picked up the saw and tried to cut a board.

"Hey! What's happened to this saw? It's so dull it won't cut."

I just walked away.

On April 8 we peeked out of the tent window when the alarm went off. Big, wet flakes of snow were settling quietly on the tents and covering the ground. Turning off the alarm we went back to sleep. At eight we roused ourselves and dressed. Alonzo went down the *rue de l'École* and called, "Boys! Wake up and see the snow. Then you may go back to bed if you want to."

It snowed until eleven o'clock, and we had an inch of wet snow on the ground and clinging to the tents. By nightfall it had melted.

The Jenks decided that they needed a vacation and left the next morning for Biskra and a good hotel. Ralph and Lloyd carried on their work at their diggings.

Chicken dinner.

We could never buy enough chickens at one time to feed everyone, so we bought one or two at a time from the local farmers or at the market. We scattered table scraps and some millet on the ground, and the chickens stayed around camp. At night they roosted on the axles of the truck and the cars.

Early one evening, the Jenks decided to drive to Berriche, the small village about five miles north of the camp. As they drove away, several of our workmen ran after the car shouting, but the Jenks had the windows closed and did not hear them.

Ferrah came to us and said, *"Patron*, one of the chickens was roosting on M. Jenks's car and went away with them."

"Well, one chicken gone." Alonzo answered.

A week later Alonzo had an errand in Berriche. He stopped at a farmhouse just this side of the village and asked if there were any chickens for sale. The woman and her young son had quite a conversation in a native dialect. Then she went into the enclosed farmyard and brought out a hen. Alonzo paid her for it and put it in the back seat of the car, finished his errand, and came home.

As he got out of the car he called, "There's a chicken in the back seat."

Komici opened the back door and took out a black hen. He and some of the others who were standing around broke into laughter. Alonzo looked puzzled.

Komici explained. "This is the chicken that rode away on M. Jenks's car. You've bought the same hen twice."

We laughed, too. One hen looked just like another to us, but our workmen recognized individuals in their livestock as we do people.

Once in a while it rained all day, and no one could work. The diggings site was a mound of mud, and the trenches had water in them. The boys stayed in their tents and wrote letters, wrote their reports, and finished sorting artifacts.

One of those evenings, we were all so bored that I dug out the one package of popcorn I had brought for a special occasion. I popped it on the gasoline stove, and then called to boys. There was only a handful apiece, but it was a treat. Some of us prolonged the pleasure by eating one kernel at a time.

From the tents where the workmen slept, we could hear them laughing and the call of *"Haddity-haddity-ha."* We knew they were playing a game similar to our childhood game of "Button, button, who's got the button," only they were using a white pebble.

The boys had gone back to their tents to get ready for bed. George L. and Mason had gone to their tent, and Alonzo and I had said goodnight to Alvan and gone back to ours. Alvan was just getting into bed when someone outside his door called, "*Monsieur*, come out quickly!"

He struggled into his trousers, took a flashlight, and stepped outside. "What's the matter?"

Several of our workmen stood there. "Prowlers!"

Alvan flashed his light around.

"We heard a noise outside, and when we went out there were two men running away."

"So," said Alvan, "they have run away."

"Yes, but they may come back."

By that time other workmen came from their tents, and Alonzo was out with Alvan. He noticed that Ferrah, Chabane, Ahmet, and Larbi were all on the outer fringe of the crowd.

"We'll go search," said the workmen, and they spread out.

The word "prowlers" went from tent to tent, and the boys all gathered around. The natives looked behind all the tents and down by the well. Alvan took the truck and Alonzo the station wagon, and each drove in opposite directions down the road and back. Some of the boys went to the diggings, and some looked under the beds in all the tents. No prowler could be found.

"But there was someone," the workmen insisted.

"Perhaps we should have two men stand guard every night."

Two of the laziest workmen offered their services.

"How will you work the next day if you stay up all night?" Alonzo asked.

"Oh, we'd have to sleep in the daytime."

Alonzo looked at Chabane. "What about this prowler?"

Chabane shrugged and smiled. Brahim loudly proclaimed that there was a prowler, but he had a twinkle in his eye.

"No guards," Alonzo said. "Everybody back to his own tent."

Some of the boys were still unconvinced that the incident was just a way of relieving boredom. They pushed tables piled with pans in front of their tent doors.

That was the last we ever heard of prowlers, but it did liven up a dull evening.

The days went on with just enough spice to keep them from being too monotonous.

31

Ferrah's Fall from Grace

*F*errah fell from grace with a thud that was heard around the countryside.

When the boys were well versed in the digging techniques, we opened two smaller camps. Six boys, with their gear and three tents, were moved to Garaet et Tarf. It was a small lake about ten miles south of Camp Logan. The natives with whom they were accustomed to work and their tents were also moved. The boys immediately named it Camp Pond.

The warm winds from the Sahara had begun to dry up the lake waters, and a dazzling white crust of salt stretched several hundred feet from the shore to the blue water. One day when I was down there, I saw a hundred pink flamingos wheel in and settle down on that blue water just beyond the snow-white crust. How I wished for George L. and his color camera, but he was away on another assignment.

The other diggings was made at a small *escargotière* about three miles north of Camp Logan. It was named Camp 51 after the site number. Only two boys were needed there, Chuck Nash and Bob Voight. The boys stayed at our camp and Alonzo or Alvan took them up every morning and went for them in the afternoon. We hired two natives, Kateb and another whose name I've forgotten, who lived nearby to help them. Ferrah often went along on those trips to explain to the workmen just what the boys expected of them. The new local workmen, especially Kateb, seemed to have a harder time than our other workmen did in understanding the excavation technique required. It seemed that Ferrah had to go more often to Camp 51 to explain and re-explain just what was wanted.

We also trusted Ferrah to buy sheep, eggs, and chickens that we needed, thinking that he would know the values better than we did.

One day when Chuck came back to camp in the late afternoon he said, "Mr. Pond, that Kateb is so stupid. He can't seem to learn about loading a wheelbarrow. He fills it too full, and the dirt, shells, and artifacts spill all over the ground as he pushes it along."

Camp Pond.

The next day Alonzo took Ferrah along with the boys to the diggings. He was impatient and had Ferrah explain again how things were to be handled. We thought the matter was settled.

However, the next day was market day, and Alonzo decided to go to town and take Ferrah with him. Alvan had taken the truck with the boys to Camp 51.

"Where's Ferrah?" asked Alonzo, as he headed for the station wagon.

"He went up to Camp 51 with the boys," answered Komici.

"Well, I wonder why he went up there."

No one said anything.

Alonzo had to wait until they came back. Then he, Alvan, and Ferrah drove off to Canrobert.

He sent Ferrah to get eggs and Alvan to get oranges, and he wandered around the market. Eventually he saw a blanket that he liked. He found Ferrah and said, "There's a blanket I'd like; go over and ask the price and come and tell me."

Alonzo wandered on, and Ferrah found him a few minutes later and gave him an exorbitant price. "Oh, I can do better than that, myself. Go back and try again."

Several times Ferrah made the trip between Alonzo and the seller, but the price was always too high. Ferrah seemed so eager to have Alonzo buy the blanket that he became suspicious and didn't purchase it.

He then went to the sheep market and priced live sheep and found that he had been paying fifteen to twenty percent more than the market value.

"Well," Alonzo thought, "so there are kickbacks."

As soon as Alonzo, Alvan, and Ferrah had driven off, Komici came to me. "*Madame*, that Ferrah. He isn't honest. He knew that the *patron* was angry with Kateb, and so this morning he went to the camp and made Kateb give him a whole day's wages for 'coffee money.' He told Kateb he would have him fired if the money wasn't paid. Kateb is just a poor farmer, and he needs the money, and he doesn't know you well enough to stand up to Ferrah.

"And that isn't all. Ferrah's done it before with the natives who can't speak French. He makes Amaroui charge you too much for the sheep you buy, and he pockets the difference. When M. Pond goes to town with the truck and takes all these country natives who want to ride in with him, Ferrah charges them two francs a ride, while M. Pond thinks he is being good to them and giving them a ride free."

I thanked Komici and then waited impatiently for Alonzo to return to camp. When I told him what Komici said, he didn't even wait for lunch but got back into the car and went to Camp 51. Somehow through sign language, he made Kateb understand that he wanted him to go to Canrobert. Then he picked up Chabane and Amaroui at our camp.

Amaroui was a native farmer who lived near us and from whom we bought our sheep. He also worked for us at the diggings. It was the growing season for the wheat, and there was little to do around his farm. Extra cash always came in handy.

They drove straight to the hotel, and Alonzo asked the owner, a good friend, to come out to the truck. The owner's father was French and his mother native Berber, so he knew the customs of both cultures well.

Through questioning our friend, Alonzo found out that indeed Ferrah had exacted a day's pay from Kateb by threatening him with the loss of his job otherwise.

Amaroui said that yes, Ferrah did take a commission on the sheep he sold because, "M. Pond could buy them from other farmers, and would, too, if I didn't pay Ferrah a few francs."

Finally Alonzo said to our hotel friend, "Please ask Chabane how the natives regard these things."

Chabane replied, "It is not honest. We workmen have been trying to tell you for weeks that Ferrah is crooked, but you trust everyone, and you wouldn't have believed us."

"I'd have believed you, Chabane," said Alonzo.

"Yes, but I mind my own business. I'm too old to want to make trouble for a no-good like Ferrah. It isn't right, though, to charge the country natives for a ride to town in the truck when you think you are being a good fellow and helping them out."

That was a really serious charge, for we had no public conveyance permit and the Algerian authorities would have frowned on any charge for riders in the truck.

We had hoped to keep Ferrah in ignorance of the affair until Alonzo could talk to him, but as soon as the car with Alonzo, Kateb, Chabane, and Amaroui pulled away, Ferrah came to me.

"Why has the *patron* gone to town again?" he asked.

I was at a loss for what to say, because I knew that Alonzo must handle this situation. Finally I said, "There is business in town, and M. Pond needs workmen for it."

Several hours later Alonzo returned. His trip to town verified everything Komici had told me.

"Alvan, I need you as a witness. Komici, please ask Ferrah to come to headquarters tent," Alonzo said.

When Ferrah came, he said, "Ferrah, I'm disappointed in you. You have betrayed our trust. You could have gotten me into serious difficulties with the government by charging the local people to ride with me. We no longer need you nor want you in camp."

"Please, *Patron*, let me stay. I won't do anything bad anymore. Just give me another chance."

"No, Ferrah, I can't. There would never be trust between us again nor between me and my workmen. You must pack your things right away, and M. Alvan will take you to your home."

Ferrah went to the tent where he slept and got his few belongings while Alvan went to the car. The year before, we had given Ferrah a small gasoline stove. He put his things in the back of the station wagon and then went to the extra cans of gasoline we carried with us and filled the stove. This was too brash even for the natives who were accustomed to his cheating. They went behind their tents and howled with laughter. Alonzo, Alvan, and I smiled, too, but we let him get away with it. After all, he had been with us for almost two years, and why should we bother about two quarts of gasoline as "severance pay."

32

Larbi's Big Moment

I t was after supper and dark. I had put Chomee to bed and gone to the headquarters tent. The tents were so close together that if she woke, I would hear her. Alonzo was checking the day's work with the boys at their tents. Alvan and I were reading the Paris edition of the *New York Herald*. Mason was running the record player.

Suddenly the tent flap was pulled aside. Larbi dashed in.

"He's going to kill me!" he cried.

"Who's going to kill you?" asked Alvan, matter-of-factly.

"That Honishe. He's drawn a knife."

"Guess I better go and get the Chief," said Alvan, and he left the tent.

Larbi was the handsomest native I had ever seen. He was tall. His white turban set off his dark brown eyes and well-groomed mustache. His white robes were always clean. He was probably the most intelligent of all the workmen we hired. Last year he had been *garde champêtre*, guarding the fields. He had often brought our mail when M. Bernard had gotten it in town.

This year when we established camp, he was without work. We hired him as a handyman for Dr. Jenks. His work was easy, as the Jenks were often away. Possibly he was envied by the other workmen.

Five or six natives had crowded into the tent after him and stood by the door. I wasn't afraid. I was too surprised. It was the first time we had violence in the camp.

"*Madame,*" continued Larbi, "he is bad. I am so afraid."

Alvan and Alonzo soon came in. Larbi was talking loudly in Arabic to the other workmen.

Alonzo broke in, "Who's going to kill you, Larbi?"

"That Honishe. Truly, *Patron*, he has drawn a knife! If I hadn't come to your tent, I would be dead."

"Why does Honishe want to kill you? Has he good reason?"

"He has never liked me, *Patron*. He always tries to make trouble for me. Last year I was *garde champêtre*. He made trouble. Now someone else has that job. It wasn't fair. He's a bad man, and I don't dare stay in camp with him. You should get rid of him."

"What's the trouble now? Honishe certainly didn't pull a knife on you because he got you fired as *garde champêtre* last year."

"Honishe sleeps in my tent. I have a little kerosene stove for making coffee. Honishe says now that it is his, but it isn't. It's mine."

I was watching Larbi, but Alonzo was watching the faces of workmen near the doorway. Finally he said, "Komici, bring Honishe in here."

Komici dashed away, and Larbi looked frightened.

"Honishe won't hurt you in our tent," Alonzo said.

We could hear Honishe talking in Arabic. He could speak French, but he was too excited to remember it. Larbi moved toward Alvan. Honishe came in and stood just inside the door as if ready to run away quickly.

Alonzo spoke slowly in French. "There are two tents out there. Honishe must move into the other tent. Larbi is to stay where he is. Now, neither of you is to go into the other tent. If I ever hear of either of you entering the other tent, I will ship both of you out of camp so fast you won't know what's happened."

"The stove is Larbi's. I was with him when he bought it. Tomorrow I'll buy another for you, Honishe, ...and I'll take the price out of your pay."

Then Alonzo turned to the workmen, "Now, all of you see that this rule is obeyed. Komici, you go and help Honishe move, and when he is in the other tent, come and tell me. Then Larbi can go back to his tent."

As the workmen left Alvan grinned and said, "It seems like a simple solution."

We thought so, too, but the next morning while we were breakfasting, Larbi came to the tent door.

"*Patron*, today is Tuesday. On Tuesdays and Thursdays Honishe brings water from the well to my cook tent. But he says you told us not to speak to each other so he won't bring the water."

The workmen did take turns bringing water from the well to both Larbi and Komici. Alonzo made a schedule of the days and number of pails of water which each man was to bring. Honishe was transferred as water-carrier for Komici.

"I think that we'll move the tent Honishe sleeps in," said Alonzo. "Alvan, will you see that two workmen move the tent to the other end of the row, perhaps over on the *rue de 1'École*."

Right after breakfast, that was done. The tents were placed at either side of the camp. Ahmet brought water to Larbi instead of Honishe. Peace settled down on Camp Logan.

33

Ghosts of Ancient Rome

*O*ur boys had worked hard for two and a half months. They had been tied pretty close to the three camps. Oh, they had attended some of the Saturday night dances at Canrobert. Twice we had taken them on Sunday to the Roman ruins, but mostly they had stayed at camp. A vacation was due them. Biskra and the Sahara beckoned.

The moon would be full the third week of May. The Jenks offered to stay at the camp for the week we would be gone. Word went out from headquarters tent that the next week we would take both the big truck and the station wagon and drive to the sand dunes beyond Biskra. The old Covered Wagon wasn't working too well, but Alvan thought he could nurse it along. Nineteen of us would go — all of our group, including Komici and Ahmet as camp helpers.

There was a busy week before we could leave. Camp Pond at Garaet et Tarf and Camp 51 had to be closed. The boys sorted their collections and wrote their reports.

I made out menus for seven days. Each day's food was to be packed in a box with paper between breakfast, lunch, and dinner supplies. There were seven boxes, each well-labeled, and holding one day's meals.

On Monday morning everyone was up at 5:30. Komici had seven chickens roasting, as well as a ten-pound roast of beef that we had been able to buy at our local market. The boys ate hurried breakfasts, washed their dishes, and made bedrolls of their sheets and blankets. George L. loaded a suitcase with cameras and films. The day before, he had printed pictures of some of the workmen and distributed them.

Some of the natives were paid off. We would not need as many of them when we came back. The better workmen were told to come back in a week.

Food boxes, bedrolls, two gasoline stoves, and two lanterns were put into the truck. Each boy took his own plate, cup, knife, fork, and spoons. Several pans and coffee pots and two dish pans were added to the supply.

Alvan got behind the wheel, and eight boys climbed into the truck, followed by Komici and Ahmet. Alvan drove away down to the main road and up over the hill. They were on their way. We were to rendezvous for lunch.

The typewriter, portable Victrola, cameras, and film were piled in the little station wagon. The Victrola and typewriter were needed for publicity pictures to be taken in the Sahara dunes. Eight of us were left to climb into the two seats and the back of the little wagon.

As I left our tent to take one last look around and see that everything we needed was packed, I said, "Where's my list of menus? I left it here on the table in the mess tent."

We spent fifteen minutes looking for that really important paper, but it couldn't be found.

"Well, never mind. The boxes are labeled one to seven, and it doesn't matter if we eat lunch food for dinner or the other way around," I said.

We left camp an hour late, but our potential speed was greater than that of the Covered Wagon, so we didn't worry. Fifteen minutes out on the road to Aïn Beïda, we had a flat tire. Those macadam roads were hard on tires. With six strong men in the car it didn't take long to change the tire, but we lost another half hour at the garage in Aïn Beïda getting the tire repaired.

Several hours later on the road south, we came upon the big truck. It, too, had had a flat tire. While the boys were repairing it, another tire went flat. We were afraid we'd never get to Timgad, our first stop, that night unless our luck improved.

Alvan and Alonzo talked over the situation and decided that the station wagon and its occupants would drive on to Timgad and pick a site for the camp. Then Alonzo would go back for a load of boys and some of the baggage. That way the truck would be lighter, and it would be easier on both the engine and the tires.

Noon came. Food was back in the Covered Wagon. We stopped at the small village of Khenchela where I had tried, unsuccessfully, to buy meat the year before. This time we bought cheese, crackers, and chocolate and munched it as we drove along. We thought longingly of the roast chickens back in the truck.

We reached the Timgad ruins in the middle of the afternoon. The Triumphal Arch stood out in sharp outline above the stony plain. Then we saw the columns. Alonzo let us off at the Museum, and we talked to the curator for a while. Then we wandered around the exhibits. There were colored mosaics taken from the floors of Roman villas. We saw many vases, although most of them were broken. After we had looked at antiques placed in the Museum, we went into the city and walked down through stone-paved streets, rutted by chariot wheels almost two thousand years ago. We went past the colonnades of town houses and through the ancient market place.

Timgad ruins; Triumphal Arch, street with chariot ruts, and columns.

It was just five o'clock when we saw the station wagon and the truck pull into the front of the Museum. The curator was very gracious and let the rest of the boys wander around through the Museum and the ruins although it was well past official closing time.

In the meantime Alvan, Komici, and Ahmet pulled the cars into the place we had chosen as a camping spot, close to a wall with the two cars making a hollow square, such as the old covered wagon trains made. The boxes of food were unloaded, bedrolls laid out, lanterns and stoves set up. Camp was ready for supper.

As we were getting supper, I said, "Komici, we had a pretty poor lunch. All the food was in the truck."

"Oh, *Madame*, this morning I put two chickens in the little car."

We looked, and there under the typewriter, Victrola, and suitcase of film was a box with two roast chickens and some bread. I wonder who supervised *that* packing!

Later on, Komici said, "*Madame*, did you see the picture Mr. Waite took of me?" He pulled a packet from his pocket and unwrapped it. The wrapping was my list of menus! For supper we had ten cans of soup, six cans of peas, two cans of apricot jam, and two roast chickens, just as the meal was planned, except for our roast chickens. The boys in the truck had eaten the other five for their lunch. I gave Komici another piece of paper to wrap his precious portrait and retrieved my menus.

After dark, when tired boys were snug in their bedrolls and Chomee was asleep on the rear seat of the station wagon, Alonzo and I slipped under the fence that enclosed the ruins of that old Roman city.

A full moon shone over the deserted city. We stumbled along the ruts made by chariot wheels so many years ago. The great flagstones which formed the street had grooves six inches deep. We strolled under the Triumphal Arch of Trajan still standing to commemorate a Roman emperor almost forgotten except by students of Roman history. We could almost hear the tramp of the victorious Roman Legion as they paraded up the street and under the Arch.

We sat on the steps of the Forum and tried to hear what the orators said in that far off time, but the sounds were only the soft breezes blowing around the columns. We walked to the marketplace and pictured in our minds the crowds milling around, the piles of fruit, the stacks of wheat, the herds of sheep, goats, and camels being put up for sale. It couldn't have differed much from the weekly markets we were accustomed to.

We sat on the top row of the theater and almost caught the shadowy forms down on the stage. Was it *Antigone* they were playing? Greek plays were popular in Roman times.

Slowly we went back to the gate, just the two of us walking in the moonlight through that city that 2000 years ago had been the center of Roman civilization in North Africa.

Sunrise the next morning saw us eating breakfast, and soon after we were on the road. Our luck held that day and we kept within five miles of the Covered Wagon all day.

At noon we pulled off the road beside a well where women in red calico dresses were washing their laundry. The boys were fascinated by the little jig the women danced to rub the soap in and the dirt out of their garments.

Camp at El Kantara.

Our lunch was a cold meal, part of the large roast beef sliced for sandwiches. Komici made lemonade.

An hour before sunset we drove into El Kantara, past the post office, past the hotel, through the gorge and into the *palmeraie*. We found a grassy spot beside a high adobe wall and once again drove the cars into a hollow square.

There was time before dinner to explore. We wandered through tiny lanes between high walls which surrounded the gardens. We peered through cracks of tall, wooden gates and saw palm trees scattered among patches of wheat. Several times we saw palm-leaf huts built into a corner of the wall, a shelter for the one who guarded the wheat from the birds. We wandered down by the River of El Kantara, which now lay in quiet, intermittent pools. The brilliant colors of the sunset were reflected in these small mirrors.

175

Hunger soon called us back to camp where Komici and Ahmet had heated canned hash and canned green beans. They made a lettuce salad and several pots of coffee. Oranges were passed around for dessert.

Later that night, after the moon had risen, Alonzo and I slipped away from camp and climbed part way up the mountain. We looked down on the dark green fronds of the palm trees which swayed in the breeze almost always blowing through the gorge. The big moon silvered the tips of the palm leaves, and the river was a ribbon of silver.

The next morning we drove on down a white road on a brown, barren plain. Waves of heat made the range of the Sahara Atlas shimmer on the horizon. At noon we drove into the small oasis of El Outaya. *El Outaya!* It was everything an armchair traveler imagines an oasis should be. Several sparkling streams meandered among grassy banks. Feathery palms threw shade on the green grass. We fairly tumbled out of the cars in our haste to get into the coolness. We stretched out in the shade while Komici and Ahmet passed around opened cans of pineapple, cheese sandwiches, and lemonade.

All too soon Alonzo roused himself and said, "It's time to go on. We have to make Biskra tonight."

We in the station wagon, waited to see that the truck started and then we sped on ahead to Col de Sfa. As we had done the year before with the girls, Alonzo stopped just on the north side of the pass. Soon the truck came along and stopped. Everyone got out, and we all walked through the pass together into the Sahara.

We had not told the boys just what they would see. No sand dunes, no camel caravans, just brown badlands, and off on the horizon, a green blur that was the oasis of Biskra. Even this barrenness was better than the view we had the year before in the drizzly rain.

We climbed back into the cars, and Alonzo told Alvan, "We will go straight through the city and drive five miles south to the dunes."

As we got south of the city our cars stirred up clouds of dust where the year before we had been mired in the mud. We drove past the café and into the dunes. Alonzo chose a place in a hollow. The little station wagon made it all right, but the Covered Wagon didn't have the power. Ten of the boys got behind the truck and pushed. It was hard work and John said, "Why can't we leave the big truck here?"

"We need to be together for the safety of our possessions," Alonzo answered. "Although there seems to be no one around, these dunes could hide even a small caravan."

At last the truck was pushed in beside the station wagon. As the bedrolls were unloaded, the boys vied with one another in finding the softest spot in the sand. Komici and Alonzo went back to the little café to make arrangements for supplying water to us.

Supper that night was eaten in a hurry. Dishes were washed quickly. It had been a long, strenuous day. Everyone was glad to crawl into bed early.

34

One Enchanted Evening

*T*he next morning Komici was up with the sun, and the good smell of coffee soon roused the rest of us. Ahmet made several trips to the well at the café, and the boys were sloshing water on their faces and arms. I put oranges, bread, and cans of jam on the tailgate of the station wagon. Komici fried a couple dozen eggs. The boys wandered over and helped themselves to food, then found a seat on the slope of the dune. I put Chomee on the front seat of the station wagon and helped her with her plate and cup.

Soon we heard the plop-plop-plop-plop of animals' feet.

"Here come the camels," I called to Alonzo. "The camels that you ordered last night are coming." Ten camels with their drivers were plodding sedately across the desert toward our camp in the dunes.

"George L., you take over," my husband said. "We will want pictures of the typewriter and a close-up of my watch and some of the Victrola." Those items had been donated to the expedition by merchants back home, and Alonzo wanted some publicity pictures.

George L. directed the boys to stand around in groups while Alonzo, his typewriter on a food box, typed a line or two. His sleeves were rolled up, and the watch showed conspicuously. Some of the boys played the Victrola. George L. made a comprehensive photographic record of everything, including camels and desert dunes. Then all of us went for short rides on camelback. All except Alonzo. His camelback ride of a thousand miles in 1924 had cured him of any urge to mount another camel.

Finally he made an arrangement with the drivers that any of the boys who wanted to could ride a camel the five miles into Biskra and spend the day. Alvan would drive the rest of them into town in the Covered Wagon.

Dune camp south of Biskra.

Alonzo, George L., and I, with Chomee, decided to take the station wagon and drive to the oasis of Sidi Okba. It was a small oasis not far from Biskra. We took Komici with us because the oasis is a shrine for Muslims.

Okba ibn Nafi, for whom the oasis was named, was the general in command of the Muslim conquest of North Africa. He rode his big, black horse from Mecca across North Africa to the Atlantic Ocean, conquering as he went. It is written that he rode his charger into the ocean, brandishing his sword as he exclaimed, "Great God, if my course were not stopped by the sea, I would still go on to the unknown kingdoms of the west, preaching the unity of Thy Holy Name and putting to the sword the rebellious nations who worship other than Thee."

The Berbers, who gave only lip service to Islam, plotted behind his back. On his way home to Mecca, he was slain and was buried in the small oasis which is named after him.

The town of Sidi Okba is a typical oasis. Our car just was able to get through the narrow street lined with adobe buildings. We made it through into the marketplace, a large, open square in the middle of the town. Wooden awnings shaded small shops that were otherwise entirely open to the street. Carcasses of sheep that hung in the meat market were black with flies. Other stores had bolts of red and yellow calico. Knives in red leather sheaths were displayed on counters.

We glanced in at the cafés and saw men lounging on straw mats sipping thick, sweet, black Arab coffee or drinking mint tea from tiny glasses.

The mosque, built over Sidi Okba's tomb, was across the square. We crossed the hard, sun-baked ground toward it. Alonzo inquired of the doorkeeper if we might enter.

"Yes, it is permitted," he answered.

We passed through the gate into a courtyard where a fountain splashed. Here the pious washed themselves before they entered the mosque to pray. Our guide told us that, contrary to the usual custom, we need not remove our shoes but must not step off the straw matting while we were in the mosque.

As we became accustomed to the dim light in the building, we saw kneeling figures all around us, but we did not see Komici. The straw carpet led us to the tomb. A structure of latticework, like a small summer house, was built around the wooden sarcophagus and painted dark green. Clusters of red, purple, and white glass grapes hung from the top of the walls. The gate was locked with a small padlock.

"It is opened once a year on the anniversary of Sidi Okba's death," explained the guide.

On the other side of the mosque was a small shrine, the wood around it carved so beautifully that it looked like lace.

"Would you like to go up into the minaret?" asked the guide.

"Very much," we answered.

He led us outside the mosque to a tall, square tower. We climbed a seemingly endless circular stairway and guided ourselves along a palm wood railing.

From the balcony, we could look over the whole oasis. The houses were low, brown buildings with flat roofs. In a corner on each roof was a little shelter of palm leaves. It was here that the women of the family came to cool off after the heat of the day. Beyond the buildings stretched a grove of feathery palms and beyond that was barren gravel plain, the true Sahara.

"This mosque is the oldest Arabic structure in North Africa," said our guide. "The supporting pillars of the building are palm trunks plastered over and then painted."

We placed a contribution in the box by the gate as we left. Komici was waiting for us.

"Komici, why didn't you go into the mosque?" we asked. We had taken him because we thought it would be a special privilege for him. At Camp Logan he had been very faithful about his prayers.

"Oh, I didn't know where to wash first," he said.

"There was a fountain in the courtyard," we replied.

He just shrugged. Komici was timid, and perhaps the idea of entering a strange mosque frightened him.

Back at our car, Komici became vociferous in scaring the little street urchins off of our car. They had swarmed over everywhere. They served to reassert Komici's self-assurance.

In a little while we were back in Biskra. We wandered through the bazaar. We met some of our boys, and the first words each of them said were, "Mr. Pond, will you loan me a hundred francs until I can get an American Express check cashed?

I've found something for my mother," or "I've got to buy this bracelet for my girl back home."

Finally Alvan and the rest of us rounded up the group and drove back to our camping place in the dunes. Komici and Ahmet soon had supper for us. The boys moved their bedrolls to a place in the sand that seemed softer than the one they had last night. Some of the boys crawled in and were soon asleep, but ten of us took a lantern and walked off a little way into the dunes to enjoy the desert evening.

There was no wood for a campfire, so we lighted a lantern and sat in a circle around it. The sun had just set behind the tawny dunes. The bright orange sky shaded to lemon yellow, to aquamarine, to pale blue. We lay back on the dune slope to watch the stars begin to twinkle. In a few minutes, the quietness was broken by the slow-rhythmic plop-plop-plop-plop of camel feet and the soft tinkle of bells. A small caravan of camels plodded along the dune crest silhouetted against the orange sky. They passed from sight, and the sound of camel bells grew faint again. All was quiet.

In the east a big moon rose, silvering the crest of the sandy ridges and casting long, deep purple shadows in the hollows. Someone at camp was playing the Victrola, and through the soft evening air came the strains of Sigmund Romberg's "Desert Song."

The moonlight was so bright that I reached out to turn down the lantern, and I must have rubbed the lamp for suddenly it seemed squat and gold-colored. Was it real or was it magic? Could it have been Aladdin's Lamp? Around the edge of the dune came two shadowy figures. Were they men or were they genii?

With a soft-spoken, "Good evening, *Messieurs, Madame*," they joined our circle. "We have treasures from all over the world. May we show them to you?"

At our murmured, "But, yes, of course," they opened their packs.

A shimmering silver and black lace scarf was tossed on the sand. "The women of Mecca wear these on Feast Days, *Madame*. It is embroidered with threads of pure silver. See how it catches the moonbeams and holds them in its folds.

"And for you, *Monsieur*, a silver dagger? There is still a spot of blood on it. It is said that a young sheik from the south slit the throat of his rival for the favors of a beautiful dancing girl."

The other man spread on the sand a bright red Chinese robe with a gold dragon embroidered on it. A string of amber beads, honey-colored as the sands of the Sahara under a hot sun, slipped through his fingers onto the robe. Gossamer scarves from India almost floated on the desert moonlight. A deep blue obi, with delicate pink cherry blossoms on it, joined the scarves. One of the merchants drew a string of crystal beads from his pack and dropped it on the obi. "Just as pure as the snows on Mt. Fujiyama," he said. They sparkled like frost crystals. Silver bracelets and anklets from "the Sultan's favorite concubine" were added to the heap.

At last, when we were almost surfeited with beauty, one of the genii said, "You will buy no more, *Messieurs, Madame*? Then we must pack up and go back to Biskra." I saw the silver sheen of a revolver as it was slipped into a coat pocket.

"Ah, yes, *Madame*. Danger lurks on the road to Biskra. Why, just last night a young sheik was killed by… ah, who knows by whom?"

Quietly the men, with their packs on their backs, stole away behind the dunes. Our lantern was tall and green again. It might have been a dream except that beside us on the sand lay the silver Mecca veil, a string of amber, a bracelet of elephant's hair, and a silver dagger.

We still sat quietly as if enchanted.

Far in the distance toward Biskra, we heard a single shot. Then the silence of the moonlit night settled down around us.

❧

The morning sun rose bright and hot. Everyone was eager to leave the desert. We hurriedly ate breakfast and sloshed the dishes clean. The food was put in the truck, but remembering our first day, we kept out enough for us in the station wagon. Bedrolls were put in the Covered Wagon, and the boys climbed in on the top of the load. "We'll see you at El Kantara at noon," called the boys as Alvan pulled away.

We gave a last look around to be sure that nothing was left and then stopped to say goodbye to the café proprietor. We went on through Biskra and up to the Col de Sfa, the true gate to the desert. On the way, we passed the Covered Wagon. It was a hard pull up the mountains, but they made it. At El Kantara we found a roadside well and waited there for the boys. It was good to be up on the plateau where it was cooler. The Covered Wagon came along in an hour, and we had our usual lunch of sandwiches, fruit, and lemonade.

During the afternoon we stayed within five miles of each other, and about five o'clock we made camp. As soon as it was dark, we went to bed and to sleep.

The following morning we were up early. Breakfast was a hurried meal, and the boys were ready to start on. We stayed together as we had wanted to get to camp together.

Late in the afternoon we pulled in at Camp Logan. The Jenks were glad to see us, and we were all glad to be back. The bedrolls were sorted out. Komici cooked a quick meal for everyone, and we settled back into the old routine.

Half of the boys liked Biskra; half of them didn't.

35

Komici and Chabane

Several days after we returned from Biskra, I gave Komici laundry to do. He took it to the well and sprinkled some water on the clothes. Instead of vigorously soaping them and dancing them clean, he sat down by the well as if he didn't have a care in the world. He sat there all morning.

When 11:30 came, I called, "Komici, please come and get the carrots ready. And bring the clothes back with you."

"Yes, *Madame*," he answered, but made no move to come back to the tent.

I was perplexed, but I got the lunch. When the workmen came back from the diggings, Komici went to his tent with them. Alonzo and the boys came back. As Alonzo came into headquarters tent, I said, "Komici won't do any work this morning. Do you suppose he is sick?"

We were used to doctoring the native workmen, but they always came to the tent, and we bandaged cuts and sores or gave them aspirin or laxatives as the need arose.

The workmen were eating outside their tents. Alonzo strolled over. "What's the matter, Komici? Why haven't you done your work this morning?"

"You are only going to be here ten more days, so I don't have to work hard any longer."

"That is where you are mistaken. We're going to be here another month. You know me well enough to know that anyone who works for me draws his pay only as long as he does his work. Now, either you get to work or leave camp!"

"All right," said Komici, and went to the tent to get his belongings.

So, once again, Alvan started up the station wagon. Komici put his things in the back and climbed in. We were a puzzled group of Americans as they drove off down the road.

The next day Alonzo stopped at the Bernard's on his way to town.

"What was the matter with Komici?" he asked our friend. "He got stubborn and lazy yesterday, and I had to fire him."

M. Bernard smiled. "Well, it's like this. You and *Madame* treated him very well. Much better than his other employers ever have. He liked working for you, but he realized that you would be leaving soon. He was offered a steady job at the grist mill with good pay. He has a family to support.

"He could not bear to tell you that he had another job and was leaving you without a cook. But he knew you would not tolerate laziness and insubordination, so he got himself fired. His leaving you was then your responsibility, not his. He stayed until the day before he told his new employer that he would go to work for him.

"It's a simple explanation, isn't it?"

When Alonzo came home and told me, I said, "Oh, why couldn't he have told us and left us with a good feeling! I'm glad you talked to M. Bernard. Now, I can still remember him as the cheerful, fairly efficient worker that he was."

So across the years, the memory remains of a Komici who, in spite of his religious taboo, helped me to cut up a pig; a Komici who replied smiling, "Very well, *Madame*" to everything I asked, but who couldn't bear to disappoint us by telling us he was leaving us without a cook.

❧

Muslims value privacy about their family lives. It is bad manners to ask about any feminine member, and rarely does one ask personal questions. Alonzo thought that he and Chabane were good enough friends so that he might ask Chabane a few questions.

Chabane always wore clothes that he bought at the local old clothes market; cast-off army trousers and blouse. His *burnous* was grimy, and his turban was always "tattle-tale gray." With his several layers of clothing, he was always warmly dressed, but he always looked ragged. We knew that he lived with his widowed sister in a dirt-floored, one room stone hut.

One day he was the last in the pay line. No one else was around.

"Chabane, what do you do with your money?" Alonzo asked.

"Oh, I buy some grain and give it to my sister to bake bread enough for a week. Also a few dates."

"But that doesn't take six day's wages?"

"Well, if I need clothes I buy a shirt or trousers at the market."

"You don't need clothes every week."

"No. I buy cigarettes enough to last a week."

"But you can't spend all your wages on that."

Chabane smiled, "No. I buy more grain."

"Well," Alonzo thought. "He's buying grain to hold for higher prices or to tide him over when he's without work."

Chabane continued, "I'm old and I can't get down on my knees to pray as often as I should. There is a young family down the street. They are having a hard time, so I give the grain to them. Perhaps Allah will accept my gift in place of my prayers."

36

Dinner at the Caid's

"The *Caid* has invited us to dinner the day after tomorrow," said Alonzo when he came home from Canrobert one day. "He's invited George L., too. I stopped at the Bernards' on the way home, and Madame will be very happy to have Chomee there for lunch that day."

"How nice of the *Caid* and Madame Bernard, too," I said. Then I had a second thought. "Do you suppose we'll have to sit on cushions on the floor and eat from a low table? I am sure I can't do that gracefully."

"We'll have to wait and see," replied my husband, who had eaten many Arab meals seated tailor-fashion on the ground.

Two mornings later we drove to the Bernards'. Madame rushed out, her arms open wide. "Come, little one, come. We'll go in and have something to eat."

She took Chomee in her arms and carried her into the house. We drove on into Canrobert.

We stopped for mail at the Post Office, then drove down the main street and turned into a side street. The way was lined on both sides with solid adobe walls. Now and then there was a heavy wooden gate. Alonzo had been there before, so he knew which gate was the entrance to the *Caid's* home.

We rapped. The gate swung open, and the *Caid's* son, about eight years old, stood there. He was dressed in short trousers and jacket, such as the French boys wore, but he wore a red fez on his head. He welcomed us, "Come in, come in, *Messieurs, Madame.*"

Across the clean-swept cobblestones of the paved courtyard was the house. The *Caid* was standing in the doorway, smiling a welcome and obviously proud at the way his little doorman greeted his guests.

"Bonjour, M. et Mme Pond, bonjour, M. Waite," he greeted us and ushered into the living room. It was also a bedroom. "Please sit down." He indicated some straight-backed chairs. Maybe I wasn't going to sit on the floor after all.

While Alonzo and the *Caid* talked about the weather and the coming wheat harvest, George L., who never picked up any French, and I looked around the room.

There were two beds, standing opposite each other in two corners of the room. Two long curtains, one at the head and one at the foot, hung from a canopy over the bed. A blue silk lining showed through a crocheted bedspread. A blue boudoir pillow with a French doll's head rested against the bed pillows. The other bed had a magenta colored silk moiré bedspread with gold embroidered pillow slips. Several velvet pillows were tossed near the head of the bed. There was a large chest of drawers near the head of one of the beds. The top held a kerosene lamp, some photographs, and several bottles of medicine.

Madame Lamine soon came to the door to say that dinner was ready. The *Caid* invited us into the dining room. I breathed another sigh of relief, because there was a standard-size dining table and chairs to match. The *Caid* seated us. True to native custom, Madame Lamine did not sit with us, but she served us as a gracious hostess.

The first course was an Arab soup called *chorba*. It was a rich meat broth, with bits of onion, tomato, red pepper, and meat.

When we finished that first course Madame Lamine removed the plates and brought in a heaping dish of couscous. And such couscous! It was the best I have ever eaten. I had never had any couscous flavored with saffron, and the herb added just the right touch. There were several dishes of carrots, peas, and bits of meat. The *Caid* passed a meat broth to pour over it. Each of us had two helpings. Then Madame brought in a potato omelet. We had all eaten our fill, but there was still dessert! Madame brought in a plate with six kinds of fruit, almonds, and cakes dipped in honey.

The *Caid* had adopted much of the western culture, and he did not expect us to belch our appreciation, as was still customary in native society. However, it would not have been difficult for us to comply with such a display of courtesy.

We went back into the living room. Madame and her sister, who was visiting her, joined us for coffee — thick, black, and very sweet Turkish coffee.

"Do you think the *Caid* would let me come and take color pictures?" asked George L.

"I'll ask," said Alonzo.

"Yes," the *Caid* agreed. He thought a minute. "Would Monday of next week be convenient?"

"Whatever time you set is convenient for us," replied Alonzo.

We got up to leave and Madame Lamine handed me a bag of the delicious apricots like those we had eaten at dinner. They were much better than those we could buy in the market.

"Thank you very much."

"*Au revoir*," said the *Caid*. "I'll see you about one o'clock on Monday."

The *Caid*'s young son appeared and once again swung open the heavy wooden gate while *M. le Caid* and *Madame* waved to us from the doorway.

37

Party Call

*T*he next Monday Alonzo, George L., Chomee, and I drove to town. Alonzo took a room in the small hotel so Chomee could have her nap. George L. and I went on to the *Caid's*.

Again, the *Caid's* son opened the heavy gate when we knocked and led us across the courtyard to the house. The *Caid* had not finished his lunch. I'm sure his timing was deliberately planned. George L. beamed his pleasure at the colorful arrangement.

The *Caid* was seated on a large cushion before a low table. His lunch was spread out on a huge round, brass tray. That lunch would have delighted a calorie-counter — a dish of radishes, a tossed green salad, a plate with two lamb chops, and a small serving of green beans.

Madame Lamine came into the room and welcomed us.

George L. said to me, "Tell the *Caid* to please stay right where he is," and went right to work setting up his camera.

Madame Lamine indicated a chair for me, then left the room, but was soon back with a china coffee service on a brass tray. Gracefully, she placed it on another low table and seated herself on the floor before it. She poured coffee for George L. and me, then got up and passed the cups to us. The *Caid* wasn't ready for his coffee so she poured a cup for herself.

I was interested in the way the family had blended western and eastern cultures. In the eastern culture, women never eat until the adult male members of the family have eaten. Nor would a woman have seated herself in the living room with men guests, but would have retired to the woman's section.

"Are you from this part of the country?" I asked my hostess.

"No, both Khalifa and I are from Biskra."

"I have been there twice," I said.

"I often go back to see my family," she replied.

That, too, was a western idea, for native women seldom see their parents once they have married and gone to another household.

"Now, Marguerite," the *Caid* said. Madame left the room at once and soon came back with a small white basin, a pitcher of hot water, and a linen towel. The *Caid* poured the water into the bowl, dipped his fingers in it, and dried them. It was a more elaborate ceremony than our use of finger-bowls at home.

"Is your name really Marguerite?" I asked. "That is not a Muslim name."

"No," she laughed. "He likes to tease me. My name is Fatima after Mohammed's daughter."

The *Caid* explained. "We have a book listing all the Muslim given names. If a child is born on the morning of a certain day he is given one name. If he is born in the afternoon, he is given another name. But, now, with western culture taking over, people name their children whatever name they like."

Then he stood up. "M. Waite, are you ready for more pictures?"

The *Caid* was dressed in a modern Muslim businessman's suit of brown wool. The trousers, made in Arab style, were very baggy in the seat and pleated around the waist, then tight below the knees. The jacket was a modern western sack suit coat. His turban was spotless white, with the traditional black cord bound twice around it to keep it securely on his head. His *burnous* was of finely spun and woven wool.

He posed in the doorway for several pictures, then took his official scarlet *burnous* from a chest and put it on over his head. Only a *Caid* may wear a red *burnous* and then only on state occasions. *Caid* Lamine's *burnous* was heavily embroidered in gold down both sides of the front and around the bottom. It was caught together at the neck with gold embroidery and decorated with six small gold tassels. The hood, too, was embroidered in gold with a tassel hanging from the point. As he tossed a corner of the cape over his shoulder, we could see the lining of blue and yellow brocade. Truly, he was a model to delight the eye of any color photographer, and George L. was making the most of it.

"Wouldn't you like to dress up in my clothes so M. Waite can take your picture?" Madame asked me.

"Oh, I would like that," I answered.

We went into another room. "Muslim men like their women plump, and you are so thin that you can put my clothes right on over yours. We won't need bloomers but all women wear them."

The pair she showed me was guaranteed to make all women look fat.

"How are they made?"

"You take eight meters (about nine yards) of cloth, lay it out flat, and fold it over so the material is double. You sew up one side and the bottom, leaving a space at each lower corner to put your feet through. The top is folded over to make a hem and a cord is run through. You step into them, pull the cord tight around your waist, and *voila*! You are plump enough to suit any Muslim standard of beauty."

I was impressed, though I gladly dispensed with the bloomers.

Marguerite took some clothes from a brightly painted chest.

"Put this little jacket on first."

It was a short jacket of magenta colored brocade. The flowing sleeves of sheer white crepe had gold flowers embroidered on them. "Now this," and she helped me into a sleeveless purple velvet coat that came to my knees. The arm-holes were trimmed with gold braid.

"Now, let's see. Which dress first?" and she searched through the chest. "This one, I think."

Over my head she drew a dress of deep wine-red moire silk. It was the style of all native women's dresses, a sleeveless jumper with deep V-neck and hung straight from the shoulders. I smoothed it. It was such beautiful material. Next, she helped me into a dress of fine white cotton material with blue flowers printed on it. It was made exactly like the red one, and it, too, went on over it.

The third dress that she took from the chest she fingered lovingly and said with pride, "This is my best dress. I wear it to weddings and on holidays."

It might even have been her own wedding dress. It was of white crepe, heavily embroidered with flowers of gold and silver. She gently placed it over my head and smoothed the folds as it fell around my feet. Then, she unclasped the purple velvet belt, also embroidered in gold, from her own waist and put it around mine.

"Now for the headdress," she said, and put a little purple velvet cone on my head fastened with a velvet chin-strap on which there were gold coins. Then she wound a white scarf with a gold and silver pattern around my head. It had a gold fringe six inches long, and the ends hung down my back.

"Now for the jewelry. Are your ears pierced?"

"No."

"We'll fix that," and she pinned a pair of gold loop earrings threaded with seed pearls to my scarf. "Necklaces? I guess this one for your scarf." A chain with pendants went around my head, the pendants hanging down on my forehead. "And this one for your neck."

It looked something like a squash blossom necklace from our own Southwest Indians, except that this was gold instead of silver.

She handed me three pair of bracelets, some silver, some gold, and I put them on. "And last," she said, as she put her own necklace of gold coins around my neck.

Then she stepped back and clapped her hands in pleasure. "M. Waite, Khalifa! Come and see *Madame* Pond."

The two men came into the room. They both laughed. George L. said, "Please go and stand in the doorway so I will have enough light to take your picture."

"*Madame* Pond," said the *Caid*, "wouldn't you like to go to the hotel and show your husband how you look as a *femme d'Arabe?*"

"I would, but it is a long way, and these clothes are too lovely to wear on the street."

"I'll call my car."

Soon his car, an open one, was at the gate. George L. and I got into the back seat. The *Caid* seated himself beside the chauffeur in front. We drove through the back streets to the hotel. Our room was on an inner courtyard. Two little gamins, recognizing the *Caid's* car, ran to open the wooden gate.

George L. helped me out of the car, and I rapped on the door. Alonzo opened it and was properly impressed, but Chomee didn't know me. She took one look, opened her mouth, and howled.

The *Caid* left us for a business appointment, and George L., too, declined to return. The chauffeur was instructed to drive me back to the *Caid's*. He decided that this was an *occasion* and drove slowly down the main street. Pedestrians stopped to stare. During that ride I felt much as Queen Elizabeth of England must feel when she drives in state with her coach and four.

Dorothy in Fatima Lamine's best dress.

38

The End of the Adventures

The first week of June came, and life at Camp Logan became a hectic rush. The weather turned almost unbearably hot. The thermometer in our tent registered 102° Fahrenheit at noon. In one of the boy's tents, their thermometer went to 120° and broke. We put up a tarp between our tent and headquarters tent. It gave some shade and created a small breeze. This open space was livable. At night the weather cooled off a little.

Dr. Jenks took his wife to Constantine where she could be in a good hotel. He then returned to camp so that he might go with Alonzo to Philippeville,[11] where the collections of artifacts were to be shipped to the museums.

The boys were busy washing and sorting stone implements. Alonzo spent most of his time overseeing them and dividing the Stone Age material. As per our agreement with the government of Algeria, half went to the National Museum in Algiers, and half went to Beloit College. Dr. Jenks, too, had to divide his collection.

The agreement also stipulated that the shell mounds were to be put back as nearly as possible into their original shape. We kept Chabane and Ahmet to fill in the trenches. Every hour Alonzo or Alvan would go up to the diggings to see that they were being filled correctly.

George L. kept busy developing and printing the last of the pictures. Besides the pictures of native life, there were pictures of the restored shell mounds for scientific publications.

---

11. Now Skikda.

The middle of May we had received a letter from Dr. Collie, the Curator of Logan Museum, saying "Our sponsor has decided not to give any more money for foreign exploration, so when you close the camp, sell everything including the truck and station wagon."

The job of inventorying the equipment fell to me. Fortunately, when the Jenks left, Larbi came to us as a cook, and he was a good one. I was freed from the task of preparing meals, washing dishes, and laundry.

In a few days the collections were packed, and Alonzo and Alvan took the boxes in the truck to the station in Canrobert for shipment to Algiers.

Some of the boys decided to go home by way of Tunis, Italy, and Paris. Mason decided to go with them. Alonzo took them to Canrobert and saw them on the train for Tunis. Later, we heard that they climbed Mt. Vesuvius, thus saving the fare on the funicular.

The next day Alonzo and Dr. Jenks started for Phillipeville with our share of the artifacts. They would go by freighter directly to America. Alvan took the rest of the boys to Canrobert where they boarded the train for Algiers, the first stage on the way to Paris and home. John and Laurie moved into the granary at the Bernards', where we had lived in June of 1929. They wanted to spend two weeks on an ethnographical study of the natives on the Model Farm. Sol went to Aïn Beïda to spend a few days with Jewish friends he had made there. Alvan, George L., Chomee, and I were left at camp.

Alvan kept our workmen busy taking down the tents. The tents, along with the stoves and lamps, had to be sent back to America since they had been allowed in duty-free if we took them out within six months.

Two days later, Alonzo was back from Phillipeville, and then we really rushed. We made two piles of equipment that was locally purchased. One was labeled "Damaged"; the other, "Good." Cots, chairs, and tables with broken legs were put in one pile, good ones in another. Fairly clean blankets and sheets went into a pile; those that had not been washed for three months went into another pile. Good plates, cups, and eating utensils were put on one table. Dented cups and forks with tines missing were put on another. Twelve dish pans added to that made quite a stack.

The next day was market day. Alonzo went to Canrobert early, and in the bar at the hotel mentioned rather loudly that the next day we were having a sale. A word to Chabane and Larbi spread the news among the natives.

Morning came, and we were up with the sun. So were our customers. Chabane and Larbi kept sharp eyes on the crowd.

"How much is this pan?" inquired a native.

"Five francs," replied Alonzo.

"I'll give you two."

"No bargaining today. This is an American sale. There are too many items; I can't take time to bargain. Everything has a fixed price. Take it or leave it."

Our first sale was a spoon for the equivalent of two cents.

The natives handled everything and walked from pile to pile. Frequently, after hours of looking, their purchase would be a plate or a cup. It was a social occasion for them.

The French came, too, and bought tables, chairs, and cots. One of the cots had been torn down the middle, but all six legs were good. We put that in the damaged pile, rolled up like others, and the tear didn't show. Most of the customers unrolled each cot and examined it carefully, as we expected them to do. One man saw the cot in the damaged pile. Alonzo saw him grab it and smile as he paid for it. Alonzo smiled back. Obviously the man thought we had made a mistake. An hour later he was back fuming.

"*Monsieur*, the cot. It is torn."

"Yes," Alonzo answered. "I saw you take it from the damaged pile."

"It is no good. I want my money back."

"No. It was in the pile of damaged goods. You could have untied it but you didn't. You were just a little too greedy. It is worth what you paid for it. Your wife can sew up the tear."

He went away muttering. I saw Chabane and Larbi have a good laugh. They knew the man. But we had been fair.

I sold a dish pan from the stack of twelve. They were all alike. Soon the native was back.

"I think this one is better," he said. "May I change it?"

"Yes. They are all alike."

He took another. Half an hour later he was back. "This one seems still better. May I change again?"

"Take whichever one you like."

A few minutes later he was back again. "This one is still better. May I exchange it?"

Wearily, I said, "Yes, but this is the last time. Take this other one and no more changing."

He picked up his choice and went off toward home.

By evening everything was gone, and we were worn out.

Dr. Fournier of Canrobert had been so good to us. He had set Danny's collarbone when Danny had fallen off a horse. He had taken care of Chomee when she was cutting her molars and running a fever. He had looked after our workmen when they needed more than the aspirin and laxatives that we gave them. All this was without charge. He and his wife had made several social calls at camp, and she had admired our air mattresses. Alonzo sent Alvan, who wanted to say goodbye to the doctor's pretty daughter, to Canrobert with two air mattresses for her mother.

When Alvan came back he brought two heavy silver bracelets crafted in Arab style, as gifts from Madame Fournier and Georgette. I often wear them.

The next morning, like Longfellow's Arabs, we folded our tents, but unlike those Arabs, we packed them in boxes with our stoves and lamps and noisily rattled away.

Chabane had slept that night in the truck in order to help us load our personal luggage in the morning, When Alonzo went to pay him, Chabane touched Alonzo's finger tips, then raised the back of his own hand to his lips and kissed it in the traditional Muslim greeting and farewell. Then Chabane put his hand over his heart and said, "Your going makes me sick here."

He climbed into the back of the truck and we took him back to his home.

We took rooms at the hotel for several days to rest and repack our luggage for the long trip home via Algiers, Marseille, and Paris. Alvan decided to go to Tunis and Italy, and we arranged to meet him in Paris in two weeks.

Alonzo went to say goodbye to the *Caid* and to thank him for the favors he had done. "*Madame* Pond sends greetings to you and *Madame* Lamine, also."

"Ah, *Madame* Pond," the *Caid* said. Then he smiled, reflecting on the two years we had been friends. "She has done what no woman, French or native, would dare to do. She has lived with her baby all alone in a tent among strange people for months and conducted the routine business of your expedition when you were obliged to be absent for days at a time." Then his Muslim upbringing overcame his veneer of Western culture, and he said, "*IF* women have courage, *Madame* Pond deserves a gold medal."

Afterword

Mary Jackes and David Lubell

Reading this memoir has been, for us, an absorbing experience because 45 years after the Ponds were there, we were doing research in the same area, under roughly similar circumstances, on the same archaeological problems. In addition, we have been working with published and unpublished documents, data and collections from the 1930 excavations at Site 12 for over 30 years (Jackes and Lubell 2014) and this memoir provides us with another perspective. We can recognize some of the background but also see great differences. As a way of illustrating this, we will make a few comments on our own experiences, but we note that because this memoir was written as a series of recollections for family rather than as an alternative record of the 1930 field research, some context is needed and we hope to provide that as well.

In 1972, 1973, 1976, and 1978, we surveyed and excavated Capsian *escargotières* in the area of Cheria, a market town about 50 km southwest of Tebessa and thus about 100km south of where the 1930 research took place. We were working primarily in and around the Telidjene Basin some 15 km south of Cheria (Lubell *et al.* 1976; Jackes and Lubell 2008) where there were a great many sites already known (Grébénart 1976). We lived in Cheria, either in housing provided by the municipality (1972, 1973) or in a rented house (1976, 1978). We hired a few local people to help us both with excavation and some household duties, but not on the scale of the Ponds. Our teams included graduate and undergraduate students from Algeria, Britain, Canada and the United States, along with professional colleagues from Algeria, Belgium, Canada, France and the United States. The maximum number was in 1978, when there were 14 of us, plus a cook seconded very temporarily from the *Centre de Recherches Anthropologiques, Préhistoriques et Ethnographiques* in Algiers, all living in a house in Cheria. With one exception, an undergraduate who had to be repatriated, the foreign students all had prior training and some were already familiar with North African prehistory, so we were not faced with Pond's need to give preliminary instruction.

The situation in Algeria in the 1970s was also very different from the 1930s. The country had been through a calamitous war, the infrastructure was not in very good condition, and the local people who were largely Berber (as was the case in 1930) were attempting to emerge from the colonial milieu which had been so advantageous for the Ponds. In fact, so far as we can judge from this memoir, the situation for the 1930 group was in several ways better than ours in the 1970s.

For one, the Ponds had established cordial relationships with the Bernard family, and this provided them with a mentor who knew the local men and spoke Arabic fluently (the workmen spoke both Arabic and Shawiya according to one of the students, Sol Tax from the University of Wisconsin, who was very interested in local matters). The choice of which students to take into the field, especially into isolated situations, is a difficult one. Pond restricted his choice to men, which caused some dissatisfaction amongst several women students as is made clear in the film *Reliving the Past* (Tarabulski and Teicher 1986). However, this avoided some of the obvious pitfalls of small isolated groups of young people. Pond had established reliable sources of good food, a most important feature for excavators. The students were well-fed, with adequate and varied diets, in a setting where they could relax by playing baseball and card games and listening to records. They were taken on excursions to survey for sites, to visit local Roman ruins, and on a trip to the Sahara. They could walk into Berriche or go by car to Aïn Beïda and Canrobert. There were dances and tennis parties with local French girls. While there were problems with vehicles, to be expected, the students were impressed by the camp equipment as new and extremely good. One of the Beloit students, Edgar Roberts, wrote in his diary: "......we hit the camp. It's about perfect. Green canvas tents with heavy cloth floors, Coleman lamps & stoves, all new cooking equipment, new canvas beds, & everything to make the life here as near like home as possible." Tax was also impressed. He wrote "We are well equipped: the tents are floored, and we are supplied with good army cots, table, chairs, an excellent gasoline lantern, and a good gasoline cook-stove." He was also impressed by the coffee, which he said "...is good, and American style."

For another, while our relationships with the two shepherds, Layesh Rahal and his cousin Lazhar Bougherara, who lived in the Telidjene Basin and became our valued field companions, were very friendly – apparently more so than the Ponds with their local assistants – our interactions with officials and people in Cheria were more distant than we intuit from Dorothy's description. Our relationships with the townspeople were more involved because we were living amongst them: a group of non-local women and men inhabiting a single house in a quite densely packed town (we were at one point told there were 30,000 inhabitants although that seemed, and still seems, an exaggeration). We had no claim to a colonial superior status and we were certainly not isolated from the local population in a very well equipped tent camp. For us, camping near the sites was not an option. It would have been insecure, there was no well nearby, and we would have been too distant from either Cheria or Tebessa to have easily supplied a field camp.

The women in our group could not comfortably walk around the town. Cheria was fairly conservative although the mayor, who was a Hadj, took an interest in local history and even prehistory. The only women to be seen were elderly and when some of the women from our team visited the wife and daughters of the local teacher, they discovered that the one son of the family, a 12 year old boy, had the job of doing all the shopping and other outside tasks for the women. The women saw only the sky above a tiny courtyard.

The men in our group could certainly not take off to a local bar or dance. While hostility towards foreigners was sometimes a problem, especially for the women, we accepted this, and we also understood that this particular town had suffered grievously during the war with the French. Our isolation, combined with the fact that our food mostly consisted of lentils, mutton and tough chickens led to some problems. The special treats we had brought with us from England and France had to be strictly rationed.

At the site, we were constantly visited by local men and boys, and occasionally we went visiting. We once went to a wedding in a tiny hamlet far beyond the site, the women inside, the men in the courtyard. A deathly ill tiny baby was brought to us for help. We could do nothing – nor for a boy brought by his father to the site, his finger slashed through to the bone, now healed over but non-functioning.

Our experiences in general, then, may have been more difficult to deal with than those of the Ponds. The relationships among our varied international excavation crew members were certainly complex: our group consisted of older and younger men and women, both foreigners and people from Algiers, and expertise and opinions were very diverse. During our final (1978) field season, we used a method of excavation that required extensive recording in three dimensions in an attempt to deal with the extraordinarily complex stratigraphy of a rockshelter. This proved too much, not only for our Algerian colleagues and students, but for one or two of the North American students.

To a certain extent we had two teams in 1978 – not socially, but academically – and it is possible that the fact that there were two parallel teams working at Site 12 in 1930 led to difficulties. Although there is no publication on Jenks' work beyond a note in *Science* (Anonymous 1930), records available at the University of Minnesota suggest that his approach was different. In broad terms, determined by equipment, both teams worked in the way which had been established at Mechta el-Arbi (Pond *et al.* 1928: 17-23) where there was a calcite crust that did not occur at Site 12. This involved the use of large picks and shovels to bring down sediment for sieving. Pond was aware that this was not the system used in France, but felt that this alternative was necessary "to obtain the little evidence which the wholesale digging here used produced." He wanted to open trenches at a number of sites and for this reason asked Collie to allow him to take a large team. As described by Voight (1930), the plan was that "…the students will each have personal charge of two Arab workmen and will work the various sites and shell heaps independently, moving on to another as soon as one has been worked." They were given 10-12 days training for this in a Site 12 trench.

Jenks' approach was very different: only one trench on one site was excavated from 8th March to 24th May. Jenks had a site supervisor, Lloyd Wilford, a man with whom he had spent the past two summers in the American southwest where their work included the excavation of hundreds of skeletons at the important Mimbres Galaz site. Wilford was himself assisted by Ralph Brown, and both kept detailed diaries and field notes which, together with photographs, provide us with a great deal of information about the Minnesota trench. Wilford also assisted the Beloit students working in the neighboring training trench.

Even the more focused work in the Minnesota trench would not be acceptable today, although it allowed observations on, for example, the distribution of ochre (contra Pond *et al.* 1938: 107). In fact, our work at Aïn Misteheyia in the 1970s, also an open-air escargotière, would be regarded as old fashioned. The external datum reference, the one meter squares and five centimeter levels would not stand up against the three-dimensional digital coordination of today. But the suggestion that Mechta el-Arbi produced "little evidence" (Pond *et al.* 1928: 23) is very questionable in comparison with the 73,000 pieces of flint (tools and debitage) and 30,000 pieces of animal bone within 19.1 cubic meters of deposit (Lubell *et al.* 1982-3) excavated at Aïn Misteheyia.

Ninety percent of the flint excavated in 1930 was discarded after examination (Pond 1931: 47), but the work of tabulation (to which Dorothy contributed, Chomingwen Pond, pers. comm.) contained in Appendix IV (Pond *et al.* 1938) records all classified material from Pond's Site 12 trenches, apparently both the collection sent to Algiers as well as that taken to Beloit. Excluding debitage, the count of lithics in Trench 1 is 1800 tools. The amount of sediment excavated from Trench 1 cannot be precisely calculated because the width was not consistent, the trench was not completely dug out to its full length of 19.5 meters, and no final profiles were drawn, but the volume of deposit removed from Trench 1 must have been around 100 cubic meters.

The Appendix IV tabulation for Trench 2 demonstrates that, with debitage excluded, 1776 tools were classified and density can be calculated because it was reported that 71 cubic meters of deposit were excavated from Trench 2 (Pond *et al.* 1938: 127). The density of tools was significantly higher in Trench 2 than in Trench 1. The difference may well reflect the fact that Trench 2 was not used as a training trench for the Beloit undergraduates: the upright screens used at the site required particularly close attention.

The Logan collection of Site 12 lithics comprises 17,662 pieces from all three trenches (W. Green, pers. comm.) and Peter Sheppard (1987) analyzed 1369 pieces from Trench 2 for his comparative study of Capsian lithic technology.

The Minnesota lithic collection has not been studied. Although 6000 lithic pieces was the published figure (Anon. 1930: 622), the collection consists of at least 23,000 flints (Anon. 2012). Based on Wilford's detailed sections, we can estimate that the *in situ* deposit excavated from that trench totaled 72.3 cubic meters, although a greater area was exposed. Since half the material had, by agreement, to be deposited at the Bardo Museum in Algiers, there can be no doubt that the site was very rich.

Despite questions about excavation techniques, the idea that all flints, faunal and human bone should be examined, and that even snails provide vital information, was an important component of prehistoric archaeology. One of us has been on sites where fauna was initially ignored and has known of archaeologists who regarded burials as no more than a nuisance.

The Minnesota team was able to benefit from the excellent facilities at Camp Logan, but they were a separate entity. Jenks had his own funding and he paid for Wilford and Brown (the student members of the Beloit team paid their own travel expenses). The arrangements for supplies were separate and Jenks started his film on the expedition with footage of Constantine, which he titled "Our provisioning base." For this reason, the Jenks took two trips to Constantine, each time just as supplies were running very low so that a delayed return, because Jenks had an eye infection and could not drive safely, caused some anxiety. The Minnesota team was also fortunate to be able to employ Larbi, recommended by M. Bernard, as a cook and general helper: he was paid by the Minneapolis group from 1st March to 25th May.

Dorothy implies that Larbi had little work to do, but in fact he was constantly with the Minneapolis group, travelling around with them on surveys, on their Sunday outings, and on their trip to the Sahara. In this context, Dorothy writes about an argument between Larbi and another man who shared a tent with him. Based on Wilford's diary this was not a unique event, but the situation was resolved. We know from the records kept by Wilford that the other man was Mazous Hanich who worked for them for only one month.

Larbi was teaching Arabic to Brown and he accompanied the older students when they walked in to Berriche for evenings off. He obviously got on with the Minnesota group extremely well and invited them to meet his family several times, each time providing them with meals. Mrs. Jenks gave a member of the family medicine, and she spent time alone with his womenfolk when Jenks and Wilford went off with Larbi, and also with the women in his wife's family. She was saddened, according to Wilford, by the lack of freedom for the local women.

Larbi remained in camp with Wilford and Brown the one time the Jenks went away by themselves for some days. They went to Algiers to participate in the *Cinquième Congrès International d'Archéologie* (14th-16th April 1930) where Jenks gave a paper on Mimbres ceramics (Leschi 1930). By a strange coincidence, other papers given in the prehistoric session of this congress were presented by Mendes Correia, a Portugese archaeologist, and by Serpa Pinto, his site supervisor, Wilford's equivalent. They were just initiating an excavation into a Portuguese shell midden with burials of the same period as Site 12. This site was studied from 1930 on, though not for long by Serpa Pinto, tragically dead from typhoid within a couple of years. We have been working on the records from this site in the same way as for the records from Site 12 and can compare the more controlled techniques used in Europe on the same type of site.

The Jenks returned immediately after the congress to Aïn Berriche, via Constantine for supplies, while other participants went on field trips in the vicinity of Tebessa and Constantine. It was at the end of these field trips that Count Begouen, who had been at the congress, visited Site 12 where the trenches had been prepared for his visit. The Count could use the Jenks' tent since they had taken their team on the trip to the Sahara.

While it was Wilford who recorded payments to the men, Mrs. Jenks was involved in the planning and paying for the provisioning of their group, including trips to Aïn Beïda and Canrobert: Wilford notes that she went over the accounts with him. She did not spend time at the excavation, although Dr. Jenks was frequently at both the Minnesota and the Beloit trenches, according to the available students' diaries and letters. Mrs. Jenks participated in all the trips to search for new sites and both the Jenks sometimes went with Pond and his students "scouting *escargotières*," as Wilford calls this activity. On one occasion, the Jenks and the Ponds, with Chomingwen, set off together so that Jenks could show Pond a cave he had visited. Mrs. Jenks stayed with Chomingwen while the others climbed up to examine the stone tools on the cave floor: she must have got on well with Chomingwen and sent a postcard to her from Algiers signed "Auntie Maud" (Chomingwen Pond pers. comm. based on Dorothy's letters). Indeed, Chomingwen was quite a favourite. She is mentioned in students' diaries as "cute," and in fact Tax mentions her twice. His later description of her as "cute and intelligent" is notable, considering that small children on archaeological excavations can come to be regarded as a nuisance.

It is hardly to be expected that Dorothy would have been involved in the excavation work. While the student diaries and letters make clear that major work around the camp was done by Small, Dobson, and Komici, Dorothy had her own responsibilities and the work of keeping up with the correspondence. Pond is mentioned in the diaries as helping with classifying stone tools – his major interest was lithics (Pond 1930; Shea1992; Sheppard 1992) – but although Dorothy says that Alonzo did all the work of checking the students' collection of flints, in fact there is evidence that she was also involved. An interesting comment comes from Tax who said that Mrs. Pond "seems to know the flints" and Pond (1938: 10) wrote that the students' "sorting and classification was checked and verified twice, first by Mrs. Pond and again by the writer." Roberts in his diary entry for 9th April wrote "In the p.m. Mr. & Mrs. Pond both came over to complete our stuff from #12. We are to set the classifications, with their help, for the entire bunch. Pretty hard work all afternoon..."

The students who worked with Pond were a disparate group. Tax saw them as falling into two groupings: those with training and a serious interest in anthropology and archaeology, and others who had no training and were there for the adventure. The first group was of men generally not from Beloit who had been recruited by Collie through his contacts at other universities. Brown and Wilford were seen by the other students as "both graduate students of considerable field experience" (Voight 1930b), and Greenlee, who was already married, had spent the previous summer working in the American Southwest at an interesting excavation which included women archaeologists (Preucel and Chesson 1994). Their eventual careers characterize the more mature students: Ralph Brown, John Gillin, Charles Nash, Lauriston Sharp, Sol Tax and Lloyd Wilford all went on to careers in anthropology or archaeology. But other students were not all without academic interests. For example, Daniel Reidel left Beloit, but graduated from Ohio State in 1933 and completed an MA in Sociology at Northwestern in 1942; Robert Voight was interested in archaeology and went on to graduate school but dropped out after a year because, as he said in *Reliving the Past*, there would be no employment opportunities; Virgil Moen became a lawyer.

Whereas our colleagues and students were not involved in food preparation and chores, the Beloit students had to cook for themselves, one of each pair of tent mates taking a one week stint of cooking in turn. Sol Tax recorded that his first Sunday was spent in "a domestic quarrel over the division of labor" with his tent mate Robert Greenlee. This was resolved by Tax taking on all the cooking (he claimed to be "recognized as by far the best culinary artist in the camp"). Greenlee did all the other chores that Tax regarded as unpleasant. Kenneth Williams' diary records that at the beginning they could not work their stove: they had three hours for lunch and needed every moment of it, since "everything went wrong with the meal." A letter from Williams to his younger sister says that he was the cook for his tent and this "takes a lot of time." He details the food and the work he has to do around the tent, but he records that the students pay "the Arabs" to wash their clothes on Sundays. Tax noted in a letter dated 20th March, that each student eventually had a servant, working at the trenches and around the tents. The main Beloit group (the Ponds, Waite, Small, and Dobson) also had a cook – this was Komici.

Although Larbi generally cooked for the Jenks, Wilford twice records chicken dinners made for them by Mrs. Jenks as "truly delicious." In fact, Brown and Wilford also did quite a lot of their own chores, week by week, preparing coffee in the morning and cooking, but sometimes eating dinners made by Larbi.

While some of the students may have found cooking difficult, others enjoyed it. Roberts especially was proud of his cooking and recorded his menus, including a meal he made for the Ponds on one of the occasions when beef was available, a Sunday. To quote his diary:

"The dinner menu was this:
        Cream of Tomato Soup -
        Roast Beef a la Logan -
        Alimentaires Salad -
        Mashed Potatoes -
        Buttered Beets -
        Date Torte -
        Hot Chocolate –
Some job! I did it alone & succeeded. It tasted pretty good though.
We messed our entire tent around to arrange for the guests."

Roberts also has an opinion (1st April) on the matter of the pig: "We've got a whole pig on our hands. It's doomed though, it can't be kept in this weather. However it tastes good for a change from mutton." Roberts became ill on 3rd April which perhaps explains his comment: "More pork for dinner, today, with macaroni & cheese. I'll be satisfied with mutton after this." Tax had words to say about the pig, too, because he had been invited out by a local man, and had invited him in return, to be presented with the social embarrassment of pork on the menu for a Muslim.

Tax provides us with some detail on food – the choice of menu for the meal he planned to give the Ponds one Sunday, his method of preparing a chicken using a Jewish recipe, the fact that they are to have beef "god knows where they found it in this country, but generally we live on mutton. We have begun to kill our own sheep (the camp has, I mean) as a matter of economy. Of course the Arab 'slaves' do it – and skin them and cut them up. The skins are dressed, and so far the Ponds have the two that have been obtained thus far..........When there is nothing else around – between meats – we eat fresh vegetables, which are numerous, and eggs. Of course we have a lot of staples, rice and such, and potatoes, which we can always use."

While Roberts enjoyed the challenge of cooking, he was not very happy. He records being homesick and not getting on well with other team members. He was very young and upon his return home was interviewed by the *Milwaukee Sentinel* for 21st June under the headline NO MORE ARCHAEOLOGY. He was not interested in the work and says in *Reliving the Past* that Pond accepted him as an expedition member because he was an Eagle Scout. He must, however, have remembered his time in Algeria with pleasure, since he attended the commemorative conference for Pond at Beloit 1985. At one point he got very behind in his work and, as recorded above, both Alonzo and Dorothy helped him to catch up with his sorting of flints. He was not alone. He records another group working in the "training trench" as being so far behind "they can hardly see their way out." In *Reliving the Past* Pond recalled of one student: "I finally discovered the notes and collections were really fouled up." The student was told to "salvage as much as he could."

Yet even Roberts could be thrilled by the idea of what he was experiencing, writing "Dr. Jenks showed me some 'Mousterian' work pieces today. They're highly interesting & date back about 60,000 years!" Tax, too, was enthusiastic: "it's great; I'm feeling tip-top, and my spirits are high. The whole thing is most interesting, and I should learn a lot of archaeology." And another time, after mentioning a problem in the camp: "but......it is an experience worth having." His high point was "a most interesting piece: a human radius fashioned into a flint-flaker. It... was a perfect specimen. Dr. Jenks said it was most remarkable, because he had never seen a human bone used for a tool...Pond was enthusiastic, too, but he said Dr. Collie had recently uncovered a human femur used as a bone flaker, also." Pond remembered in *Reliving the Past* that Gillin told him that actually handling the stone tools and classifying them was worth more than hearing about them in lectures.

Dorothy does not write about the Jenks – they were, after all, very much older. But some background will provide context. Jenks had for years been developing an interest in archaeology, had often been in Europe, and planned further work in Algeria (a plan which could not be realized, so he continued excavating in the United States for some years). After the work at Site 12, the Jenks set off for a month's exploration for sites, and then went on to Europe to work at the famous site of La Quina. Jenks (1869-1953) was an important anthropologist at the time, but some of his opinions, unacceptable today, have to be judged within their historical context (Soderstrom 2004). He was clearly more interested in field work and teaching than in administration, given that he turned down the offer of the directorship of the Bureau of Ethnology (Johnson 1992: 47).

Maud Huntley Jenks graduated with a BA from University of Wisconsin in 1898, married in 1901 and – against the wishes of her parents – went with Jenks to the Philippines. It was just a few years after the Spanish had been expelled from the Philippines, and yet the Jenks went to live in a highland village for many months. After her death in June 1950, her letters and diaries were of sufficient interest to be published (Jenks 1951), and they are commented on (Roma-Sianturi 2007) as displaying an unusual feature: Maud Jenks was not simply acting in a domestic role, she was participating in her husband's research. That research produced a detailed monograph (Jenks 1905), magnificently illustrated with about 150 photographs, many of them taken by Jenks. Jenks was a keen photographer and took still and movie cameras with him to Algeria, making a delightful movie. Details of Maud's later life are not available, beyond the fact that she had a son, born in the Philippines in 1905, who died in 1918, no doubt a victim of the Spanish flu which raged through Minneapolis and St. Paul late that year (Ott *et al.* 2007).

Maud's letters are lively and fascinating, illustrated with beautiful photographs. She spent months living a difficult journey of several days from any other American women, on one occasion by herself when Jenks went off on an expedition with head hunters. It is clear that Maud liked and admired the people they lived amongst, the Igorots, and did not mind the fact that her living space was at all times shared with many Igorot visitors.

The Jenks had several seasons experience of large excavations in New Mexico. Jenks and Wilford's work in 1929 digging the Mimbres site (Anyon and LeBlanc 1984) was done together with five students, supervising local workmen. It is no wonder that Pond several times brought his students across to the Minnesota trench to note the techniques used.

Dorothy's memoir, together with the surviving diaries and letters of the students, provides an interesting background to this early attempt to take North American students on an overseas excavation. Both Alonzo Pond and Albert Jenks were experienced in overseas work. Pond had excavated and explored in France and Mongolia as well as North Africa. Jenks had years of experience as one of the first Americans with a PhD in anthropology, had worked overseas and in North American anthropology and archaeology.

It was not, in the strict sense, a field school. Pond certainly did not see it as such, and while some of the students from other universities received academic credit for their participation, none of those from Beloit did. Wilford and Brown had extensive field experience already, and in 1929 Greenlee was on the Tecolote Project in New

Mexico run by A.V. Kidder (Preucel and Chesson 1994). Following the Algerian work, Greenlee, Gillin, and Tax all went on to the 1930 summer field school of the American School of Prehistoric Research in France directed by George Grant MacCurdy to which Pond had gone on a scholarship in 1921 (Bricker 2002). Jenks also had connections with the ASPR.

The "connections" are interesting but beyond the scope of this short contribution. Clearly, the concept of field training was not exclusive to Beloit, but the fact that this season was as successful as it was is certainly due to the careful preparations of Alonzo and Dorothy Pond. They had established relationships with the Bernards of Medfoun Experimental Farm and with individuals in Canrobert. They had done preliminary work on Capsian *escargotières* in the region and they chose a good location for a major excavation at Aïn Berriche (Site 12). The camp was established near a well, close to a main road, a few kilometers from Berriche and not many more from Aïn Beïda.

One of us has previously assessed the significance of Alonzo Pond's archaeological research (Lubell 1992) and there is no need to repeat that here, other than to reiterate that it was in many ways ahead of its time, although by today's standards the excavation methods as described (Pond *et al.* 1928 and 1938) would not be thought appropriate. Other papers by Sheppard, Johnson, and Shea in that same 1992 volume provide further details.

Sheppard (1987: 54) was able to use Site 12 material for his study of Capsian lithics, examining the Beloit sample deriving from the more controlled work done in Trench 2 by the advanced students (Tax, Greenlee, Gillin, and Sharp). It was his opinion that the technique used allowed even small microliths to be collected, so that the sample is usable and relatively unbiased by the techniques. The work at Aïn Berriche, and above all the publication on the lithics, bone tools, and fauna (Pond *et al.* 1938), was an important contribution, providing the impetus for our work in Algeria in the 1970s and beyond.

References Cited

Anon. 2012. North African catalogue, University of Minnesota Department of Anthropology, courtesy W. Green.

Anon. 1930. Archeological field work of the University of Minnesota in 1930. *Science* 72(1877): 622-623.

Anyon, R., and LeBlanc, S. (eds.) 1985. *The Galaz Ruin, a Prehistoric Mimbres Village in Southwestern New Mexico.* Albuquerque: Maxwell Museum of Anthropology and University of New Mexico Press.

Bricker, H.M. 2002. George Grant MacCurdy: an American pioneer of palaeoanthropology. In: D.L. Browman and S. Williams (eds.), *New Perspectives on the Origins and Americanist Archaeology.* Tuscaloosa and London, University of Alabama Press, pp. 265-285.

Grébénart, D. 1976. *Le Capsien des Régions de Tébessa et d'Ouled-Djellal, Algérie: contribution à son étude.* Études Méditerranéennes 1, Éditions de l'Université de Provence, Aix-en-Provence.

Jackes, M., and Lubell, D. 2008. Environmental and cultural change in the early and mid Holocene: evidence from the Télidjène Basin, Algeria. *African Archaeological Review* 25(1-2): 41-55.

Jackes, M., and Lubell, D. 2014. Capsian mortuary practices at Site 12 (Aïn Berriche), Aïn Beïda region, eastern Algeria. *Quaternary International* 320: 92-108.

Jenks, A.E. 1905. *The Bontoc Igorot.* Manila: Bureau of Public Printing.

Jenks, M.H. 1951. *Death Stalks the Philippine Wilds: Letters of Maud Huntley Jenks,* Edited by Carmen Nelson Richards. Minneapolis: Lund Press.

Johnson, E. 1992. A.E. Jenks and the University of Minnesota Algerian excavations. *Logan Museum Bulletin (new series)* I(1): 45-48.

Leschi, L. Le cinquième Congrès International d'Archéologie (Alger 1930). *Journal des savants. Juin 1930*: 272-275. http://www.persee.fr/web/revues/home/prescript/article/jds_0021-8103_1930_num_6_1_2385.

Lubell, D. 1992. Following Alonzo's trail: paleoeconomic research in Algeria since 1930. *Logan Museum Bulletin (new series)* I(1): 49-57.

Lubell, D., Hassan, F.A., Gautier, A., and Ballais, J.-L. 1976. The Capsian escargotières. *Science* 191: 910-920.

Ott, M., Shaw, S.F., Danila, R.N., and Lynfield, R. 2007. Lessons Learned from the 1918-1919 Influenza Pandemic in Minneapolis and St. Paul. *Minnesota Public Health Reports (Association of Schools of Public Health)* 122(6): 803-810.

Pond, A.W. 1930. *Primitive Methods of Working Stone, Based on Methods of H.L. Skavlem.* Logan Museum Bulletin III.

Pond, A.W., Romer, A.S., and Cole, F.-C. 1928. *A Contribution to the Study of Prehistoric Man in Algeria, North Africa.* Logan Museum Bulletin, I (II).

Pond, A.W., Chapuis, L., Romer, A.S., and Baker, F.C. 1938. *Prehistoric Habitation Sites in the Sahara and North Africa.* Logan Museum Bulletin, V.

Preucel, R.W., and Chesson, M.S. 1994. Blue Corn Girls: a herstory of three early women archaeologists at Tecolote, New Mexico. In: C. Claassen (ed.), *Women in Archaeology.* Philadelphia, University of Pennsylvania Press, pp. 67-84.

Roma-Sianturi, D. 2007. At Home in the Cordillera Wilds: Colonial Domesticity in the Letters of Maud Huntley Jenks, 1901-1903.*Asia-Pacific Social Science Review*, 7(1): 59-74.

Shea, D.E. 1992. Peet, Collie and Pond: the establishment of Beloit College Field Studies in Anthropology. *Logan Museum Bulletin (new series)* I(1): 25-31.

Sheppard, P.J. 1987. *The Capsian of North Africa: Stylistic Variation in Stone Tool Assemblages.* BAR International Series 353.

Sheppard, P.J. 1992. Snail shells and paradigms: the role of the Logan Museum expedition in North African prehistory. *Logan Museum Bulletin (new series)* I(1): 33-44.

Soderstrom, M. 2004. Family Trees and Timber Rights: Albert E. Jenks, Americanization, and the Rise of Anthropology at the University of Minnesota. *Journal of the Gilded Age and Progressive Era* 3(2): 176-204.

Tarabulski, M., and Teicher, B. 1986. *Reliving the Past: Alonzo Pond and the 1930 Logan African Expedition* (film).

Voight, R. 1930a. *Round Table* 75, no. 31, 8 February 1930.

Voight, R. 1930b. *Round Table* 75, no. 55, 14 May 1930.